LEGENDARY
— OF —
WOODSTOCK
NEW YORK

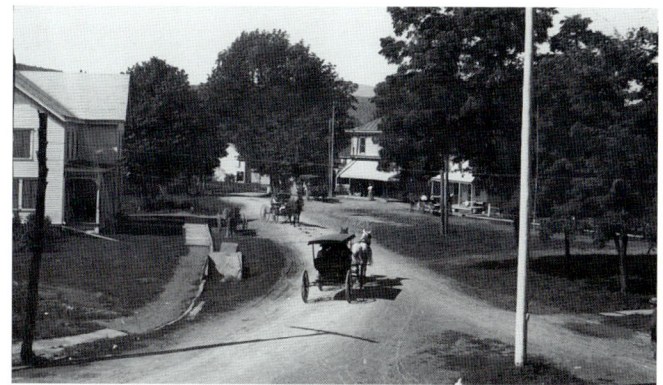

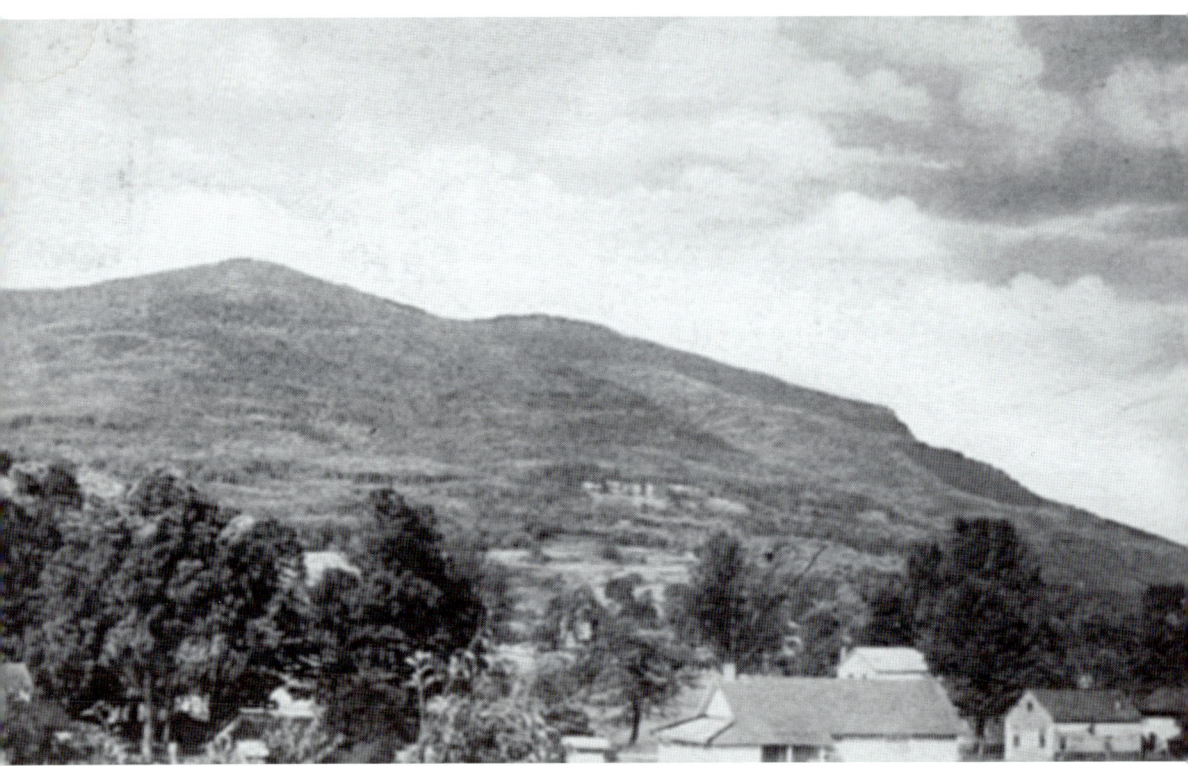

Overlook Mountain
The village of Woodstock lies at the base of Overlook Mountain, which over the years has been at the heart of Woodstock's economic and creative development. First traversed by Native Americans and remarked upon by Henry Hudson's first mate in 1609, Overlook has served as an inspiration to all who have lived and worked in its shadow. (Courtesy Janine Fallon-Mower.)

Page 1: Village Green
Woodstock and the village green are pictured as they appeared at the time artists began to arrive in the early part of the 20th century. Throughout the years, the village green has served as the focal point for town celebrations, protests, music, and, each year, Woodstock's most cherished tradition, Christmas Eve and the arrival of Santa Claus. (Courtesy the Historical Society of Woodstock.)

LEGENDARY LOCALS
OF
WOODSTOCK
NEW YORK

RICHARD HEPPNER AND
JANINE FALLON-MOWER

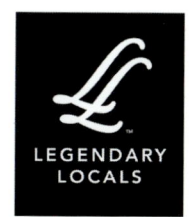

Copyright © 2013 by Richard Heppner and Janine Fallon-Mower
ISBN 978-1-4671-0067-0

Legendary Locals is an imprint of Arcadia Publishing
Charleston, South Carolina

Printed in the United States of America

Library of Congress Control Number: 2012950194

For all general information, please contact Arcadia Publishing:
Telephone 843-853-2070
Fax 843-853-0044
E-mail sales@arcadiapublishing.com
For customer service and orders:
Toll-Free 1-888-313-2665

Visit us on the Internet at www.arcadiapublishing.com

Dedication
Special thanks to my family, especially John Mower, who gives me the encouragement and the space needed to pursue my lifelong interest in the research of local history. Also, to the people of Woodstock, who are always willing to share their stories and photographs.
—Janine Fallon-Mower

To my wife, Deborah, who offers patience and understanding (a lot of it), and to the citizens of Woodstock, who make history every day. Thanks also to the Historical Society of Woodstock, which continues to keep faith with its mission.
—Richard Heppner

On the Cover: From left to right:
(TOP ROW) Albert Grossman (Courtesy Sally Grossman; see page 13), Jane Neher Keefe (Historical Society of Woodstock Archives; see page 54), Christian Baehr (Historical Society of Woodstock Archives; see page 15), Wilna Hervey (Historical Society of Woodstock Archives; see page 117), George Mead (Historical Society of Woodstock Archives; see page 21).
(MIDDLE ROW) Holley Cantine (Courtesy Jay Wenk; see page 122), Bluestone Quarryman (Historical Society of Woodstock Archives; see page 102), Hervey White (Historical Society of Woodstock Archives; see page 12), John Wigram (Historical Society of Woodstock Archives; see page 28), Ralph Whitehead (Historical Society of Woodstock Archives; see page 11).
(BOTTOM ROW) John Pike (Historical Society of Woodstock Archives; see page 24), Sarah MacDaniel Cashdollar (Courtesy Jean White; see page 109), Lee Marvin (Courtesy Jay Peterson; see page 94), Teddy (Courtesy Deborah Heppner; see page 107), Luke Klementis (Courtesy Esther Baldwin; see page 95).

CONTENTS

Acknowledgments 6

Introduction 7

CHAPTER ONE   Legendary Leaders: Power, Influence, and Change   9

CHAPTER TWO   Community Legends: Crafting a Better Woodstock   41

CHAPTER THREE   Legends Recalled: Tales and Stories that Remain   85

Index   126

ACKNOWLEDGMENTS

All images in this book, unless otherwise noted, are from the archives of the Historical Society of Woodstock and/or the private collections of the authors. The authors gratefully acknowledge the assistance of the Historical Society of Woodstock and the important work it does to preserve Woodstock's history.

Special thanks and appreciation also goes to Jean White, Sally Grossman, Sasha Gillman, Jay Wenk, Cornelia Rosenblum, Weston Blelock and WoodstockArts, Esther Baldwin, Alan Van Wagenen, Carl Van Wagenen, JoAnn Margolis, Karen Vos, John Mower, Deborah Heppner, Tina Bromberg, Brian Hollander, the *Woodstock Times*, Ellen Povill, Marcia Weiss, Happy Traum, Adam Traum, Donald Allen, Kathy Longyear, Audrey Klinkenberg, the Pierpoint family, Leslie Koehn Fertel, Jackie Earley, Rosemary Croissant, Jeremy Wilber, Dion Ogust, Jon Elwyn, Amy Raff, Jean Gaede, the Forno family, Bill Harder Sr., Marion Cunningham, Mary Elwyn, Beverly Sweeney, Adele Varney Rose, Jill Peacock DeLisio, the Baumgarten family, Ken Peterson, Jeanne Shultis, Lorin and Shirley Rose, Craig Balmer, Gary and Sharon Reynolds, David Rose, Judson Smith, the Van Kleeck family, the Volz family, Rowena Wilber Koester, the Snyder family, Denise Clark, Woodstock Library, Frank Engel, Barbara Vos Moorman, Ray Bryant, and Brett Munson.

Please note that due to space limitations, lack of biographical detail or photographs, and an effort to provide a broad view of the history of Woodstock, some historical figures have not been included in this book. For example, it was impossible to list every important artist or musician who has graced Woodstock's cultural scene over the years. As a result, we have chosen to include those Woodstockers whose vision and efforts fundamentally impacted the arrival and growth of the arts in Woodstock or whose work in other areas of community service provided a vital contribution to the welfare of Woodstock. This work also does not feature, for the most part, those of us lucky enough to currently enjoy the fruits of Woodstock life. It is our hope that a second edition will, some day, include all those deserving individuals who have helped shaped the full character of Woodstock.

The reader is encouraged to further explore Woodstock's past through the works of Alf Evers and by visiting the Historical Society of Woodstock, the Woodstock Library, the Woodstock Byrdcliffe Guild, or the Woodstock Artists Association and Museum. Additional works by the authors of this book are also available.

INTRODUCTION

Woodstock, New York, is both a physical place and a state of being. Carved from the original Hardenbergh Patent by Robert Livingston and created by an official act of the New York State Legislature in 1787, the fabric that is the history of Woodstock has been intricately woven from the threads of lives that have lived and labored beneath the face of Overlook Mountain in the heart of New York's Catskill Mountains.

Born out of a wilderness that was, at the time, the western frontier of a new nation, Woodstock is a town that has uniquely known both isolation and the impact of worldwide attention. Internally, it has born the battles that come from change and from the age-old conflict between old and new. As a result, Woodstock's "legendary locals" have emerged from a variety of backgrounds and unique circumstances.

Many of the individuals cited in the pages that follow were lifelong residents of Woodstock, members of proud families that sustained themselves during the town's early years through farming and such labor-intensive industries as timber, glassmaking, tanning, and quarrying. As Woodstock's population grew and a community rose around churches, one-room schoolhouses, taverns, blacksmiths, and general merchandise stores, the stories their lives wrote began to fill the pages that became Woodstock's history and remain, even today, deeply lodged within the town's collective memory. The legendary tales they bequeathed were built mainly on the backs of hard work, faith, caring for families—their own and their neighbors—and nurturing a growing community that could sustain them all through both good times and bad.

In the early 20th century, as farmhouses gave way to boardinghouses, Woodstock became known more for what others saw in the land than what could be stripped from it. In doing so, the door opened to a new cast of locals who, inspired by the beauty and solace Woodstock's physical environment offered, arrived in the form of artists, musicians, writers, actors, and even a few "legendary characters." As a result, the recipe for the dynamic and eclectic town Woodstock would become in the 20th century was set. As newcomers began to settle in alongside founding families, each influencing the other, new legends began to take root and grow within the shadow of Overlook Mountain.

Woodstock's legendary locals are a diverse blend of people. Indeed, if there is one word that could be descriptively applied to the Woodstock experience of any generation, it would be "individualism." From its earliest settlers to its most innovative artists and freethinkers, Woodstock's primary strength has been its willingness to accept, albeit sometimes grudgingly, the unique quality of spirit found in each of its citizens. A fundamental respect for the individual has enabled this small mountain town to evolve and endure throughout the years. As a result, each life offered here can be viewed as a transition, both epilogue and prologue, within the pages of Woodstock history. Taken within the context of its own era, each individual story, forged by the past, moved forward to shape the future. As those lives intertwined with others and the landscape, the community of Woodstock was constructed. It is that community and its ability to transcend change that so intrigued one of Woodstock's most noted citizens, Dr. James T. Shotwell, when, in 1958, he told the *St. Louis Dispatch*, "This is the amazing thing about the Woodstock community, that in all the changes of these changeful years, it still keeps in touch with its original purpose. There is nothing like it anywhere else in America for richness of content, beauty of form and color, and the enduring, irrepressible note of freedom."

Grounded in the hard-earned liberties of the 18th and 19th centuries and renewed through the self-expression of 20th, the individuals to be found on these pages provide the reader with a unique social and cultural study quite unlike most small towns in America. From Woodstock's founding fathers to the founders of the Woodstock generation, the lives of Woodstock's legendary locals offers a reflection not only on where the town of Woodstock has been but on the long road this nation has traveled as well.

—Richard Heppner
Janine Fallon-Mower

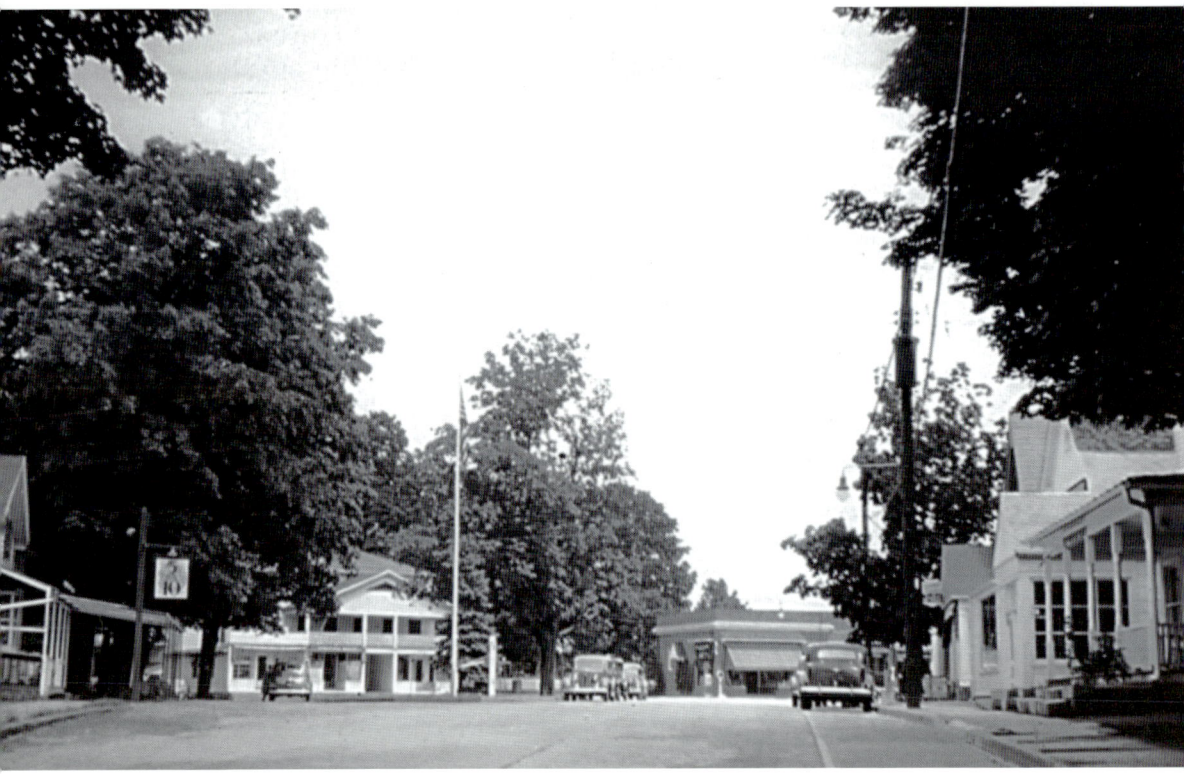

Tinker Street
Though the architecture along Tinker Street has changed little over the years, Woodstock has had a front-row seat to the ever-shifting political, social, and cultural climate of the past century.

CHAPTER ONE

Legendary Leaders: Power, Influence, and Change

Community leaders come in different forms. There are, for example, those who guide or direct the political evolution of a town. Similarly, there are those who, though divorced from the political, exercise important influence over a community's evolution and development nonetheless. Throughout its history, Woodstock has been fortunate enough to know individuals in possession of such remarkable abilities. From its earliest days on the edge of American wilderness, through the economic struggles of the 19th century, to the cultural upheavals of the 20th, a selective parade of individuals has come forward to leave its imprint on the growth and direction of the small town it called home. While their uniqueness as individuals offers a testament to the rich diversity in Woodstock's history, they all possessed the singular characteristic of vision and the ability to see beyond where their lives—and the lives around them—were and what they might become.

It is a trait found, for example, in the life of Elias Hasbrouck, Revolutionary War soldier and, as Woodstock's first supervisor, the man who transformed the idea of a town into reality. It is seen in the writing and works of Alf Evers, whose love of Woodstock and its people led to his gift of the town's history. It is found in men such as George Mead, who saw Woodstock's unique landscape as a resource to be appreciated and shared. That same respect for Woodstock's natural setting is also what brought men such as Ralph Whitehead, Hervey White, and Albert Grossman to Woodstock as each, in their own way, sought to alter the cultural norm in art and music from this small corner of the Catskill Mountains. Meanwhile, that same spirit found its voice in women such as Marion Bullard and Val Cadden as their causes and hard work altered the perception that legendary Woodstockers needed to be of the male variety.

These and the others have been a part of a unique journey. Though mostly separated by the interval of time, they are forever linked in the pages of Woodstock history.

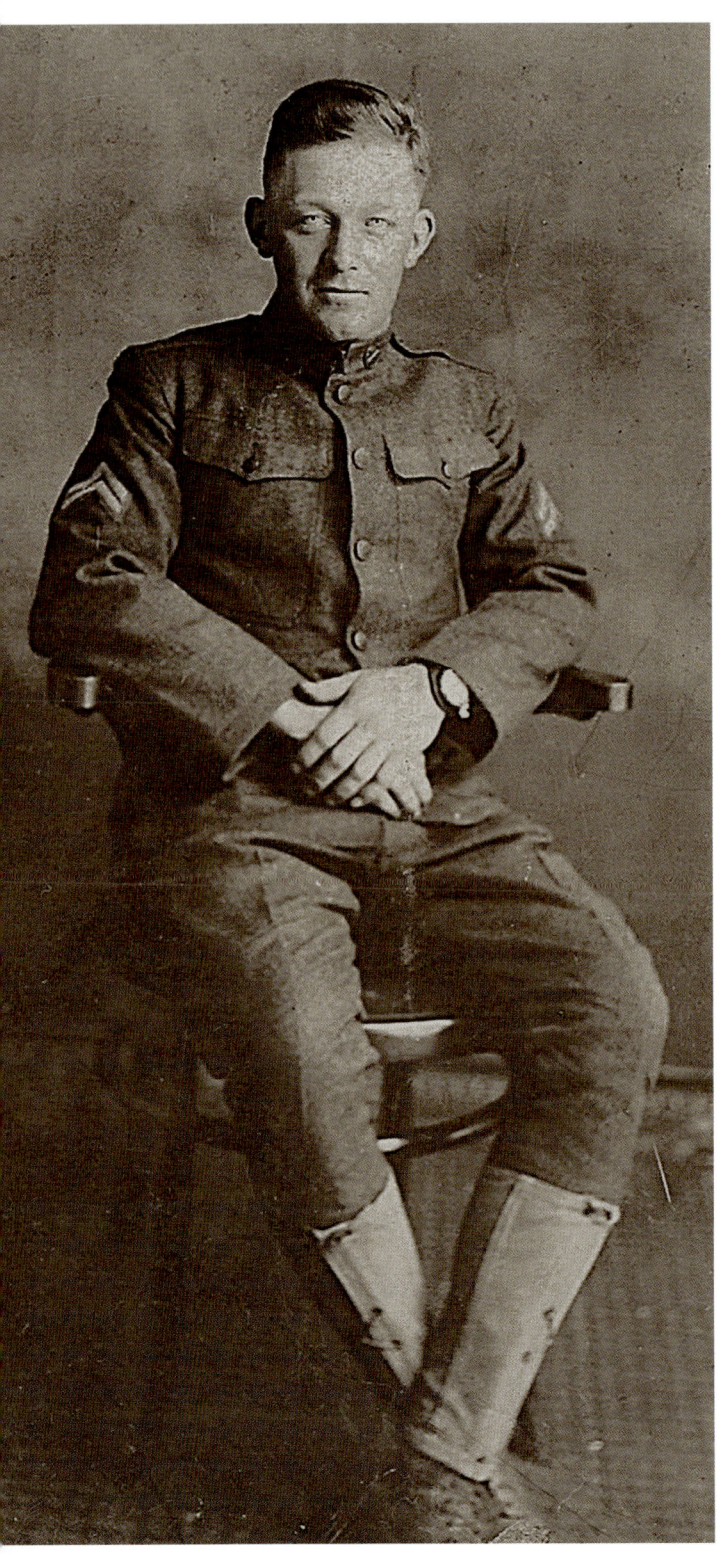

Albert Cashdollar

When the United States entered World War I in 1917, Albert Cashdollar, a member of the US Army, left Woodstock and headed for Fort Dix, New Jersey. In a letter home to his mother, he remarked that a phonograph near where he was resting was playing *Nearer My God to Thee*. He went on to tell her, "I hope I will live to see the end of this war and be back in Woodstock to hear it sung again." Cashdollar would go on to fight in a number of major battles during the war, serving in field communications. Wounded during one of the Argonne battles, he continued fighting until replacements came to his aid. Born in 1891, Cashdollar opened the first garage in Woodstock at the age of 18. The horseless carriage was growing in popularity, and he had a hunch that servicing cars just might pay off in the future. During the war, a large building known as the Griffin Herrick Building had been built on the corner of Mill Hill Road and Mower's Lane. Cashdollar purchased the building to increase the service area for his business. In addition to his commercial interests, Albert Cashdollar wore many public hats during his long career. As a Republican, he was elected supervisor of Woodstock for six consecutive terms and, during World War II, headed the Ulster County Defense Council. He also served as Ulster County treasurer and superintendent of highways in Woodstock. He was a member of Woodstock Fire Company No. 1, a member of the Kingston Elks Lodge, and a charter member of Woodstock American Legion Post No. 1026. He was married to Olive Reynolds, and they spent their years together in a home on Meads Mountain Road directly across from the former Reynolds Boarding House. (Courtesy Jean White.)

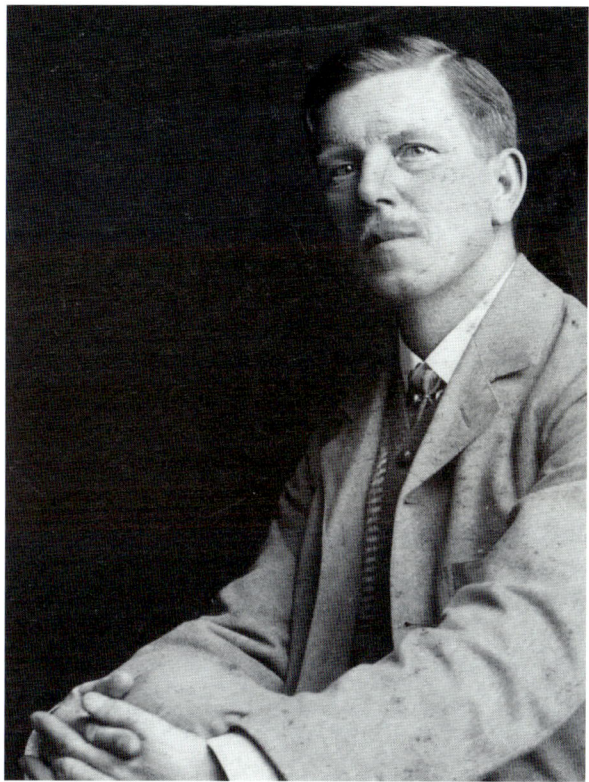

Ralph Radcliffe Whitehead

Ralph Whitehead's vision eventually led to the arrival of artists in Woodstock. Born in England in 1854, Whitehead, the son of a wealthy British industrialist, attended Oxford University, where, as a student of John Ruskin, he was first introduced to the concept of a utopian society centered on the arts. Arriving in the United States in 1892, Whitehead married Jane Byrd McCall, who shared his interest in creating an arts colony. Early attempts to build such a community in California and Oregon, however, met with little success. So it was that Whitehead employed Hervey White and Bolton Brown to seek out an environment conducive to his vision. With Brown's "discovery" of Woodstock, a new chapter in the life of a small town began. Summoned by Brown to Woodstock, Whitehead, after viewing the possibilities, agreed that the 1,500 acres along the base of Overlook Mountain would be an ideal location for Byrdcliffe—a name derived from combining the middle names of both Whitehead and his wife. The goal for Whitehead's art colony, inspired by the ideas of Ruskin and William Morris, was to become self-sufficient by creating beautiful and useful objects that could be sold to support the community. At first, creativity flourished as Byrdcliffe artists excelled at works in weaving, furniture making, painting, pottery, and photography. Within a few years, however, pressures began to build on, and within, Byrdcliffe. Furniture crafted at Byrdcliffe proved too costly for commercial success and, from within, the authoritative nature of Ralph Whitehead led to increasing conflicts between himself and members of the colony. So it was that some began to abandon the dream of Byrdcliffe. Whitehead carried on until 1928, when his son Ralph Jr. was lost in a disaster at sea. Never fully recovering from the loss, Ralph Whitehead died in 1929. Following his death, Jane took over managing Byrdcliffe. Under her direction, crafts, painting, writing, and acting continued to be a part of Byrdcliffe life. Following Jane's death in 1955, her surviving son, Peter, would eventually bequeath the historic site to the Woodstock Byrdcliffe Guild. Though the ultimate reality of Byrdcliffe may not have equaled the vision Ralph Whitehead began with, his commitment to his ideals forever changed Woodstock. More than a century later, artists still work, create, and share in Whitehead's vision of Woodstock.

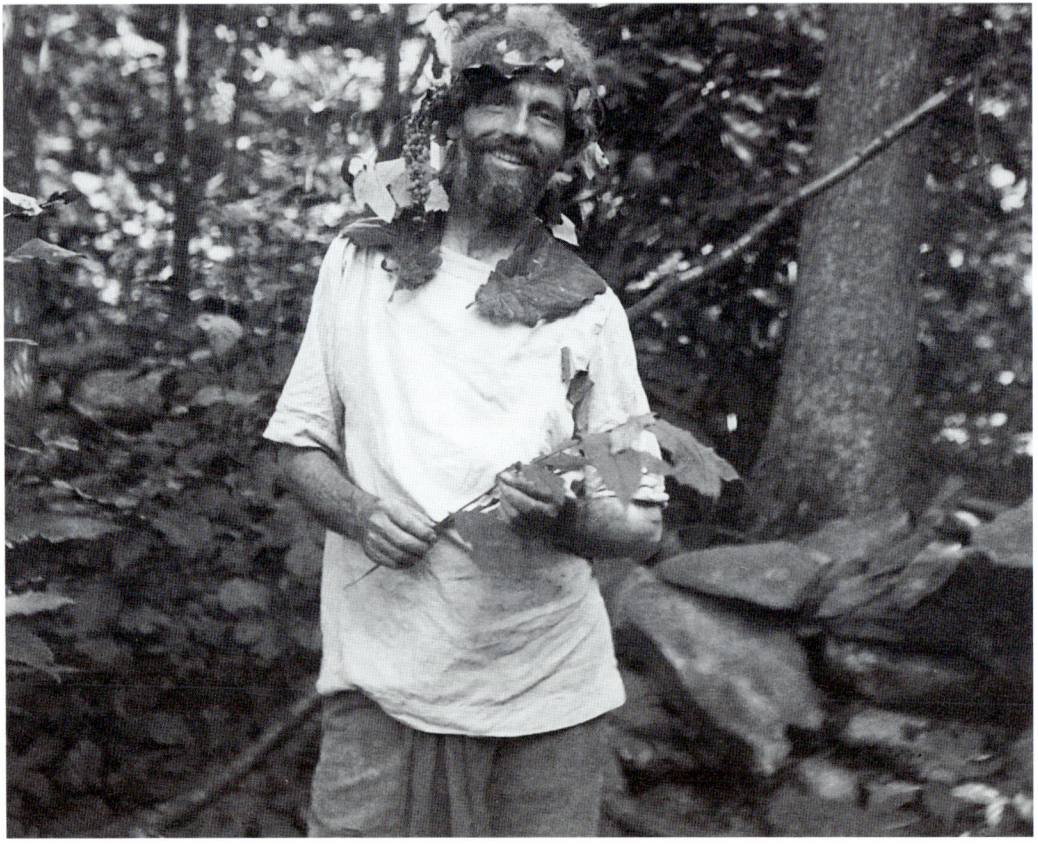

Hervey White

Few people, in both spirit and deed, are as important to Woodstock history as Hervey White. Born in New London, Iowa, a graduate of Harvard, and a part of Jane Adams's social service work at Hull House in Chicago, White, along with Bolton Brown, was selected by Ralph Whitehead to join him in the search for the ideal location for Byrdcliffe. Four years later, unsettled by Whitehead's operation of Byrdcliffe, Hervey White would go on to establish the Maverick Colony. A romantic on one hand yet practical on the other, White's own dream for an art colony centered on providing those artists willing to work with an environment in which they could create. None, however, created more than Hervey White. White initiated a series of summer concerts known as the Maverick Concerts. Still active today, the Maverick Concerts are the oldest continuous chamber music series in the nation. For many years, the Maverick was also home to a summer theater. Actors such as Edward G. Robinson and Helen Hayes performed there early in their careers. Most notably, it was Hervey White who, in 1916, first associated the idea of a festival with Woodstock. His Maverick Festivals, which were a major source of income in support of the colony, attracted thousands each year. Unfortunately, as the sheer size of the festival continued to grow, so too did local concerns over rowdiness. With the onset of the Depression and dwindling attendance, the last Maverick Festival was held in 1931. An author in his own right, White created the Maverick Press, which published his work and the works of others. He also served as editor of *Plowshare* and *Wild Hawk* and publisher of *Hue and Cry*. Despite concerns over the festivals, few newcomers were more respected by old Woodstock than Hervey White. Having grown close to local physician Dr. Mortimer Downer, for example, White served as his nurse when needed and, during the influenza epidemic of 1918, risked his own health to be of service to Downer and the citizens of Woodstock. Often referred to as Woodstock's first hippie, White's generosity and service to others, as well as his love for music, art, and the written word, are reverently recalled by Woodstockers today.

Albert Grossman

Like Ralph Whitehead and Hervey White before him, Albert Grossman fundamentally changed Woodstock and altered the perception of Woodstock held by the world at large. As the manager of Bob Dylan, Janis Joplin, the Band, Peter, Paul and Mary, Richie Havens, Paul Butterfield, and numerous others, Grossman's arrival in Woodstock established not only a new chapter in Woodstock's creative journey but also helped lay the foundation for Woodstock's fame. Born in Chicago in 1926, Grossman entered the music world in the 1950s. Spurred by the growth of folk music, he opened the Gate of Horn "listening room" in the windy city. Coming east, he would eventually team with George Wein to launch the Newport Folk Festival. In the early 1960s, while in New York and establishing himself as one of the premier managers in the music industry, Grossman began buying property in Woodstock. Not long after, he would purchase a home in Bearsville where his new wife, Sally, would eventually join him. Soon, others within Grossman's orbit began arriving. Dylan would be a guest at Grossman's home and eventually purchased his own place in Woodstock. The musical migration to Woodstock was underway. But the "Baron of Bearsville" had a greater vision. Eventually, work would begin on a recording studio. From there, Bearsville Records was born. Purchasing additional land in Bearsville, Grossman sought to reshape his new property through further construction. A devotee of fine food, Grossman envisioned and built the complex of restaurants that remains today, including The Bear and the Little Bear. Eventually, a theater was also constructed. More important than the physical construction Grossman undertook in Woodstock, however, was the sense of transformation that his activities brought to Woodstock. Where once artists found their way to the foot of Overlook Mountain to share in Whitehead's vision of a creative community, Grossman's own work and presence in Woodstock opened a similar door for musicians. And, though the Woodstock Festival was never held here, the spirit and the energy that led to its birth were certainly conceived here, in large part through the visionary leadership of Albert Grossman. Albert Grossman died in 1986. Surrounded by pine trees, his grave lies near the stream that flows through the heart of his beloved Bearsville. (Courtesy Sally Grossman.)

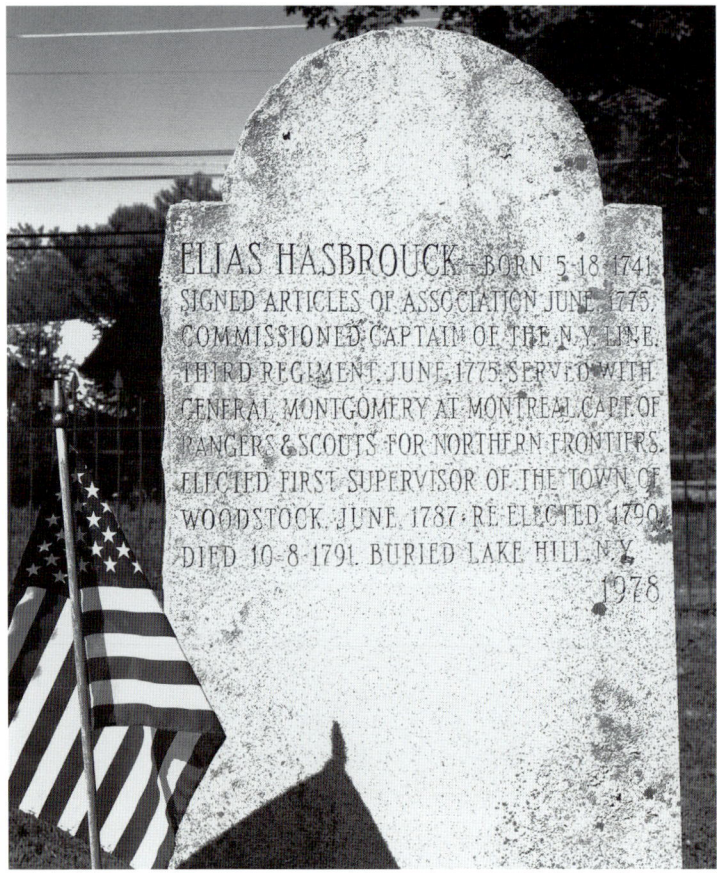

Elias Hasbrouck

Elias Hasbrouck came to Woodstock ultimately by way of New Paltz and Kingston and the events of the Revolutionary War. Born in May 1741, Hasbrouck was the youngest of eight sons born to Huguenot parents, Solomon and Sara Hasbrouck. In the early fall of 1757, a young Elias Hasbrouck was apprenticed to the Livingston family. By the mid-1760s, Hasbrouck had established himself as a merchant in Kingston, New York, where he sold such items as teapots, spectacles, writing paper, and snuff. Hasbrouck also steadily came to believe in the case for American independence and would put both his name and his life on the line for that cause. Following the outbreak of hostilities at Lexington and Concord, Hasbrouck, along with more than 200 other citizens from New Paltz and Kingston, lent his support to the Colonial cause by affixing his signature to the Articles of Association, expressing alarm and concern over increasing taxes and the bloody events in Massachusetts. In June 1775, Hasbrouck received a commission as captain in the 3rd Regiment. In addition to serving with Gen. Richard Montgomery, he also served as a quartermaster in charge of supplying troops protecting the Hudson Highlands, sought out spies and conspirators, and additionally transported supplies on the Hudson for both American and French troops. On October 16, 1777, Hasbrouck, along with other outnumbered Colonials, fought in the defense of Kingston as the British took the war, and their torches, to the heart of Ulster County. In 1785, Hasbrouck moved to the Lake Hill area of Woodstock and established yet another shop and inn at the corner of what is now Route 212 and Mink Hollow Road. Two years later, on June 5, 1787, Hasbrouck became Woodstock's first supervisor following the official creation of the town by New York State in April of that same year. Though elected twice as supervisor, Hasbrouck would not see the end of his second term. Elias Hasbrouck, having borne witness to the birth of a nation and a small town in the Catskills, died on October 8, 1791.

CHAPTER ONE: LEGENDARY LEADERS: POWER, INFLUENCE, AND CHANGE

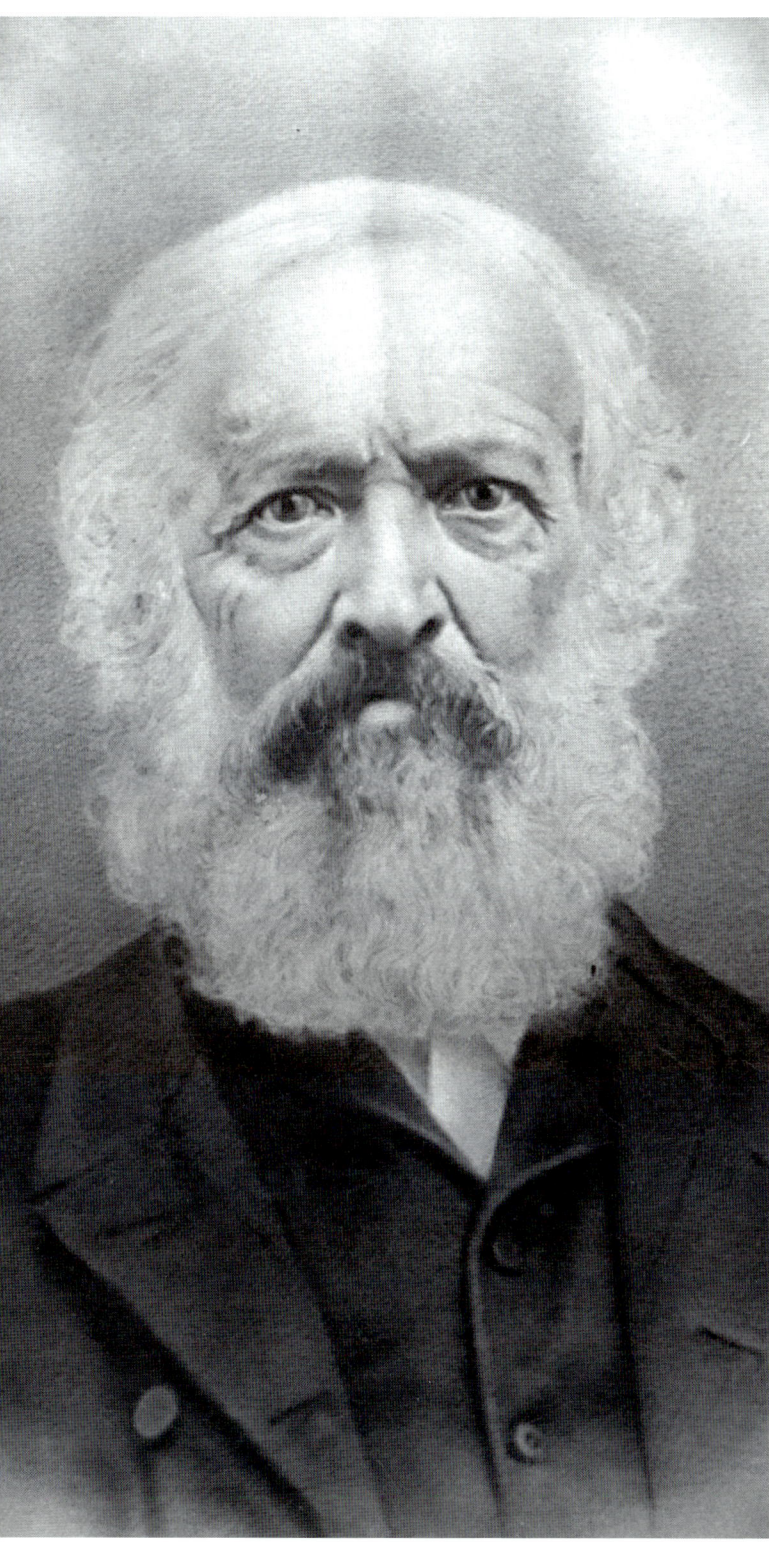

Christian Baehr

When most visitors to Woodstock pass through the hamlet of Bearsville, they instinctively believe that the name must have derived from a former abundance of bears in the area. While bears are, to this day, no strangers to Bearsville, the hamlet's name actually comes from the last name of one of Woodstock's more eminent citizens, Christian Baehr. Born in Germany in 1797, Baehr arrived in the United States at the age of 23. In 1839, he married Catherine Daily of Greene County. Their daughter Wihelmina was born in 1846. For many years, Baehr ran a store in the area that would eventually carry his name. At one time, he was also the partner of Wesley Shultis, a Woodstock farmer of means. Baehr would eventually lead the push to establish a post office in Bearsville and, when his effort succeeded, was named as the hamlet's first postmaster. A Democrat in a decidedly Republican town, Baehr would later move to Saugerties, New York, and finally to Malden, New York, where he would live out the remainder of his life on a 150-acre farm. Christian Baehr died in 1882 and, along with his wife, who died 10 years later, is buried in the Woodstock Cemetery. His great-great grandson Birge Simmons was a locally well-known farmer and insurance agent who also resided in Bearsville.

Alf Evers

Through his classic work of local history, *Woodstock—History of an American Town*, Alf Evers shaped Woodstock's sense of place like no one else. In addition, through his other major works, Evers did much the same for the Catskills and the city of Kingston, New York. In *The Catskills, From Wilderness to Woodstock*, he underscored the sense of shared history of the region. And at the age of 99, not long before his death, his work *Kingston—City on the Hudson* did much the same for New York's first capital. Arriving in Woodstock in the 1930s, Evers began his writing career as an author of children's books. His *Treasure of Watchdog Mountain*, for example, was an attempt to teach children about the relationship between humans and the land and is illustrative of the concern for ecology found in all his works. Throughout his life, in fact, Evers's voice was an important part of efforts to preserve Woodstock and the Catskills. Alf Evers was Woodstock's first town historian and also served as president of the Historical Society of Woodstock for many years.

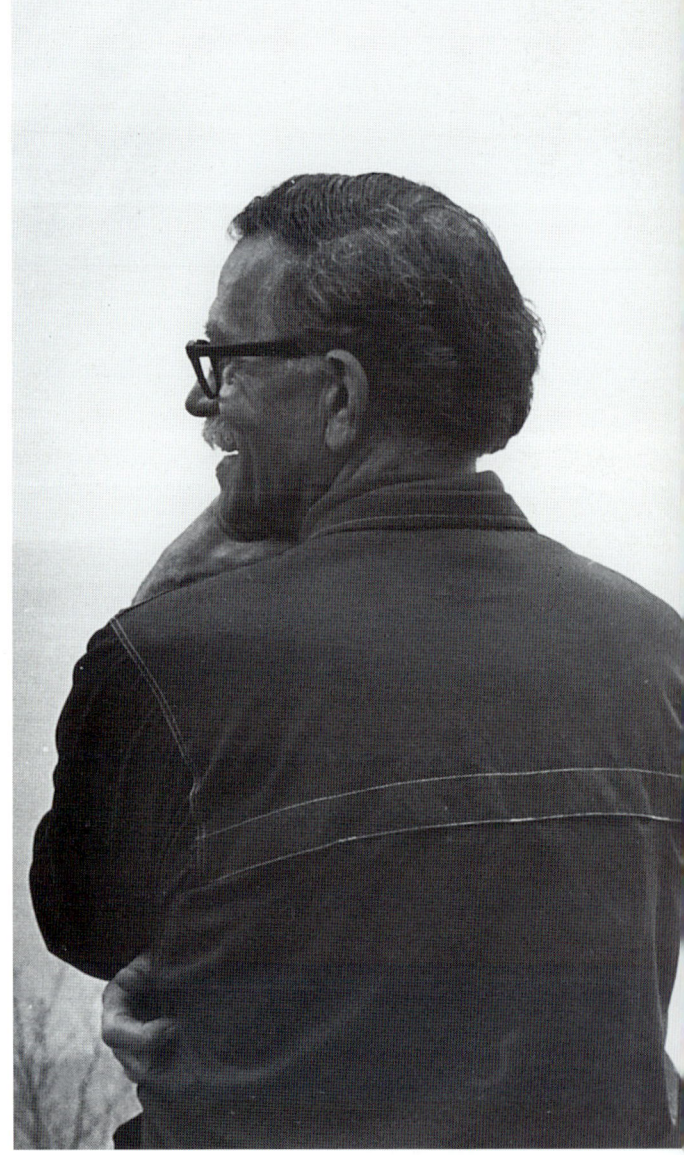

Always the ultimate historian, Evers immersed himself in research, folklore, oral histories, historical architecture, myths and legends, and how things worked. Needless to say, his talks, presentations, history walks, and the exhibits he assisted with were must-attend events in Woodstock. Alf Evers died just shy of his 100th birthday in 2004. He worked right up till his death, putting the finishing touches on his Kingston book. And even at 99, he had plans to continue writing. Through his essays, stories, and major works, Alf Evers constructed the foundation upon which Woodstock's story continues to build. Beloved by all who ever had the opportunity to talk with him or who heard him speak, the Town of Woodstock, following his death, honored Evers's memory with the park that now bears his name at the site of the Historical Society of Woodstock and, each year, by bestowing the Alf Evers Volunteer of the Year Award on one Woodstocker who, over his or her lifetime, has given back to the community.

CHAPTER ONE: LEGENDARY LEADERS: POWER, INFLUENCE, AND CHANGE

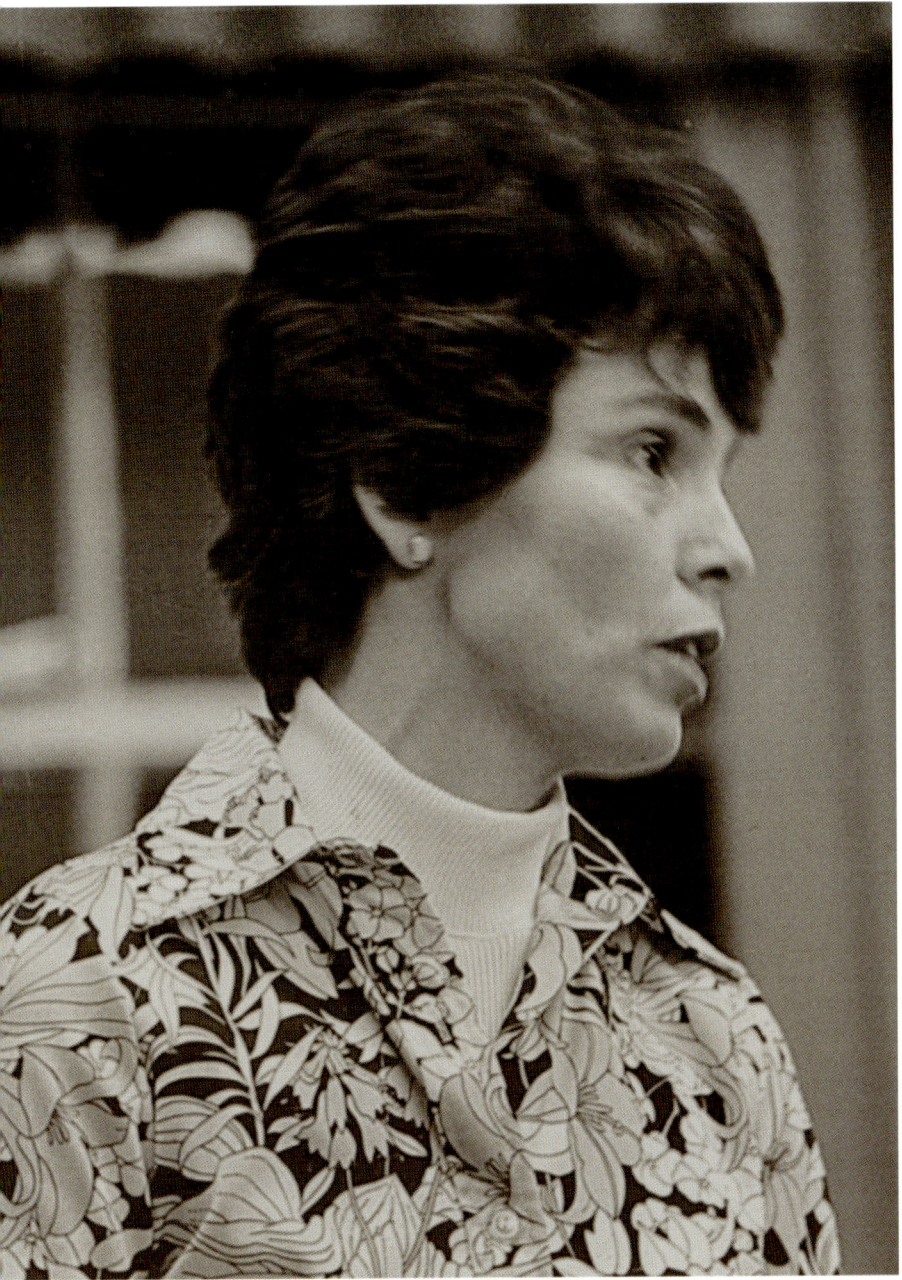

Carol Harder

Born in New Jersey, Carol Harder grew to know Woodstock during summer visits to the town that would eventually become her home. Following her marriage to Bill Harder, who went on to become Woodstock's water superintendent and highway supervisor, Carol began a local political career of her own when she was appointed to the town board following the resignation of Richard Hilton. Entering local politics at a time when Woodstock's political sands were shifting from a Republican-dominated town to a Democratic one, Harder, a Republican, held forth on the Woodstock Town Board for eight years before resigning at the end of 1986. During her service to Woodstock, she participated in the decision by the board to purchase the 78-acre Comeau estate for use by the town and its citizens.

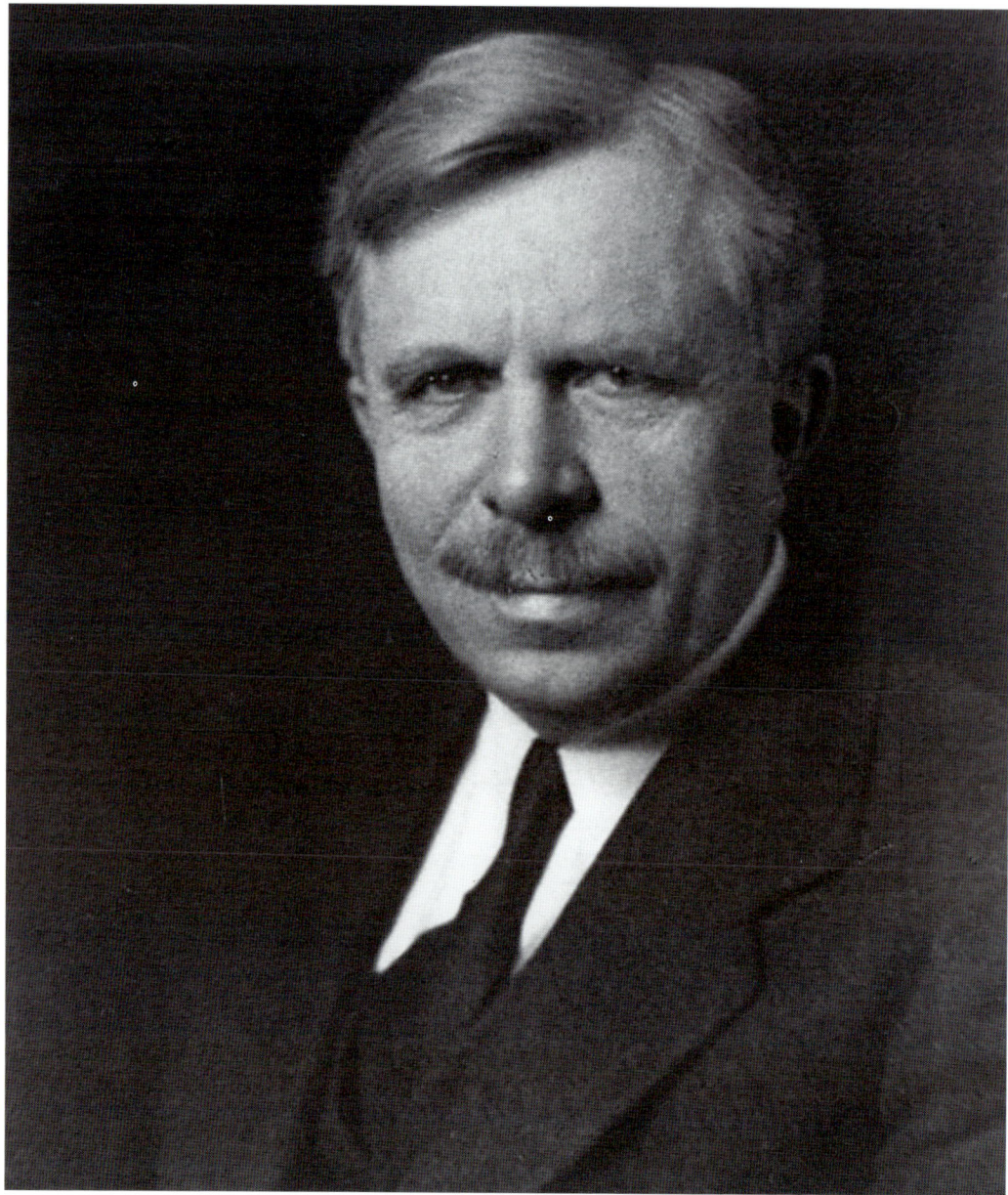

Dr. James T. Shotwell
A longtime Woodstocker, James Shotwell's life was dedicated to the pursuit of peace. Shotwell traveled with Woodrow Wilson to the Paris Peace Conference at the end of World War I as part of Wilson's foreign policy group. His work with French foreign minister Aristide Briand helped lead to the Kellogg-Briand Pact, an ill-fated attempt between nations to outlaw war. A professor at Columbia, Shotwell also served as the president of the Carnegie Endowment for Peace and was in attendance in 1945 as the world convened to draft the charter that would create the United Nations and include, through his influence, a declaration of human rights. As Woodstock's leading citizen, Shotwell was called upon to address the gathered townspeople on the village green as they celebrated the end of World War II. Born on August 6, 1874, Shotwell died in Woodstock on July 15, 1965.

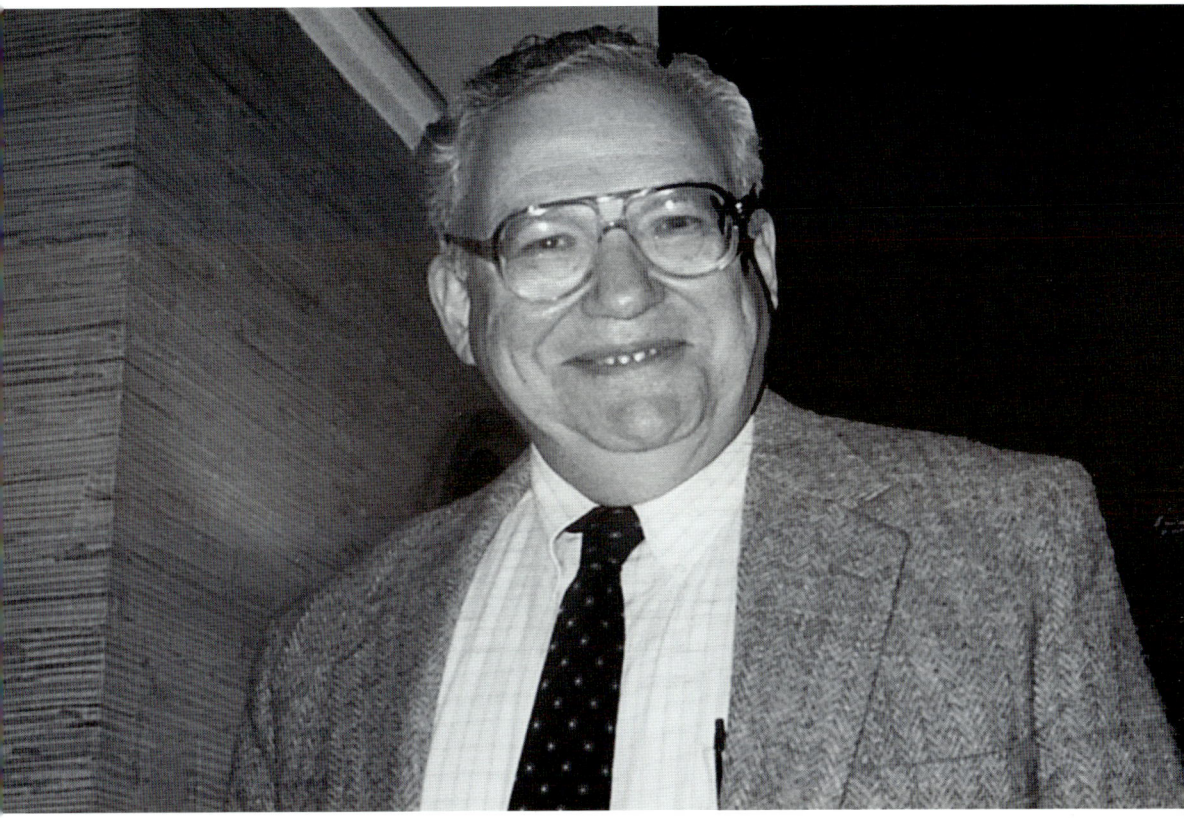

Dr. Norman Burg

A Brooklynite by birth, Dr. Norman Burg was a true Woodstocker at heart. Like many country doctors of the past, no one, regardless of their ability to pay, was turned away from his door. And he made house calls. Dr. Burg and his wife, Sandy, came to Woodstock in 1962 and established his medical practice at 114 Tinker Street. He would later move the ever-expanding practice to a house on Glasco Turnpike. Barbara Vos Moorman was his first receptionist, and Barbara Breitenstein was the first office nurse. Sandy Burg filled the multiple roles of wife, mother, and office nurse when needed. Because of his love of children, Burg found time to serve Woodstockers as the president of little league and also coach several teams. He was also the school physician for Onteora Central School. Himself an Eagle Scout, Burg was very active in Scout Troop No. 34 in Woodstock. He also received the Woodstock PTA Jenkins Award for Service in 1981. Through 1964 and 1965, he could be found leading forums on Medicare throughout New York State. In need of his expertise, Woodstock's community leaders reached out to him during the summer of 1969 and appointed him chair of the Woodstock Narcotics Guidance Council. He was also a founding member of the Woodstock Rescue Squad. When the Burgs came to Woodstock in 1962, they soon realized that he was going to be Woodstock's only doctor for quite some time. By the mid-1970s, the practice had grown such that a larger facility was needed. Believing that Woodstockers would be better served if they had local access to x-ray and laboratory services, Burg set about the quest to receive zoning approval for a facility that he wanted to build on Ricks Road. After about a year and a half, approval was given for a family health center to be built. Known to always have a resident or medical student following him on rounds, Dr. Burg was a cofounder of the resident training program in family medicine in Kingston, later becoming the Mid-Hudson Family Health Institute. He was on the staff of both Kingston and Benedictine Hospitals and held academic appointments at New York Medical College, Albany Medical College, and New York College of Osteopathic Medicine. (Courtesy Sandy Burg.)

Calvin "Cal" Cunningham

Cal Cunningham arrived in Woodstock via Long Island in 1980. Following a brief career in nursing, he earned an MBA in public administration. Considered a natural leader, Cunningham was drawn to local government and served as deputy county executive for Long Island's Suffolk County. Politics being politics, a future election outcome in Long Island led to his arrival in Ulster County to serve as the county's first county executive. In 1987, he took over as head of the United Way of Ulster County. His love of politics, however, insured he would remain active in the leadership of both the Ulster County and Woodstock Republican parties. Cunningham served on numerous boards, including the Children's Home of Kingston and the Woodstock Planning Board. A former director of Kingston Hospital, Cunningham also served on the Ulster County Charter Commission. (Courtesy Marion Cunningham.)

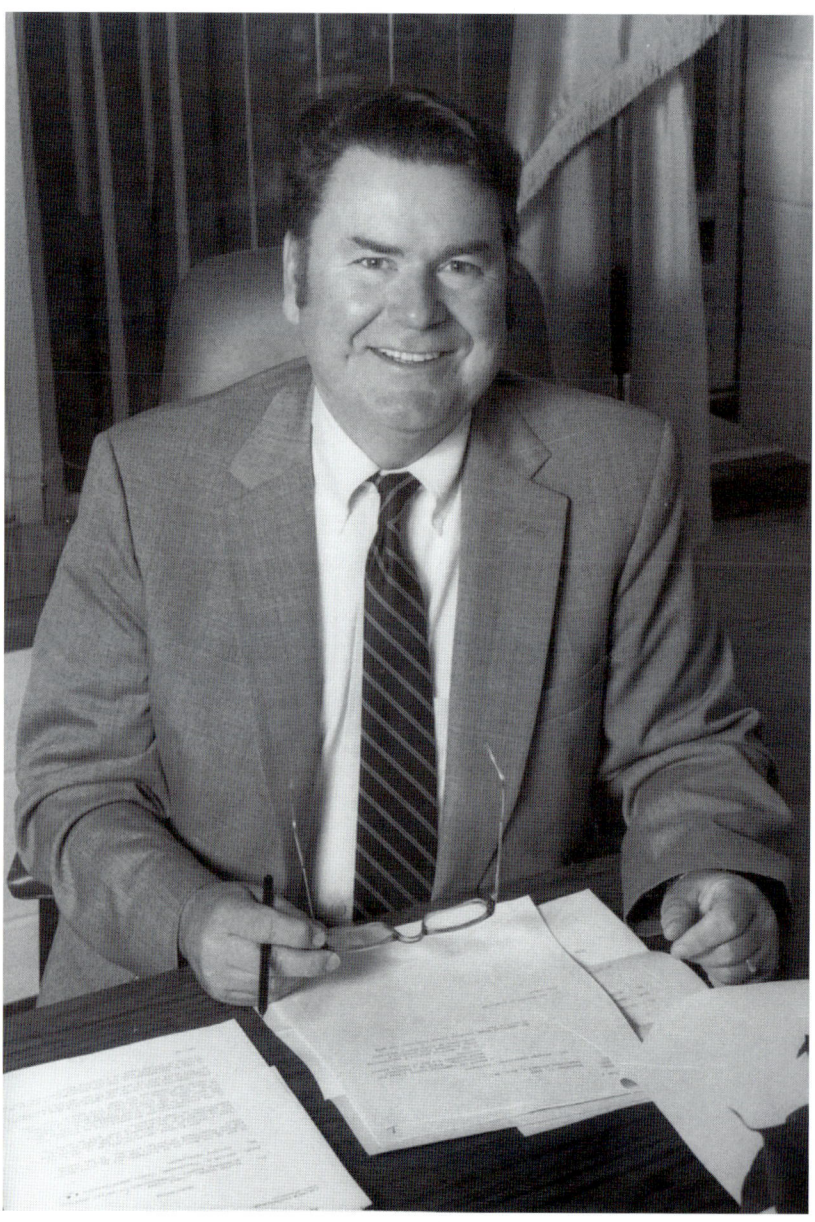

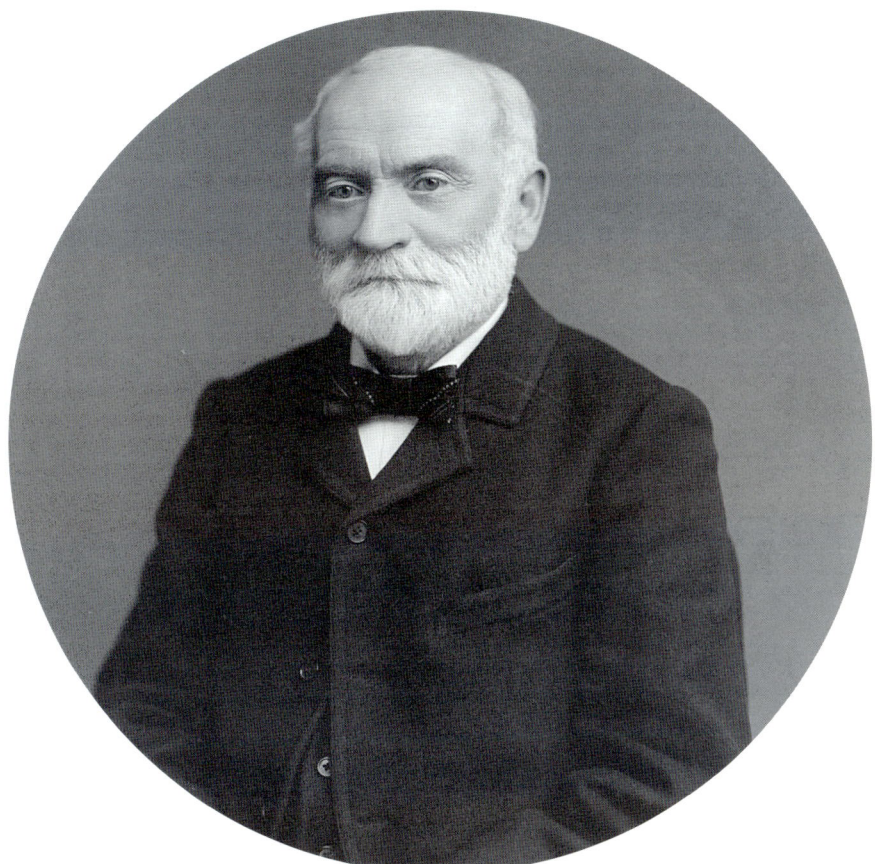

George Mead

In 1865, George Mead purchased property and a wood-beamed structure owned by Henry Fuller on the Wide Clove section of Overlook Mountain. Originally constructed in the early part of the 19th century, Fuller's "halfway house" offered those making their way up Overlook a "rustic" place to rest and have their horses cared for. At the time of the purchase, Mead, who originally hailed from Connecticut, operated a business in Kingston, New York, producing silver plating for harnesses. Sensing the potential for a profitable boardinghouse that would attract visitors climbing Overlook or wishing to fish Shue's Pond (Echo Lake), Mead began construction on what would become Mead's Mountain House. As the business of catering to summer visitors began to become a mainstay of Woodstock's economy, Mead continued to expand his building. In 1880, he undertook construction of an 80-by-30-foot addition, and upon completion, the mountain house could host up to 50 guests. In 1891, recognizing the need for mountain visitors to have a place of worship, he built the small chapel that still stands nearby. (Now a New York State historical landmark, the Church of the Holy Transfiguration of Christ on the Mount continues to conduct services there.) In time, with the establishment of the Byrdcliffe art colony, Mead's often hosted a number of artists and intellectuals. It was, in fact, George Mead who Bolton Brown first encountered while in search of a physical location that would match Ralph Whitehead's plans for an art colony. Coming upon Mead at work in his small apple orchard, Brown asked the older gentleman what village lay below. Mead simply responded, "That is Woodstock village, sir." In 1948, the mountain house passed to Capt. Salvo Milo and his wife, who maintained the building until it became the site of the Karma Triyana Dharmachakra Monastery in 1978. Following an unsuccessful effort to receive historic designation from the State of New York, the mountain house that Mead had nourished through the years was demolished in 2011.

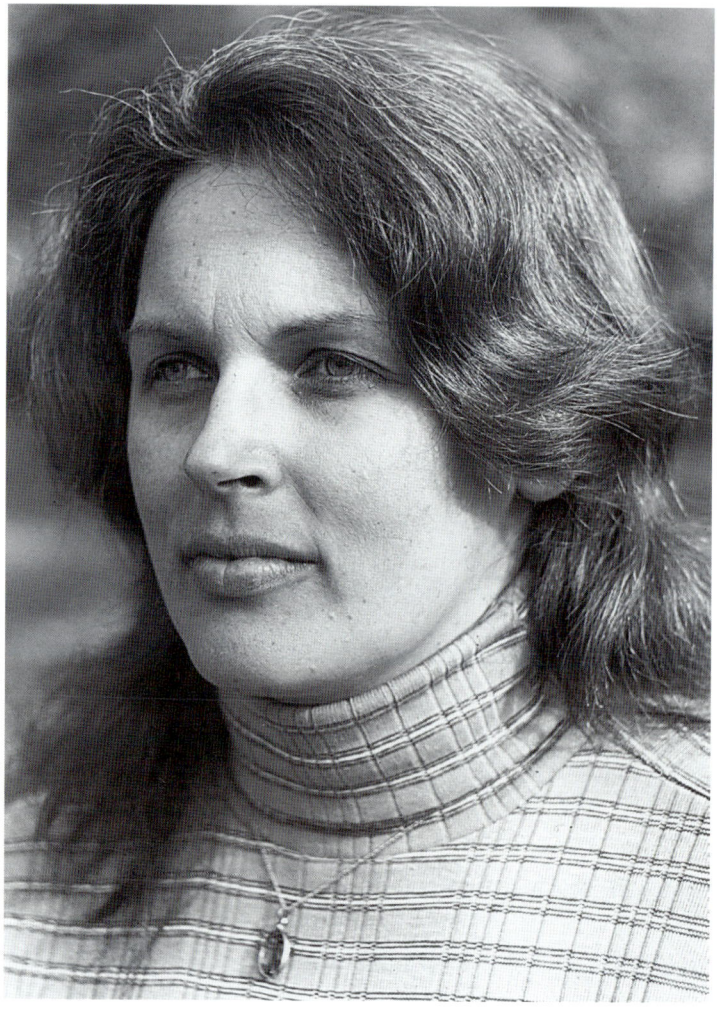

Jane Van De Bogart

Following her death in 2009, the New York State Senate honored Jane Van De Bogart with the following words: "Armed with a humanistic spirit and imbued with a sense of compassion, Jane VanDeBogart leaves behind a legacy which will long endure the passage of time and will remain as a comforting memory to all she served and befriended." As a member of the Woodstock Town Board, Jane served nine years and, among the many important changes seen during her tenure, none was more critical to the town's environment that the construction of a sewer system within the village. She also served as secretary to the planning board, as the assistant to the town assessor, and as president of the Woodstock Library Board of Trustees. A lifelong activist, Jane could be found holding vigil most weekends on Woodstock's village green as a member of Women in Black, a global peace organization. Her commitment to the peace movement was underscored further by her support for Doctors without Borders, Veterans for Peace, RESIST, and the War Resister's League. Jane was also a founding member of Health Care STAT, where her advocacy for reproductive rights led her to oppose a proposed merger between two local hospitals, one with a religious foundation. Similarly, she lent her voice to associated causes such as Planned Parenthood, NARAL, and the Abortion Conversation Project. Married to the late Aaron Van De Bogart, a Woodstocker of note as a forester and naturalist, Jane Van De Bogart was also a vital member of the area's quilting community, having been a member of the Wiltwyck Quilters Guild and Quilters for Peace.

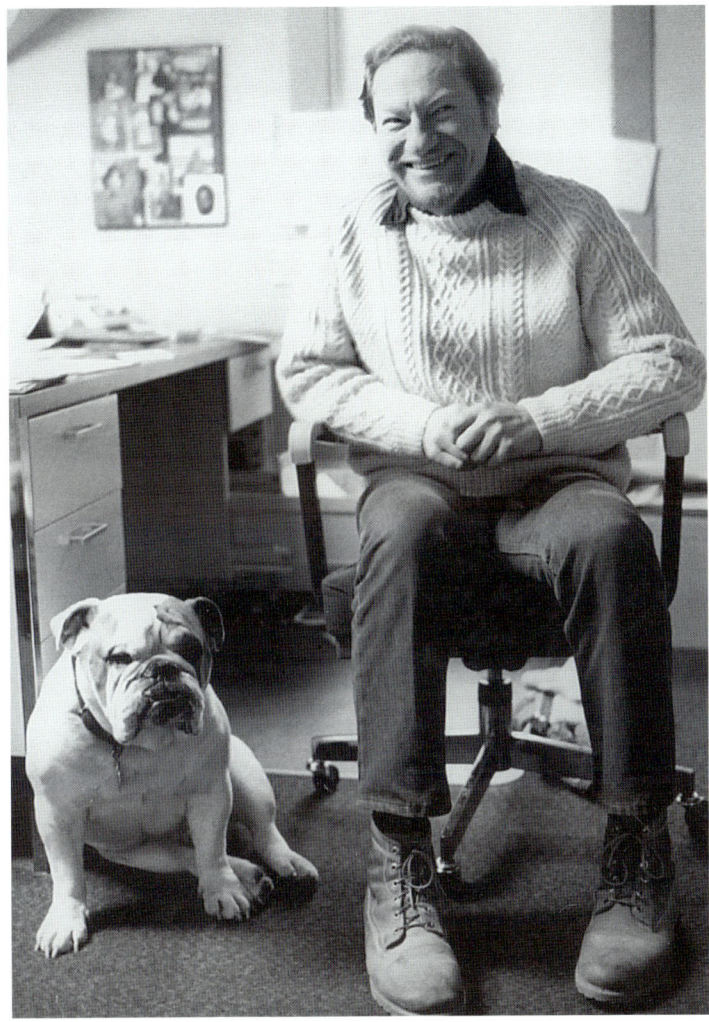

Jerry Gillman

The son of Jewish immigrants, Jerry Gillman was raised in Brooklyn. A navy veteran, he studied English literature at New York University and psychology in Vienna. Gillman began his career as a speechwriter, having once written a speech for Harry Truman. Entering the field of public relations, he worked for the Federation of Jewish Philanthropies and, later, the public relations firm of Ruder and Finn. Gillman and his wife, Sasha, arrived in Woodstock in 1970, first purchasing a cabin in Shady. His inability to find a decent radio station on the air at the time launched a decade-long struggle to fill that void. Over the next 10 years, Gillman made his way through the FCC's technical and legal maze until, in 1980, WDST was finally launched. In a tribute to Jerry Gillman following his death, Brian Hollander, editor of the *Woodstock Times* and first "morning voice" of WDST, recalled the station's launch: "When it finally came forth, what a glorious chaos it was, a bursting, bustling expression of creativity that carried with it the pent up voice of a Woodstock that we all believed the world needed to hear." Not to be outdone by the voices that fed the airwaves over his station, Gillman could also be heard daily. Each morning, at precisely 11:00 a.m., the *Bookstall* hit the air. For the next hour, the audience needed only to sit back and listen as the voice of Jerry Gillman transported their imagination into the wonderful world of literature. Jerry Gillman was a man of many skills and talents. He rode horses, flew planes, trained in karate, and was, as this photograph with Winchester indicates, an unabashed lover of bulldogs. More importantly, he and Sasha were married for 54 years. (Courtesy Sasha Gillman.)

LEGENDARY LOCALS

John Pike
Born in 1911, John Pike would become one of the nation's foremost watercolor artists. In addition to his paintings, his illustrations graced the covers of *Life*, *Colliers*, and *Reader's Digest*. He established the John Pike Water Color School in Woodstock in 1960. Pike would also serve as a member of the town board—becoming the first Woodstock artist to do so—and designed Woodstock's logo and street signs.

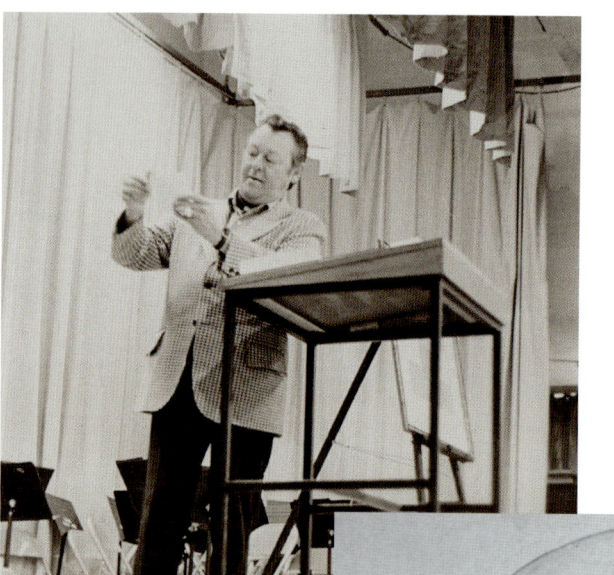

Grant Elwyn
During World War I, Grant Elwyn was part of an Army detail assigned to protect the Ashokan Reservoir. A member of the Woodstock men's baseball team with his friend Bernie Lapo, the two also operated the Nook restaurant. Prior to World War II, Elwyn worked as a commercial artist in New York. Following duty in the Navy during the war, Elwyn served as Woodstock's town clerk. (Courtesy Mary Elwyn.)

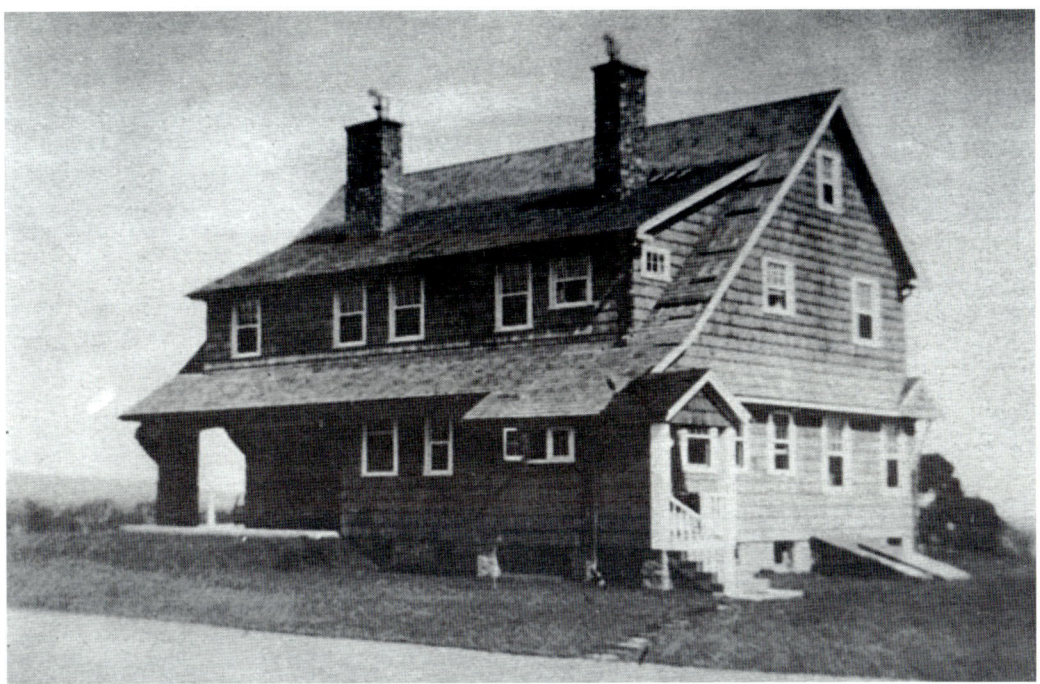

Edgar and Kate Eames and the Comeau Property

In 1979, the Town of Woodstock purchased what is now known as the Comeau Property, 78 acres of fields and forest. While a small portion of the property plays host to town offices, the property, under a conservation easement, offers Woodstockers a remarkable natural setting to be forever enjoyed. The name of the property, however, is a bit of a misnomer. In reality, the estate would be better served were it the Eames Property, after Edgar and Kate Eames, who originally owned the land and built their home there. Both Edgar and Kate were born just prior to the Civil War, in 1858. Meeting 20 years later, they were married in Wilmington, Massachusetts. Their only child, Marion, was born two years later. Edgar's business was textiles. The family moved to Montclair, New Jersey, so Edgar could commute to the New York office of Arnold Printing Works—the world's largest printer of designs on cloth. During the course of his work, Edgar became acquainted with a young designer named Margaret Goddard. At the time, Goddard was also studying landscape painting in Woodstock under her future husband, John Carlson. Inspired by Goddard's description of Woodstock, the Eameses decided to make the trip north to explore. Falling in love with what they found, they began, in 1909, construction on a new home on land that included part of the old Rick's farm. Designed by the noted architect Frank E. Wallis, the exterior of the Eames home incorporated the Dutch Colonial style of the Hudson Valley while the interior carried the Arts and Crafts style of Byrdcliffe. Despite their wealth, the Eameses socialized little. Except for their relationship with John and Margaret Carlson and an occasional appearance at soirees hosted by Jane Whitehead, townspeople had little association with the folks on the hill. When the Eames family did leave their estate, however, people took notice. For, on such occasions, the family was usually seated in their six-passenger, 12-cylinder National touring car driven by their chauffeur, Courtney Rodney. Edgar Eames died in 1917. Kate would live another 12 years until her death in 1929. Their daughter, Marion, who was 49 at the time, inherited the property from her mother. Two years later, at the age of 51, she would marry a 34-year-old lawyer named Martin Comeau.

Martin Comeau

Besides lending his name to the town-owned Comeau Property as the result of his marriage to Marion Eames in 1931, Martin Comeau wore numerous hats during his time in Woodstock. Comeau served as Woodstock's civil defense director during World War II, overseeing scrap drives, blackout drills, and victory gardens. A lawyer, he also worked as Woodstock's town attorney, negotiating an agreement that would forever keep the Woodstock Golf Club as open space should it cease operations. Comeau also served as a US marshal and as vice commander of the local American Legion. Sadly, when Marion died, so too did Martin Comeau's connection with Woodstock. Closing his law practice, he became the image of the lonely widower on the hill. With curtains drawn, he no longer entered the living room of the home he and Marion had shared.

Dr. John Kingsbury

Born in Kansas, John Kingsbury would become a resident of the Woodstock hamlet of Shady. Kingsbury served in a number of positions on the national level, including administrative consultant to Harry Hopkins and the Works Progress Administration, commissioner of Public Charities of New York City, general director of the New York Association for the Improvement of the Poor, and executive director of the Milbank Memorial Fund. At the time of his death, he was chairman of the National Council of American-Soviet Friendship. He was a champion of a national health plan for all Americans, and his support for some aspects of socialized medicine led to charges against him as a subversive. Following the tragic death of his son in 1934, Kingsbury purchased and developed the property that became the Woodstock Memorial Society, better known as the Artists' Cemetery.

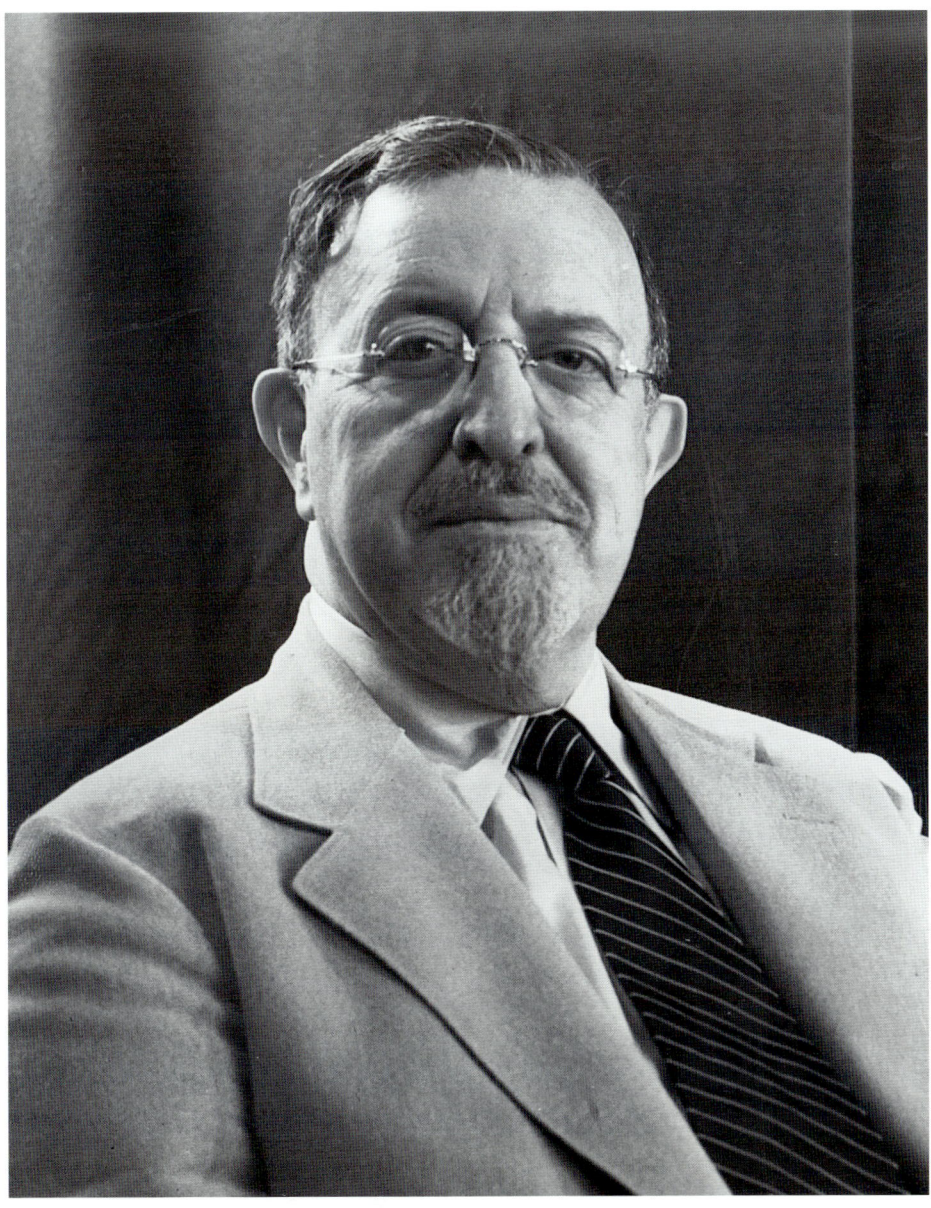

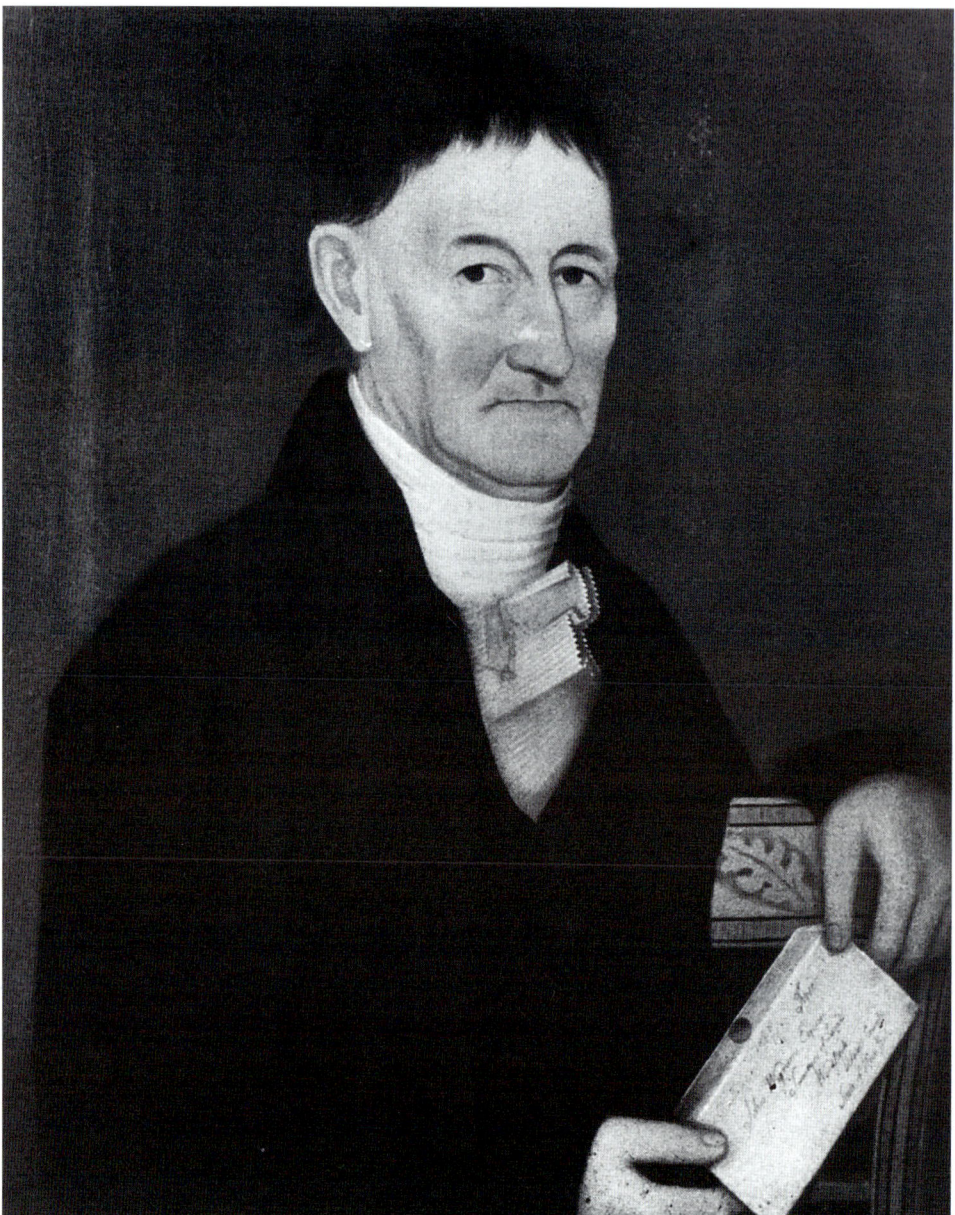

John Wigram
In many respects, John Wigram was one of Woodstock's founding fathers. Hired by landowner Robert Livingston in 1806 to serve as his rent collector, Wigram, in essence, ran Woodstock as the protector of Livingston's vast interests. While most Woodstock tenants were leery of their powerful landlord, Wigram was said to be a fair overseer, organizing rent parties at times or checking on tenants to work out the best possible terms. As a surveyor, Wigram also mapped many of the farms in the area, providing more accurate maps than had been previously known. In 1814, as the town grew, Wigram petitioned for a post office in Woodstock and would serve as postmaster beginning in 1819. Despite his employment by Livingston as a rent collector, Wigram was popular enough to be elected to several terms as Woodstock's supervisor.

Jane and Victor Allen

When Jane Bradshaw was dating Victor Allen, she lived in Highland and worked in Kingston. As a result, in the years right after World War II, it was not always easy for her to get to him in Woodstock, or for him to pick her up. That problem was solved when local undertaker Victor Lasher offered to give her a ride to Woodstock on Friday evenings in his hearse. Once married, Victor would carry on the family business, Allen Electric and Supply Company. Jane settled into the community and would become a force behind many committees and local politics. Her time spent on town committees included 22 years (1962–1984) on the Woodstock Recreation Committee, service on the Woodstock Public Health Committee, Meals on Wheels coordinator, and operation of the Loan Closet, providing medical equipment such as wheelchairs and walkers to those in need. Additionally, she taught Sunday school at the Overlook Methodist Church, volunteered at the Woodstock Library Fair, and was a member of the Woodstock Fire Department's Ladies Auxiliary. In her later years, as Parkinson's slowed her, the Allen living room saw a steady stream of Woodstockers coming and going with the latest news, gossip, and candidates seeking her support in a local election. In addition to receiving the Jenkins Award from the Woodstock Parent-Teacher Association, Jane Allen was honored in 1983 as Citizen of the Year by the Woodstock Rotary and Lions Club. When not working or supporting his wife's efforts, Victor could be found on the Woodstock golf course. His more-than-60-year membership was a source of great pride for which, at age 81, he was rewarded when his tee shot on the forth hole found the cup for his first ever hole-in-one. (Courtesy the Allen family.)

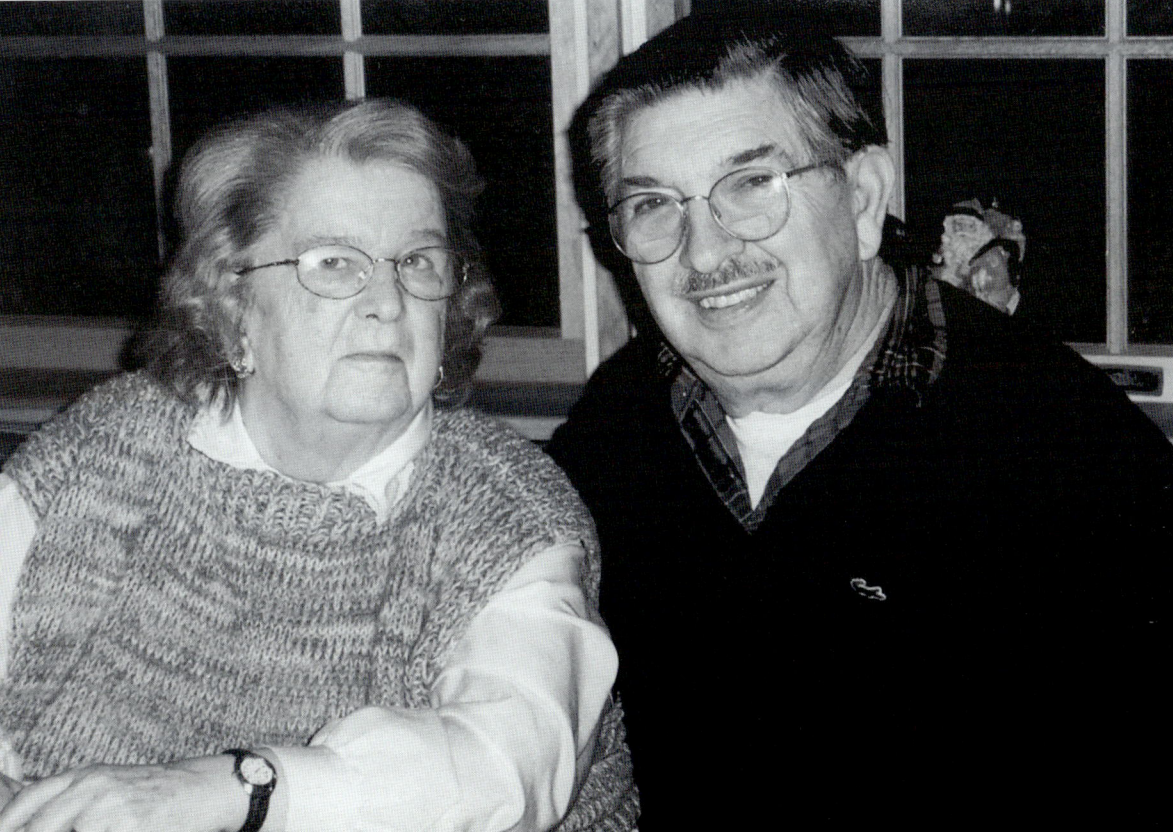

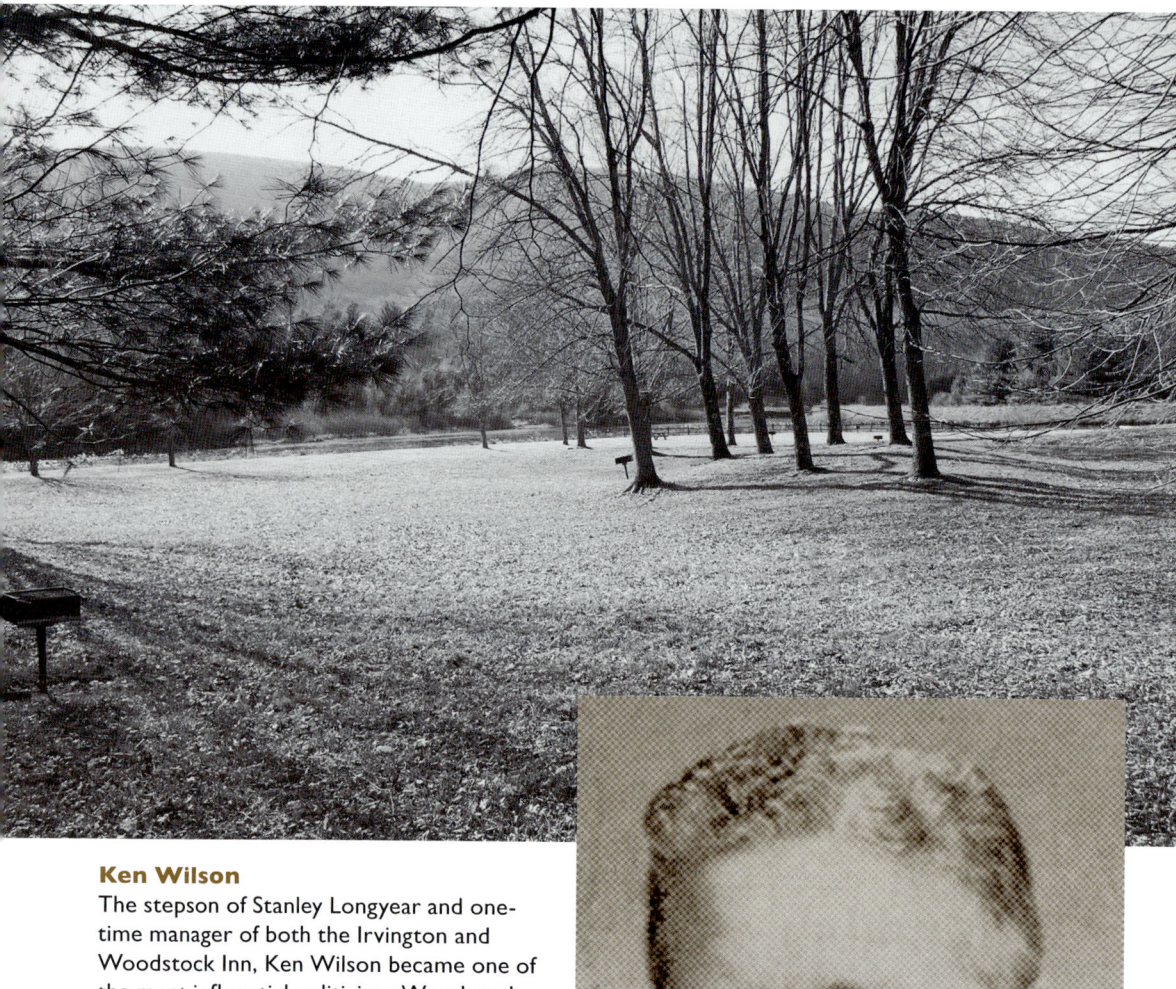

Ken Wilson

The stepson of Stanley Longyear and one-time manager of both the Irvington and Woodstock Inn, Ken Wilson became one of the most influential politicians Woodstock ever produced. A protégé of another powerful politician, Sen. Arthur Wicks of Kingston, Wilson emerged in his own right following his election to town supervisor in 1944, replacing Albert Cashdollar. He would serve as supervisor until 1954. Under his administration, Woodstock would see a number of postwar advancements, including a municipal water system. After 10 years as supervisor, Wilson successfully ran to for state assemblyman. He held that position until 1968, accomplishing, among other things, the establishment of Belleayre Ski Center. Like his mentor, Wilson served as chairman of the county's all-powerful Republican Party. Today, Wilson State Park in Wittenberg bears his name. (Wilson photograph courtesy Kathy Longyear.)

CHAPTER ONE: LEGENDARY LEADERS: POWER, INFLUENCE, AND CHANGE

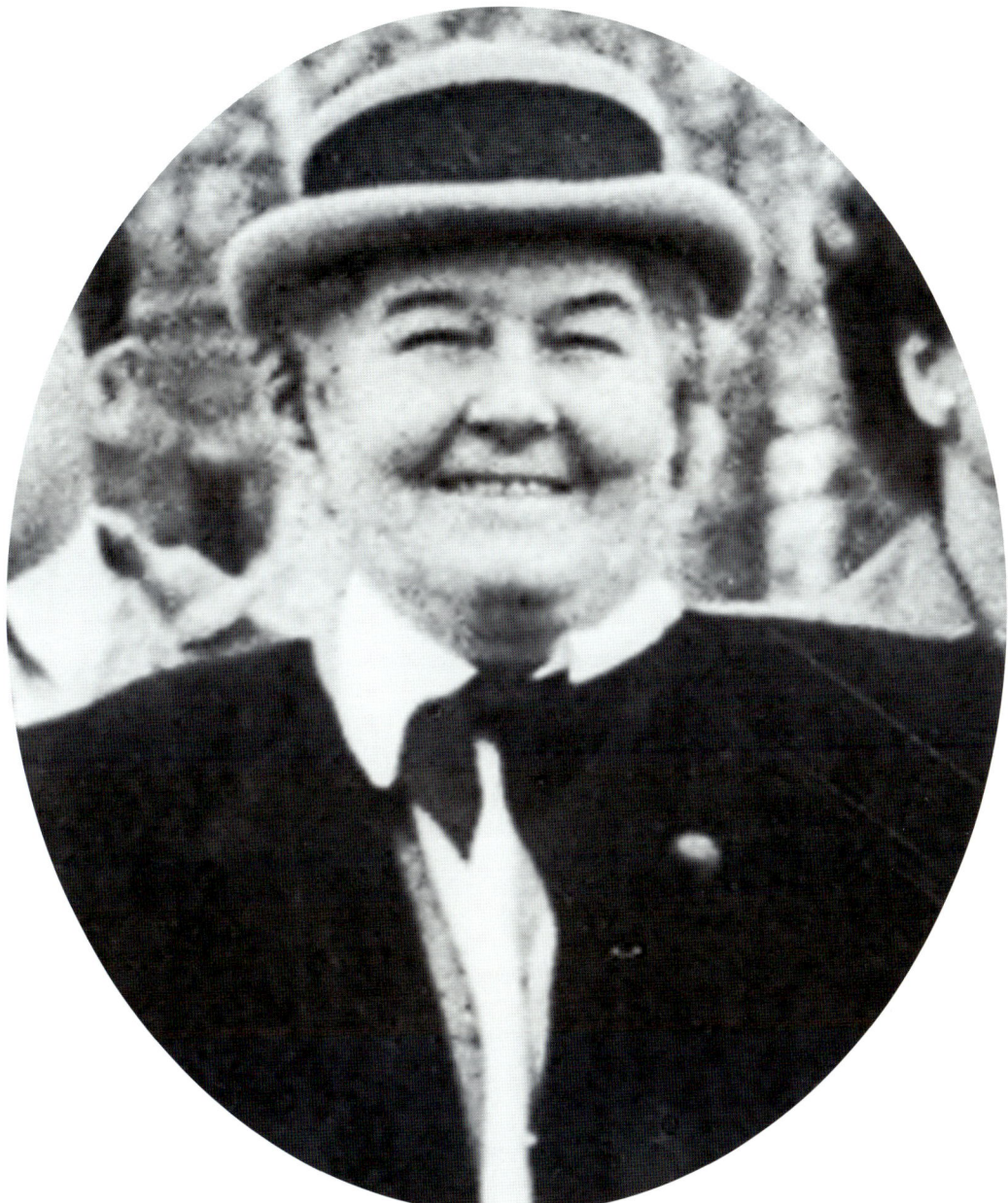

Marion Bullard

Marion Bullard was born in Orange County, New York, and arrived in Woodstock in 1911 to study at the Art Students League. In addition to her artwork, Marion Bullard was also a well-known writer and illustrator of children's books. Uniquely, her characters were all animals who lived in Woodstock. Her love of Woodstock led her to become a strong community activist, fighting for open government, a water system, the elimination of billboards, and a proper elementary school. In an era when Woodstock was a decidedly male-dominated, conservative town, Bullard was one of the first female voices to speakout against the status quo. Tragically, that voice was silenced in December 1950. Noticing newspapers accumulating on her porch, neighbors entered her home to find Bullard dead in her bathtub.

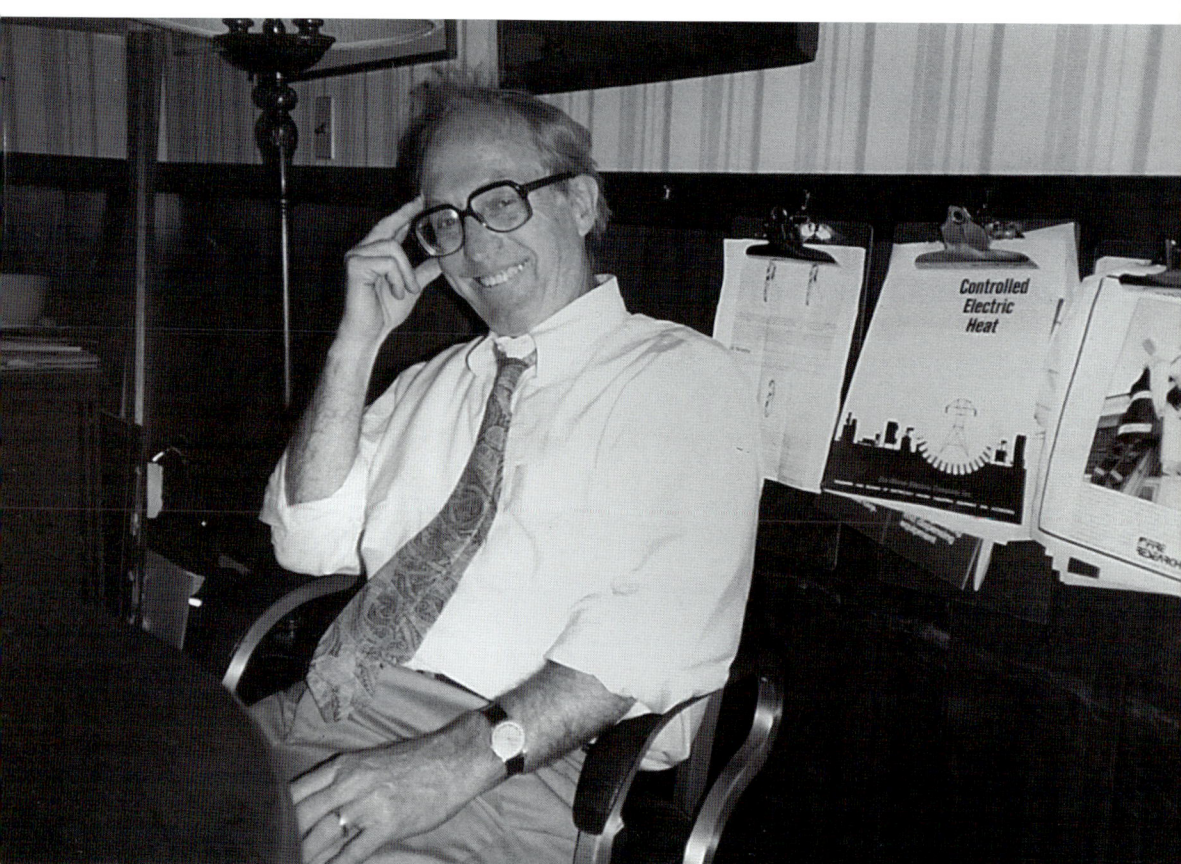

Kevin Sweeney
In many ways, Kevin Sweeney's life was Woodstock; he immersed himself in business, politics, and volunteering. Arriving in Woodstock in 1948, Sweeney, following a stint in the Army and graduation from Columbia, dedicated his efforts to a new venture that began in a small shed in 1963. That venture was Simulaids, and over the years, he would turn the making of simulated injuries and wounds into a successful business, second only to Rotron as Woodstock's largest employer. A member of the fire department, Sweeney, despite opposition, led the fight to create the Woodstock Rescue Squad in 1974. His service to the community also included time spent as town justice and as a member of the town board. Kevin Sweeney was at home in Woodstock, giving back to the town as much as Woodstock gave him. (Courtesy Beverly Sweeney.)

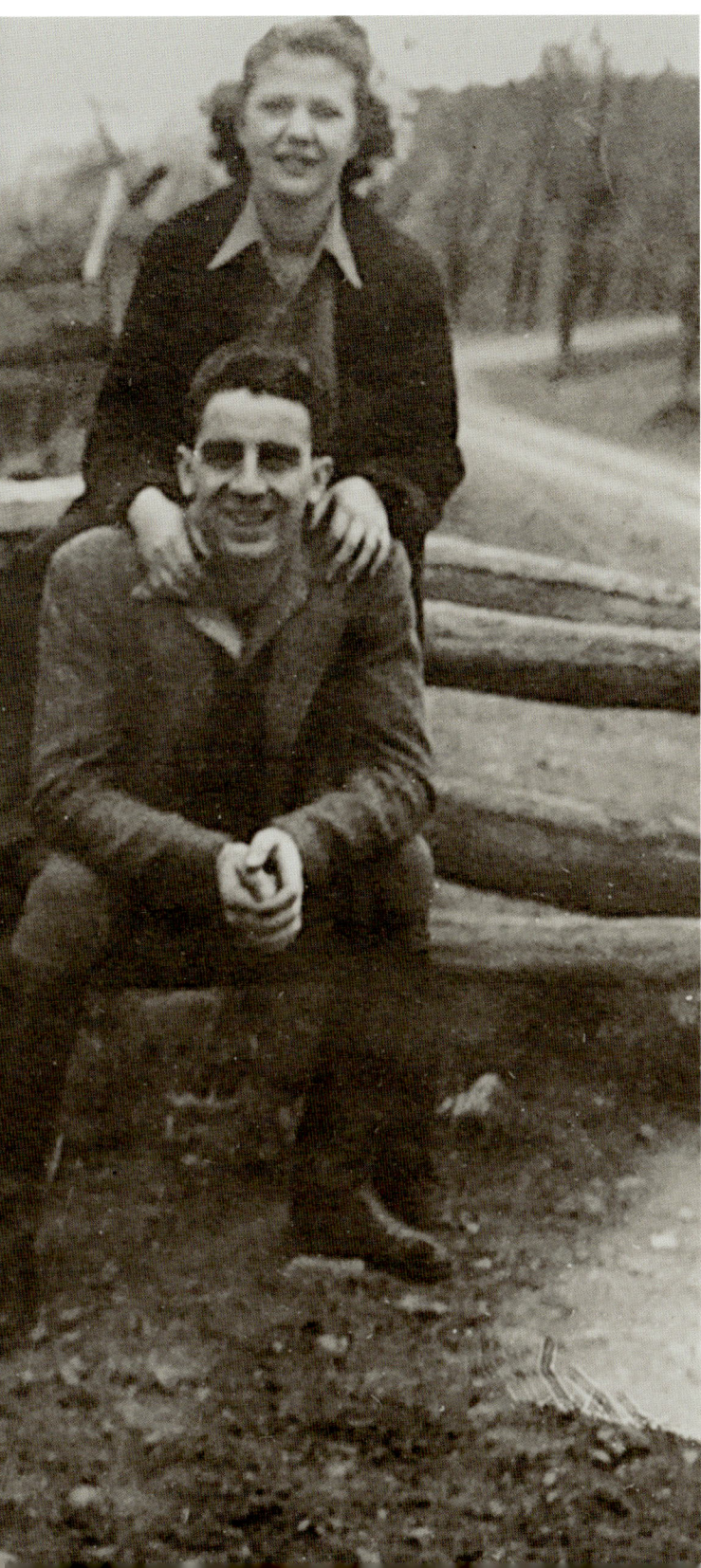

Joe Forno and Barbara Shultis Forno
Considering all Joe Forno did for Woodstock and the multitude of organizations and committees he was involved with, it is surprising he had time to run Colonial Pharmacy. But run it he did, 24 hours a day, seven days a week. Opening the pharmacy on Tinker Street in 1947 and moving to Bradley Meadows in 1968, Forno managed to find the time to serve as a town councilman and two terms as town justice. He also served as president of Woodstock Rotary, a member of the town's Recreation Committee, president of Woodstock Little League, and a member of the Woodstock Little League Old Timers Committee, the Christmas Eve Committee, the fire company, and the Woodstock Republican Committee. Honored for his generosity and concern for Woodstock's children, Forno received the PTA's Jenkins Award in 1958. In 1984, the Rotary and Lions Clubs tapped him as Woodstock's Citizen of the Year. Equally as important, the couple founded the Woodstock Easter Egg Hunt. Sponsored by the Forno family from 1947 to 1994, the Easter egg hunt is an annual tradition in Woodstock that continues today. While the above list is impressive, Woodstockers will also say that Forno and his wife, Barbara, quietly did so much more. Not ones to seek publicity or to promote themselves, they never hesitated to come to the aid of an individual or organization in need. (Courtesy the Forno family.)

Walter Van Wagenen

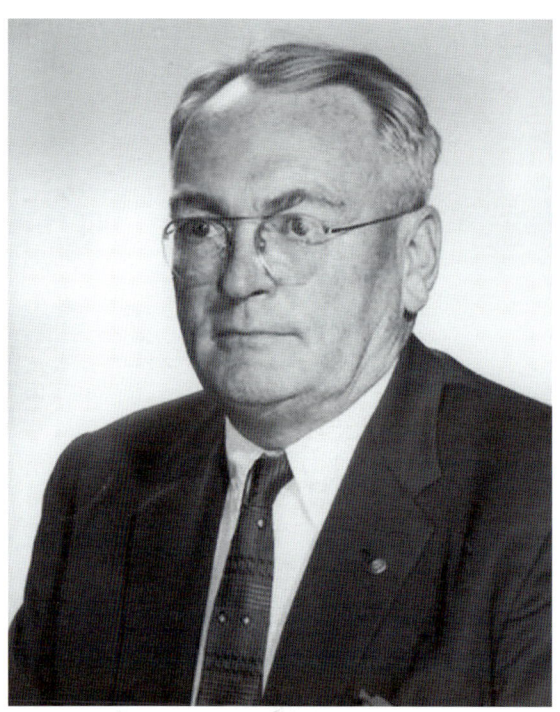

On April 25, 1941, Woodstock's *Overlook Press* reported that Woodstock school trustees Clark Neher, Walter Hastie, and Warren Hutty had hired Walter Van Wagenen as the new principal of the elementary school. At the time, Van Wagenen was 36 years old, married to "Sally" Drury, and the father of three sons. His initial salary was $2,500. Van Wagenen would serve as principal until 1968, making Woodstock the last stop in a distinguished career. During Van Wagnen's tenure, Woodstock's one-room schoolhouse era ended with the construction of the Woodstock Elementary School in 1950 (pictured). Walter Van Wagenen dedicated much of his free time to Woodstock's children through involvement in the Boy Scouts, youth baseball, and basketball. His commitment to community also included charter membership in Woodstock's Rotary Club. (Courtesy Carl Van Wagenen.)

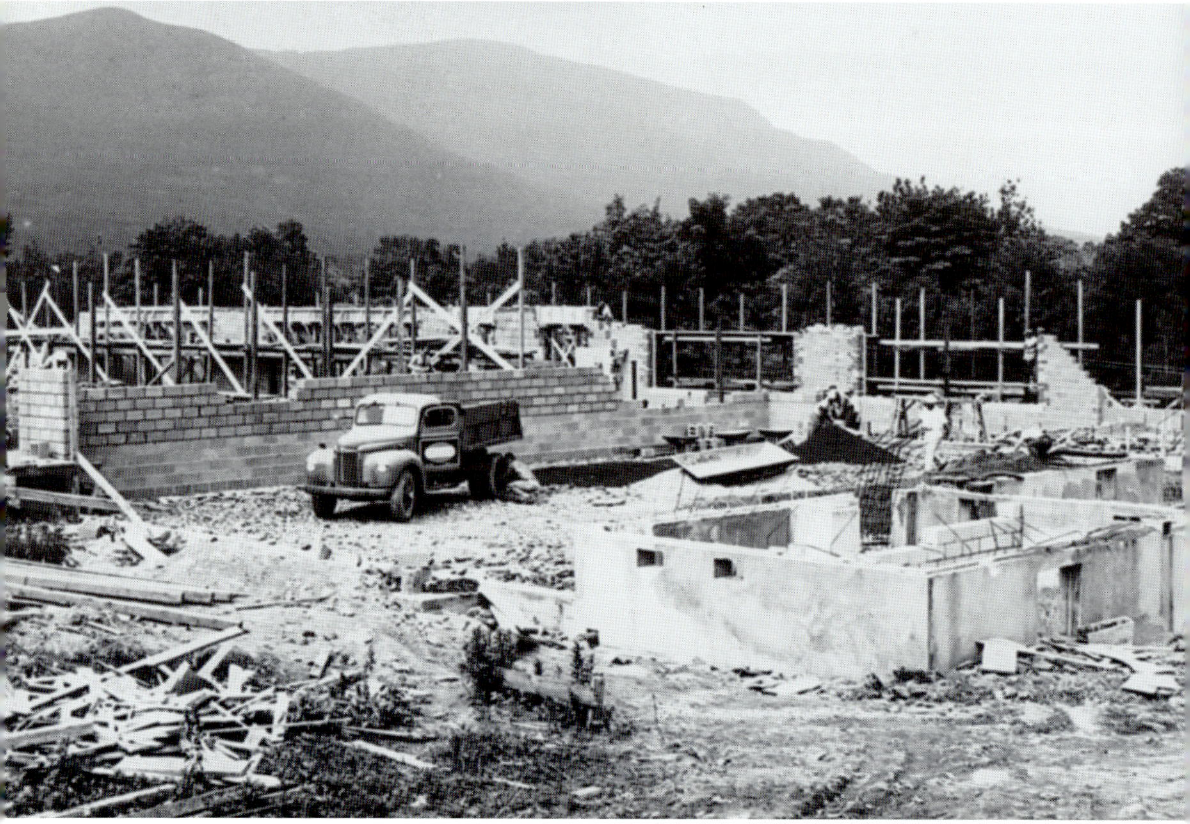

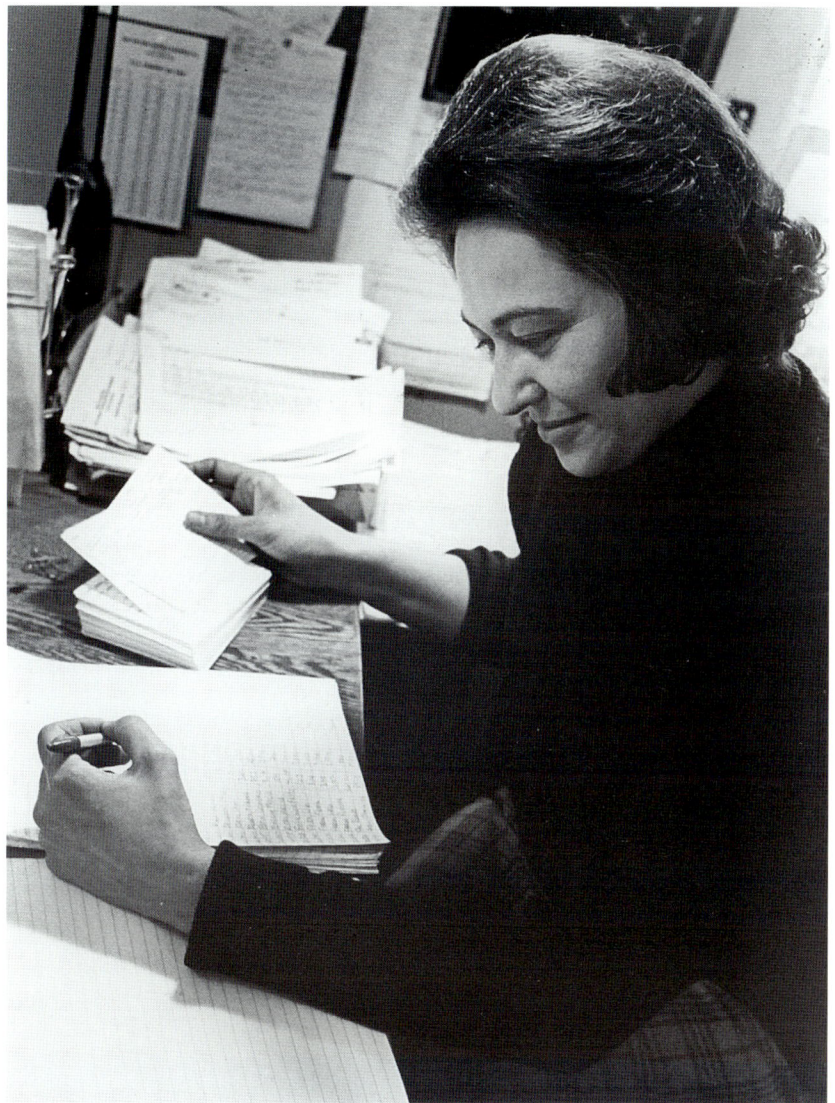

Valerie Cadden

Sidewalks, a town sewer system, and the purchase of the 78-acre Comeau Property—as town supervisor, Val Cadden was the driving force behind all of the above. A shy but determined woman, Cadden first served as a town councilwoman prior to becoming supervisor. Local history will also long note that she was the first woman supervisor ever elected in Woodstock. As supervisor, she found herself in the national spotlight when she grappled with the issue of "home relief" and her refusal to issue checks to home relief recipients who would not work. One such recipient, as the relief rolls swelled with the influx of young people into town following the Woodstock Festival, refused his job of cutting grass because "it would destroy the homes of the bugs who lived there." Val Cadden was born in Roselle, New Jersey, in 1931 and arrived in Woodstock in 1965. In addition to her work as councilwoman and supervisor, Cadden worked to found the Zena Recreation Park and served as treasurer of Woodstock Meals on Wheels and as chair of the Board of Directors of the Woodstock Rescue Squad. She was a member of the Woodstock Rotary Club and volunteered her time on behalf of the Woodstock Food Pantry. Val Cadden died in 2002 having left a lasting mark on her beloved Woodstock.

Mescal Hornbeck

Mescal Hornbeck was long at the center of activism and volunteerism in Woodstock. Most remarkable was that most of her career as a volunteer and activist took place over the span of her senior years following a 39-year career as a nursing instructor, private-duty nurse, and public health nurse. Upon returning to Woodstock to care for her aging mother, Olive Toms, many of Hornbeck's activities centered on improving opportunities for seniors, including working towards the establishment of Ulster County's Office for the Aging and Woodstock's Senior Recreation Committee and serving as a member of the New York Senior Action Council. Along the way, she also found time to serve four years as a member of the Woodstock Town Board, was instrumental in the establishment of the town's community center that now bears her name, and worked to build Woodstock's Meals on Wheels program. Not limiting her concerns to local causes, Mescal Hornbeck was also a strong advocate for recycling programs, ecological responsibility, family planning, and universal health care. Most Woodstockers fondly recall picking up their copy of the *Woodstock Times* each week and finding her letters to the editor titled Mescal's Message, offering her thoughts and opinions on the issues of the day. In 2007, the Town of Woodstock celebrated her efforts by honoring her with the Alf Evers Award as volunteer of the year.

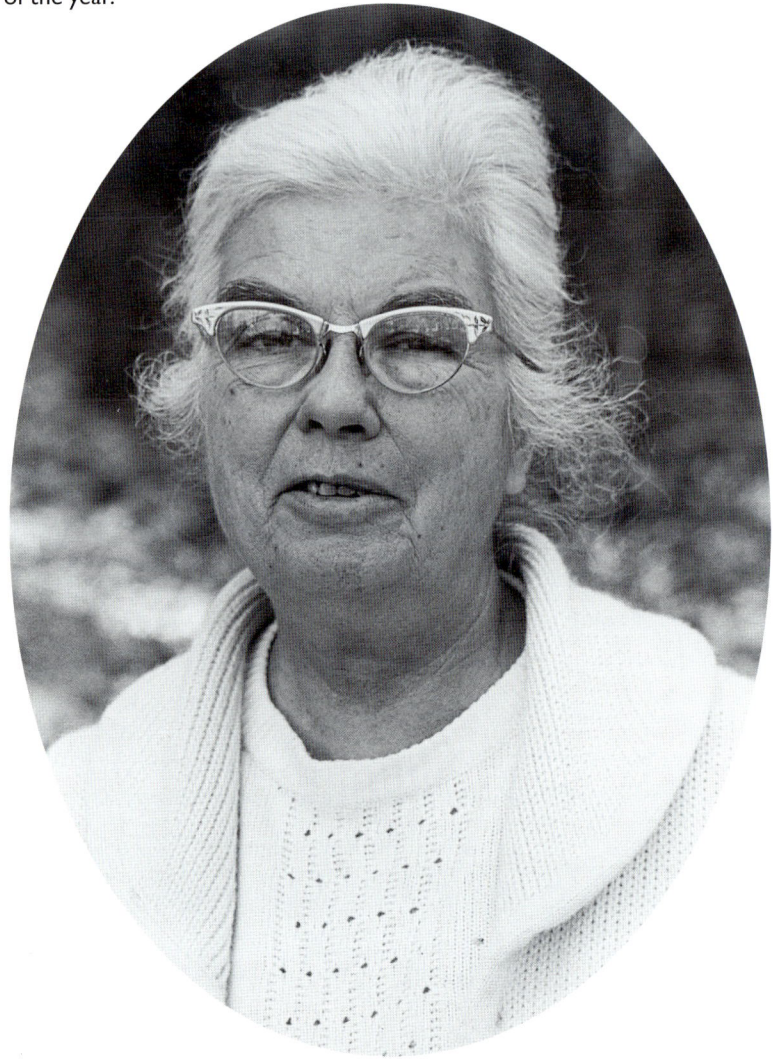

J. Constant van Rijn

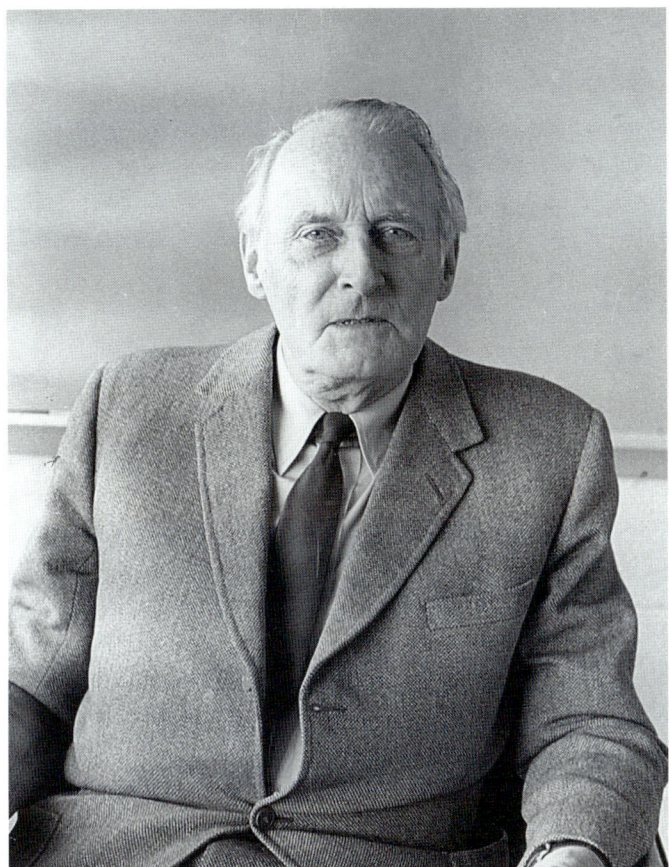

During World War II, J. Constant van Rijn, a Dutch engineer and refugee, settled in Woodstock. Recognizing the need for small, reliable fans for the expanding electronics industry, van Rijn founded Rotron Manufacturing in 1947. The business grew from utilizing a chicken coop as an office and a barn for engineering work to the eventual construction of a new engineering facility in 1961. In the process, Rotron would become Woodstock's largest employer. By all accounts, van Rijn was a man who appreciated aesthetics. As a result, he employed many Woodstock artists while also commissioning their work for the company's lobby and offices. Actively involved in town affairs, van Rijn helped found the Woodstock Association, leading to the first planning board and zoning ordinance in 1965. He was also a founding member of the Woodstock Tree Trust.

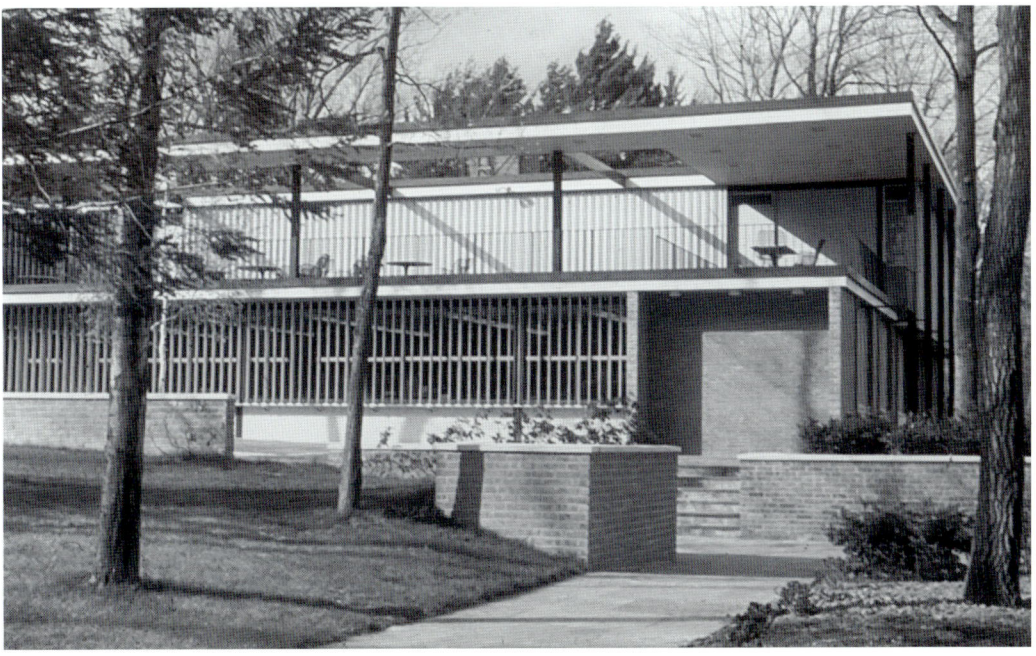

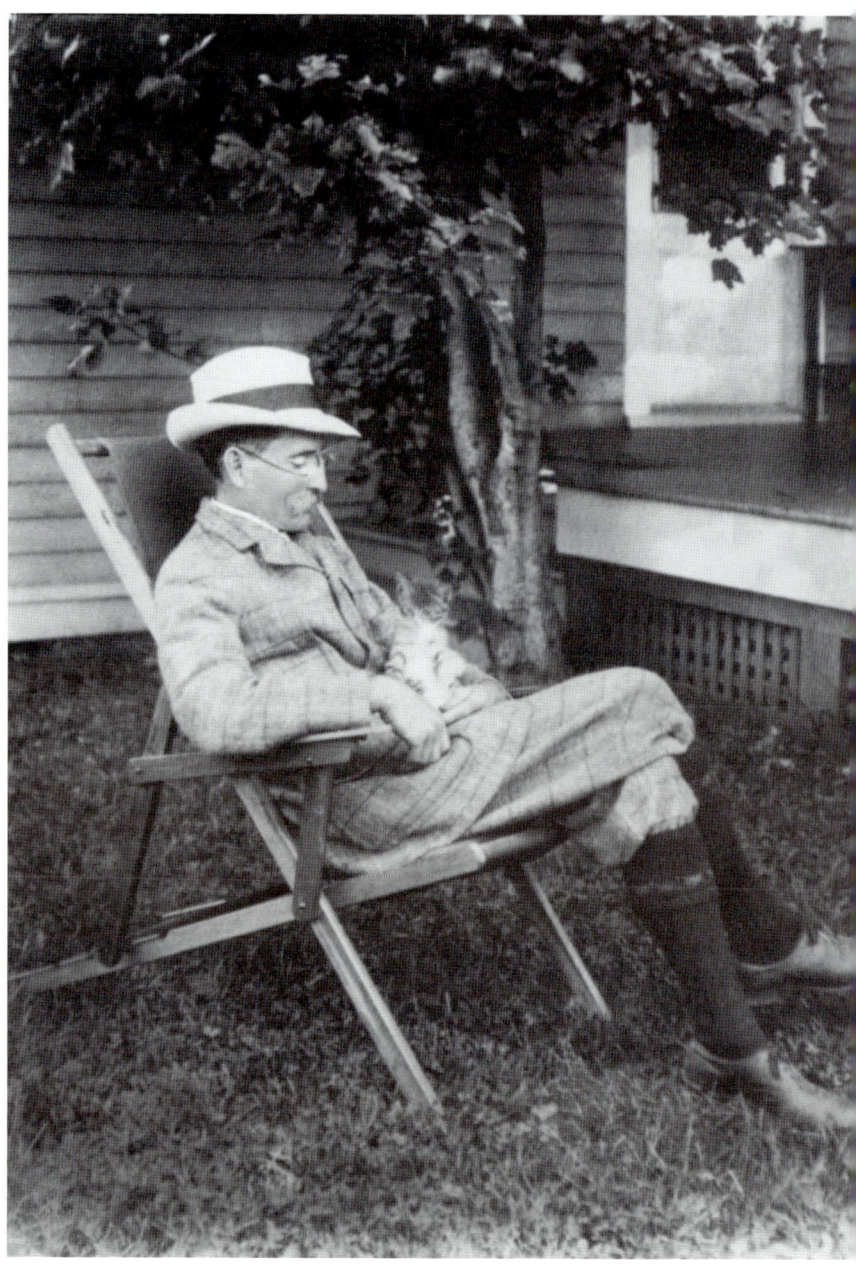

Birge Harrison

In 1906, following a decision by the Art Students League to bring its summer school to Woodstock, Birge Harrison agreed to become its head. A noted landscape painter in his own right, Harrison arrived in Woodstock during Byrdcliffe's second summer of operation. A friend of Ralph Whitehead, Harrison was viewed as a man of great warmth and an excellent teacher. Like others, however, his stay at Byrdcliffe was brief, ending in 1905. Under Harrison, the Art Students League succeeded in establishing Woodstock as a desirable place to study art. In the process, it also began to reshape Woodstock's sense of place as young artists, attracted by Harrison's published accounts of the landscape, made the journey to live and study in the shadow of Overlook. Harrison headed the school until 1911, when John Carlson took his place.

CHAPTER ONE: LEGENDARY LEADERS: POWER, INFLUENCE, AND CHANGE

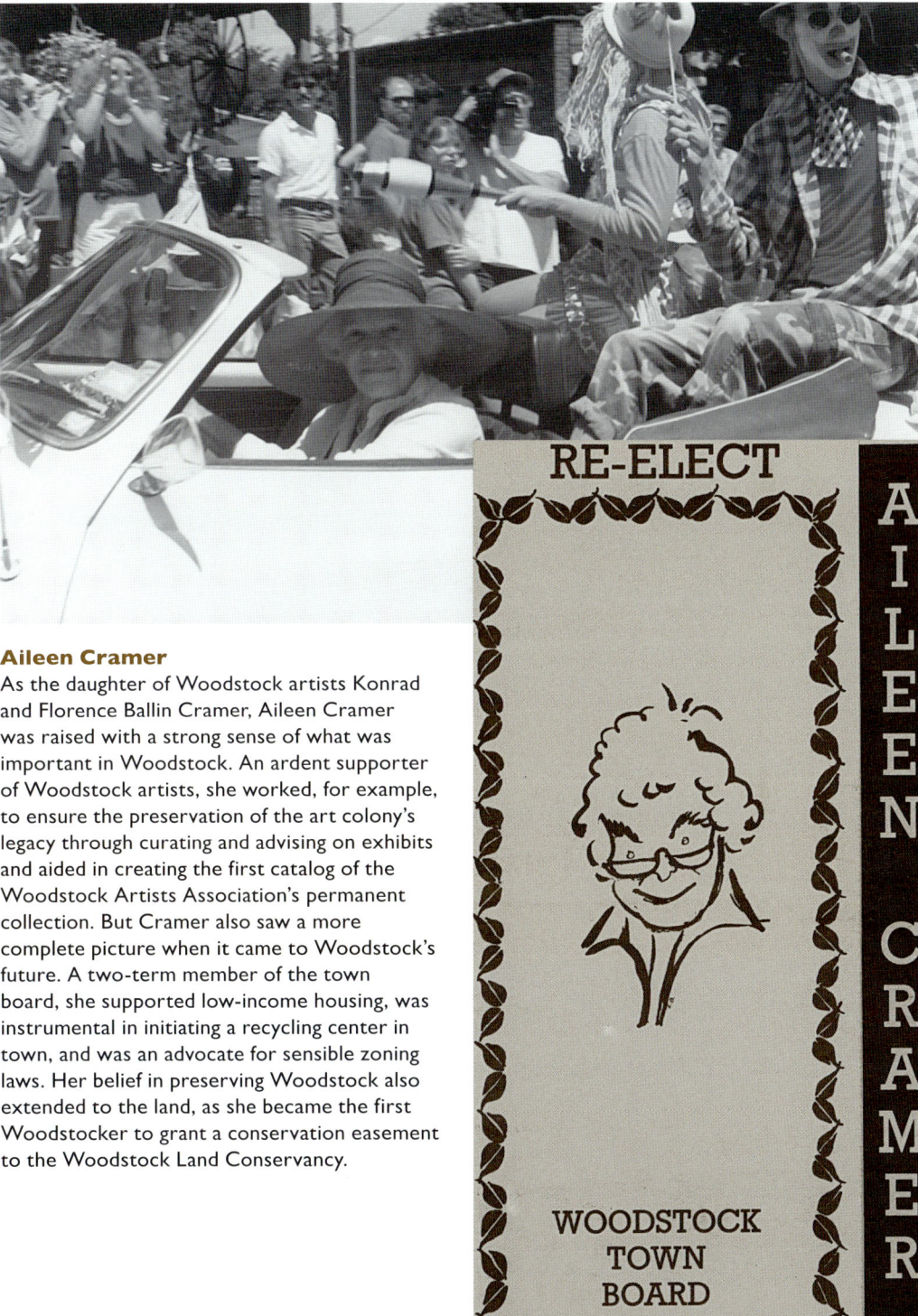

Aileen Cramer

As the daughter of Woodstock artists Konrad and Florence Ballin Cramer, Aileen Cramer was raised with a strong sense of what was important in Woodstock. An ardent supporter of Woodstock artists, she worked, for example, to ensure the preservation of the art colony's legacy through curating and advising on exhibits and aided in creating the first catalog of the Woodstock Artists Association's permanent collection. But Cramer also saw a more complete picture when it came to Woodstock's future. A two-term member of the town board, she supported low-income housing, was instrumental in initiating a recycling center in town, and was an advocate for sensible zoning laws. Her belief in preserving Woodstock also extended to the land, as she became the first Woodstocker to grant a conservation easement to the Woodstock Land Conservancy.

Sid Slayton

No one is quite sure how many weddings Sid Slayton officiated during his years as town justice, but each was most likely unique. A resident of Lake Hill with his wife, Freda, Slayton left a mark on Woodstock justice that will be long remembered. While some thought him too liberal, many will say that he was the right justice for a diverse town like Woodstock. A defender of individual rights, Slayton was not afraid, when warranted, to rule against local authority. In fact, he did just that, twice, when he ruled against the Town of Woodstock for attempting to prevent worshippers of the full moon from gathering in Magic Meadow on Overlook by ticketing their cars for illegal parking. Slayton determined that the town's actions were unconstitutional, denying worshippers their religious freedom and the right to assemble.

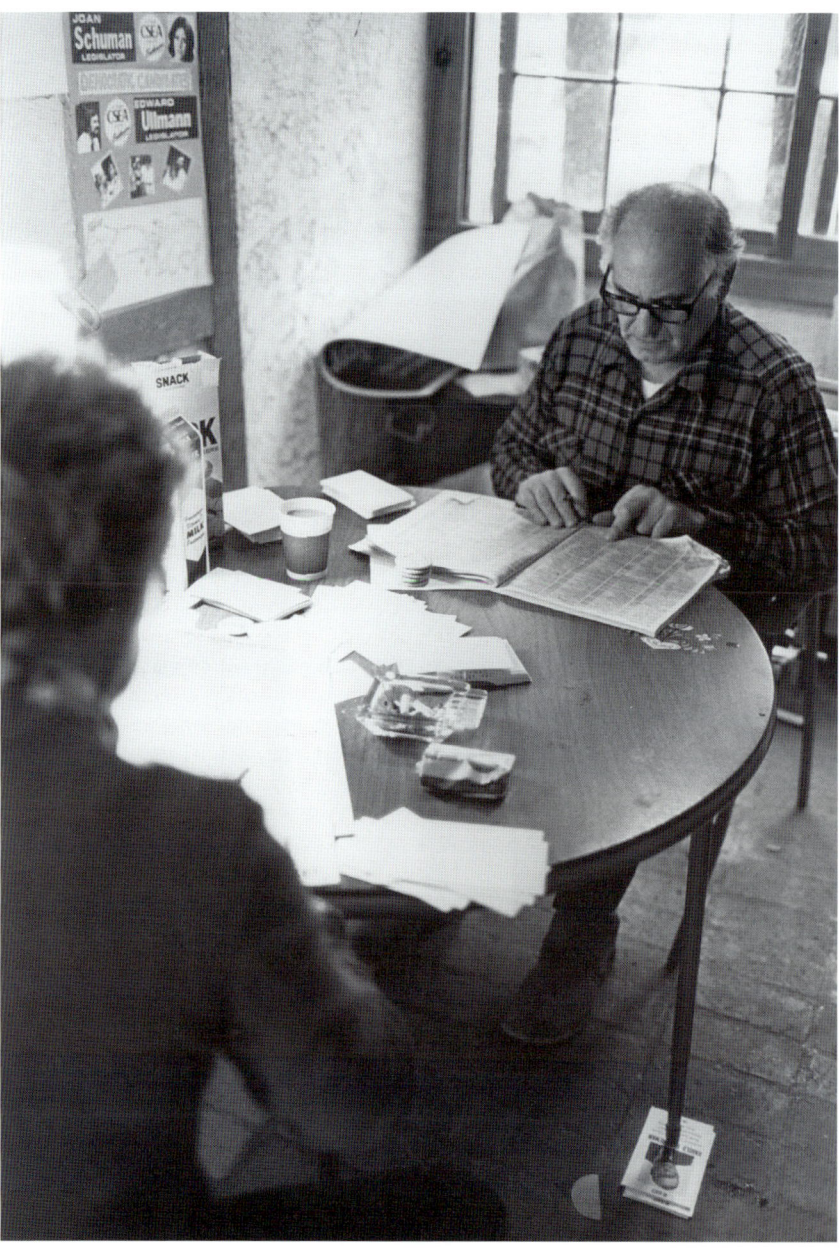

CHAPTER TWO

Community Legends: Crafting a Better Woodstock

More than a physical place—the roads, the buildings, the fields and streams, and the mountains—Woodstock is a collection of people who, over the generations, have chosen to build their lives here and call it home. Too often, however, those living in the present fail to appreciate that others came before, raising families and building a community. People tend to forget that before they expressed present-day concerns over the direction of the town, others, in their time, did the same; that before they volunteered their time to the library or Meals on Wheels of today, those who came before committed themselves and their resources to the same. As a result, there is a continuum that current citizens are but one part of. And, as heirs to what went before, they remain connected to other days and other individuals in ways they may not fully appreciate.

The individuals on the pages that follow represent those who chose to offer of themselves and give back to the community of Woodstock. While the context of their time shaped them differently than citizens are moved today, their desire to make Woodstock a better place was no less than the many who currently drive to evening meetings, supervise various activities and events for children, care for others, or have committed themselves through artistic or cultural endeavors to further Woodstock's creative lineage. Efforts today echo those of people like Sam Mercer, for example, who not only had a family to support but also worked to insure that Woodstock was taking care of its children through his efforts on the school board or his nightly little league games, or Father Francis and Rev. Harvey Todd, who tended to the spiritual needs of a diverse community. They also recall individuals such as Deanie Elwyn, whose hospitality made his restaurant not only the center of Woodstock evenings but also the primary place for social, cultural, and political mingling, or the Longyear and Elwyn families, who over the generations have long been at the center of Woodstock's political and economic life. These and so many other people gave life to the town of Woodstock throughout the years.

Woodstock is not a town whose history rests on great battles or sending a politician to the White House. Rather, its history is found in the lives of individuals who extended themselves on behalf of the town they loved and attempted to live their lives in ways that offered respect to their neighbors and to the physical environment that surrounded them. In many respects, they symbolize the essence of local history, serving and building a community through collective effort. As a result, it is the combining labors of the individuals cited on the pages that follow that ultimately fill the chapters of Woodstock's story.

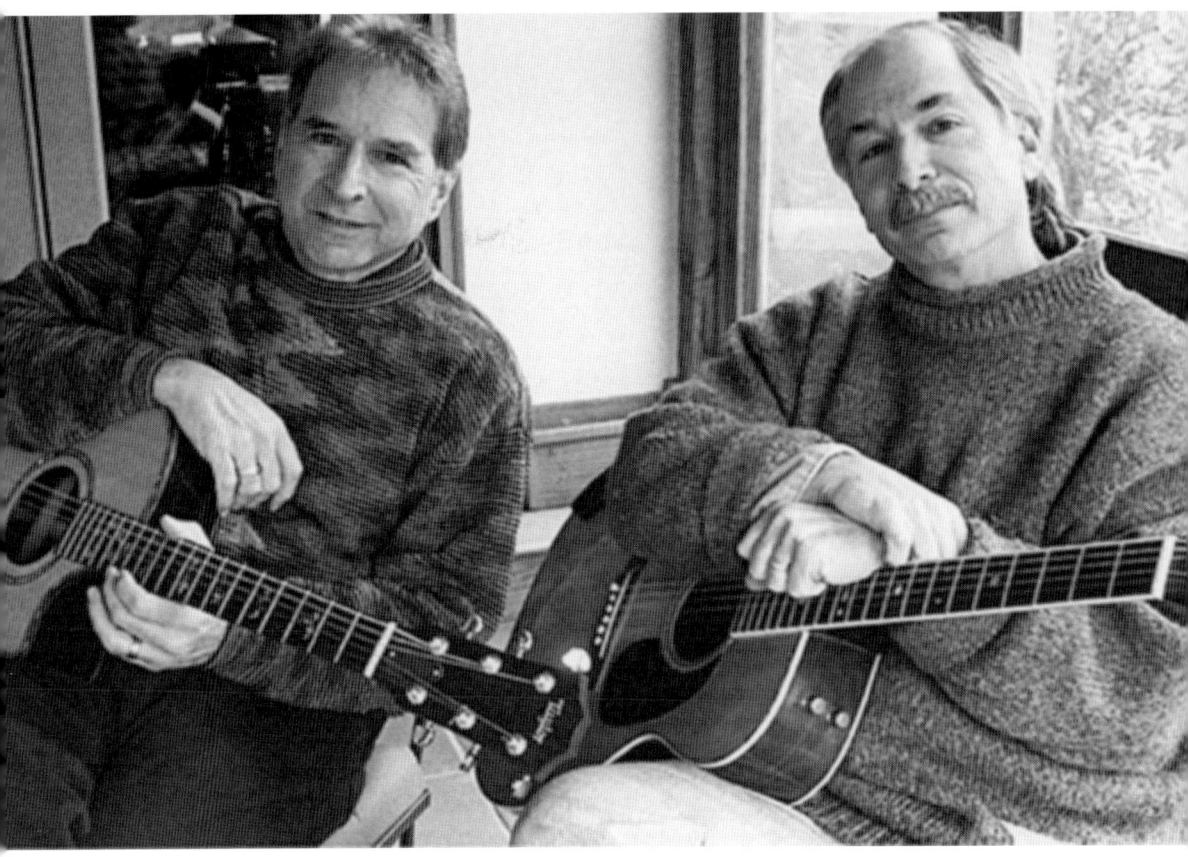

Artie Traum
Countless musicians have passed through Woodstock. But musicians Artie Traum (right) and his brother Happy made Woodstock their home. That difference not only shaped their music but shaped Woodstock as well. Happy Traum first arrived in Woodstock in 1963 to play at the Café Espresso and moved here permanently in 1967. Artie Traum would soon follow, originally house-sitting in a home owned by Bob Dylan. Joining their musical talents, the brothers, represented by Albert Grossman, toured as an opening act for many within Grossman's stable of talent. A record deal with Capitol Records led to their first albums, including *Happy and Artie Traum*, *Double Back*, and *Hard Times in the Country*. When in Woodstock, the Traums began hosting a series of performances at the Woodstock Playhouse featuring a number of friends from the area. From that experience, Artie Traum developed the idea of assembling many of those friends as a recording group. The result would be a series of recordings featuring Woodstock-made music on such albums as *Mud Acres: Music among Friends* and *More Music from Mud Acres*. The core group, including John Herald, Bill Keith, Pat Alger, Jim Rooney, Roly Salley, and Larry Campbell, would also take to the road as the Woodstock Mountain Revue. Joining in on the music at times were such artists as John Sebastian, Paul Butterfield, and Eric Anderson. Artie Traum would go on to enjoy a distinctive solo career as well. A pioneer in acoustic music, Traum's versatility would see him move easily from folk to jazz and back again throughout the various stages of his career. In 1988, along with Happy, he began hosting *Bring It on Home*, a pubic radio program for WAMC in Albany, while also producing instructional guitar tapes for Homespun Tapes, a company cofounded by Happy and his wife, Jane. More importantly, Artie Traum and his brother Happy never paused when it came time to give back to the community. Few Woodstockers, musicians or otherwise, have ever donated more time and talent when a cause called out for support. Unfortunately, Artie Traum was lost to Woodstock far too early, dying of cancer in 2008 at the age of 65. (Courtesy Adam Traum.)

Robert Elwyn

Robert Elwyn, a descendent of one of Woodstock's oldest families, emerged as an actor, director, and theater manager under the eye of Hervey White and the Maverick Theater. Desirous of his own facility, he was determined to construct his own theater and, with design by architect Albert Milliken and construction by Arthur Wolven, the Woodstock Playhouse opened in 1938 with a performance of *Yes My Darling Daughter*. Following World War II, Elwyn sold the theater and went on to direct both feature and short films for such Hollywood studios as MGM. Elwyn is pictured here with actress Elissa Landi, who appeared at the Woodstock Playhouse in the role of Elizabeth Barrett in *The Barretts of Wimpole Street* in 1947. The original Woodstock Playhouse was destroyed by fire in 1988.

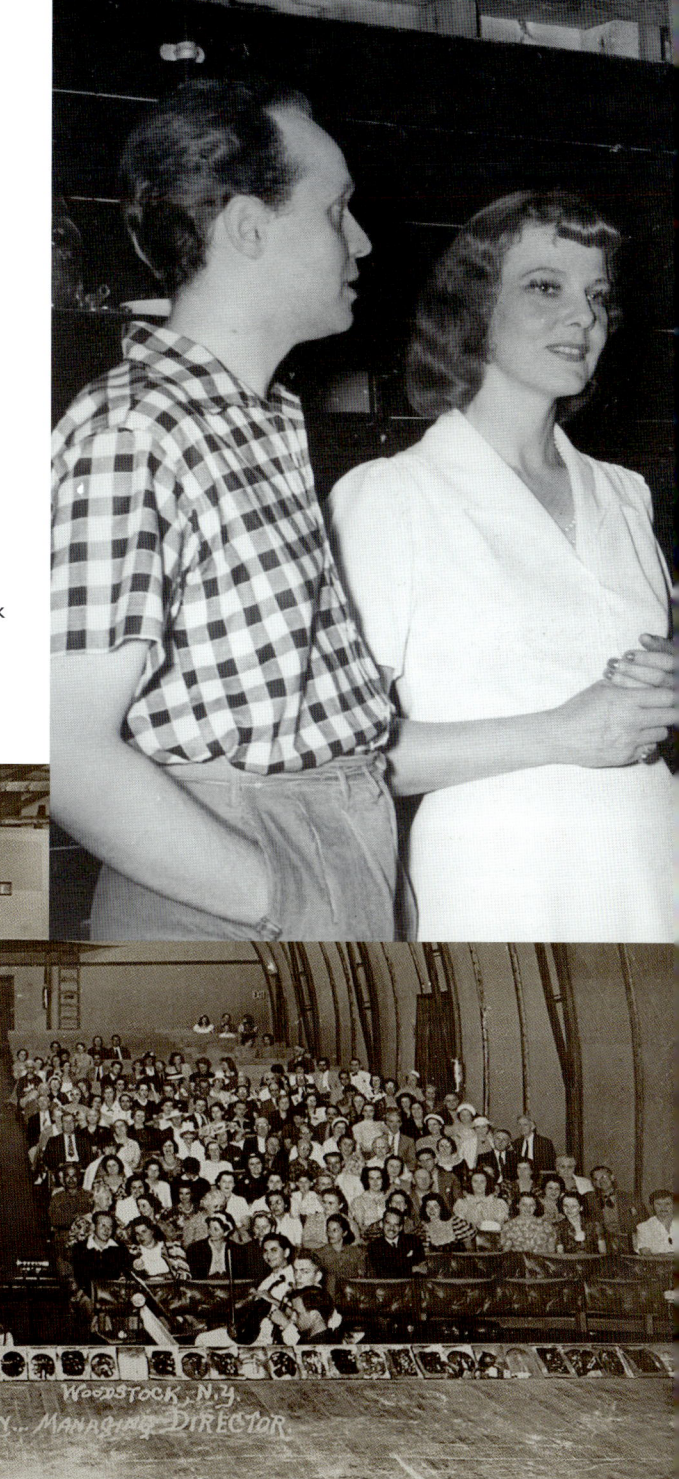

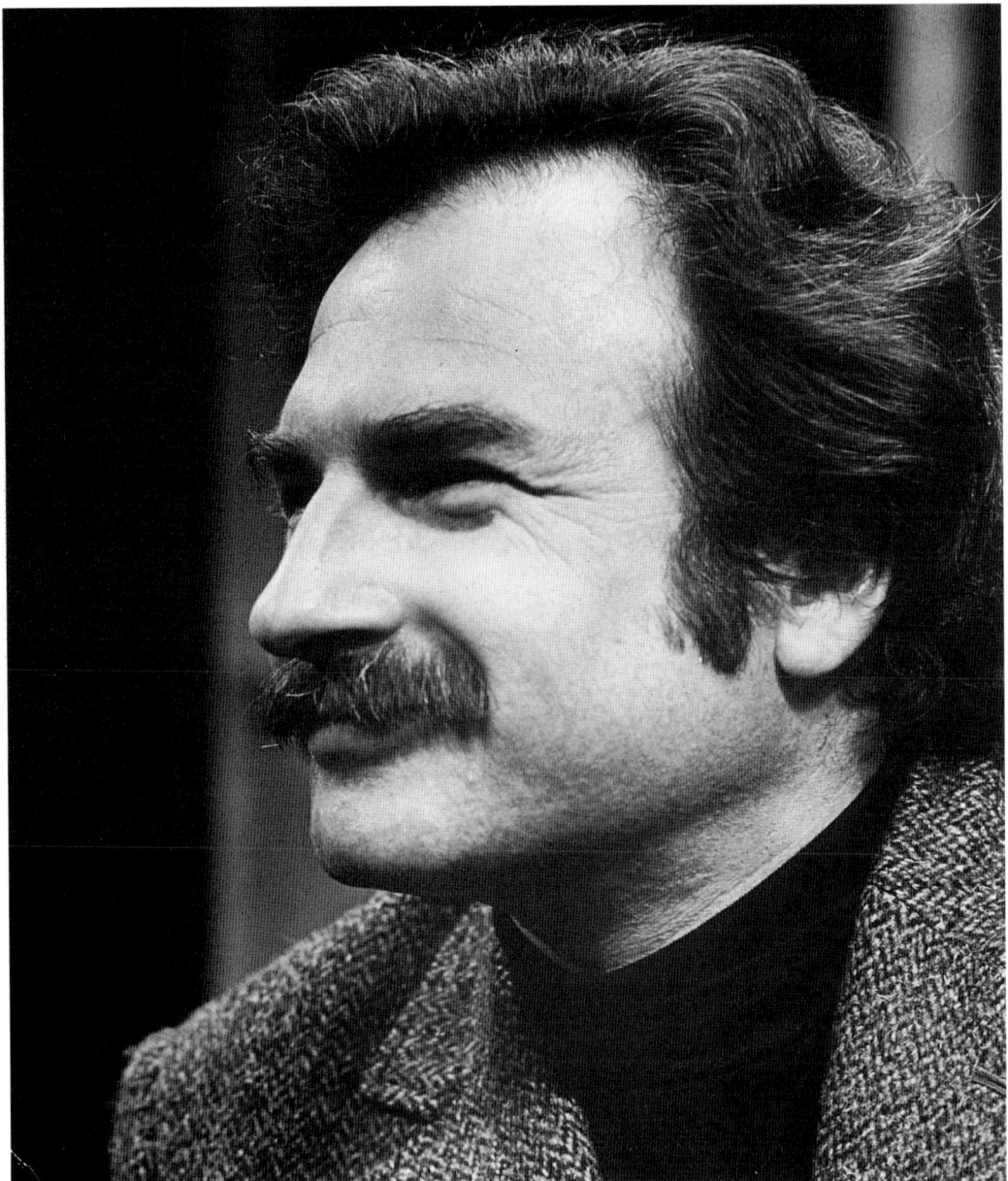

Edgar Rosenblum

Born in 1932, Edgar Rosenblum began a career in arts management in New York in the 1950s. In 1957, he established the Polari Gallery in Woodstock and, in 1960, purchased the Woodstock Playhouse. For the next 12 years, under Rosenblum's leadership, the playhouse became the cultural center of Woodstock, offering the best in summer theater and attracting such quality actors as Estelle Parsons, Diane Keaton, and Judd Hirsch, to name a few. Hoping to expand professional theater beyond the summer season, he created the Hudson Valley Reparatory Theater in 1967. During his tenure, Rosenblum also developed Saturday morning children's programming and presented midnight concerts at the playhouse with the likes of Pete Seeger and Tom Paxton. Appointed as executive director of New Haven's Long Wharf Theater in 1972, Rosenblum sold the Playhouse to Harris Gordon. (Courtesy Cornelia Rosenblum.)

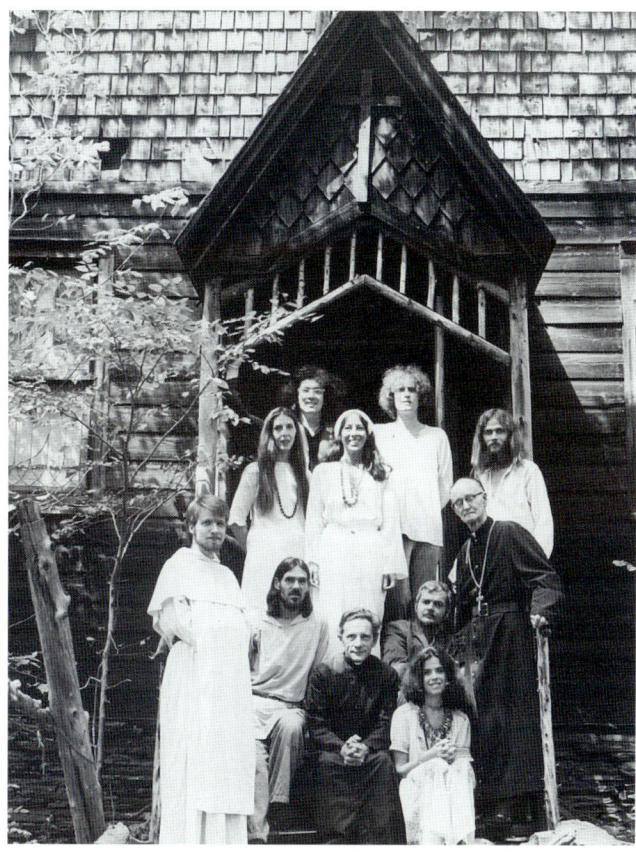

Father Francis

William Henry Francis Brothers (right, in dark frock) was born in England in 1885. His family immigrated to the United States when he was 12. As a child, he counted among his friends the likes of Clarence Darrow and Carl Sandburg. A part of the Old Catholic Church movement, which separated itself from the Roman Catholic Church over such policies as papal infallibility, he was consecrated a bishop in 1916 and as archbishop in 1917. Father Francis was unafraid to follow his convictions. He supported the suffragettes and their battle to gain the right to vote for women, campaigned with Margaret Sanger in support of birth control, served as a theological advisor to Darrow during the Scopes trial, and was asked to marry the Duke and Duchess of Windsor. In 1936, Jane Whitehead, concerned about the spiritual direction of her son, urged Father Francis to come to Woodstock and take up ministry in the former Episcopalian chapel on Overlook Mountain that once served visitors to the Mead's Mountain House. When the Episcopal diocese objected to a prominent member of the Old Catholic Church practicing on Episcopal property, Jane purchased the property, and Father Francis set about rebuilding the structure known as the Church on the Mount. Difficult winters, however, often made church attendance at the top of the mountain impossible. As a result, Father Francis renovated an old barn in town to serve as a more accessible chapel. He called his church St. Dunstan's. During the war years, he held services there while also leading efforts to aid the people of Poland and the Jews of Europe. Towards war's end, however, fire destroyed St. Dunstan's, and Father Francis returned to the Church on the Mount. As time passed on the mountain, events would converge to bring new visitors to Woodstock and to Father Francis' flock. As members of the counterculture began to arrive in the 1960s—many of them taking up residence in Woodstock's fields and forests—the town became uncharacteristically hostile, and residents and officials tried to stem the tide of hippies. It was then, through the humanity of Father Francis—who became known both in terms of praise and derision as the "hippie priest"—that his chapel found new life as a place of welcome to those who, not unlike Father Francis himself, chose to question the status quo.

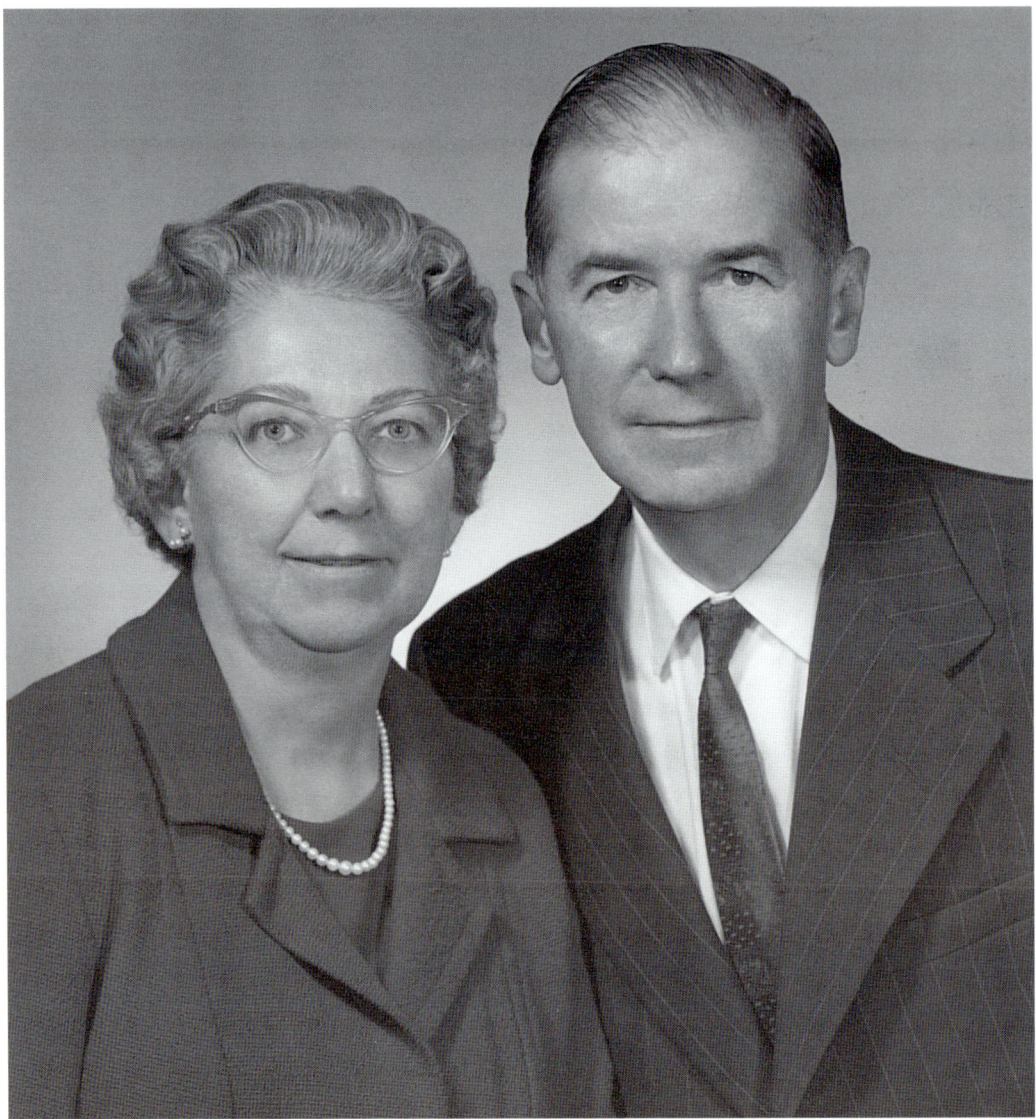

Elbert Varney
As Woodstock began to enjoy the prosperity of the postwar years, Elbert Varney became the man who helped make it possible. A manager of Woodstock's first bank, the Bank of Orange and Ulster, Elbert Varney was the person Woodstockers went to for a mortgage or business loan. A native of Long Island, Varney came to Woodstock in 1955 with his wife, Dorothy. In addition to his banking interests and helping Woodstock grow, Varney was active within the community. A member of the local Rotary Club, he also served as treasurer of the Library Fair and as a member of the committee that worked to build the new Methodist church on Route 212 in Bearsville where both he and his wife were lay leaders. (Courtesy Adele Varney Rose.)

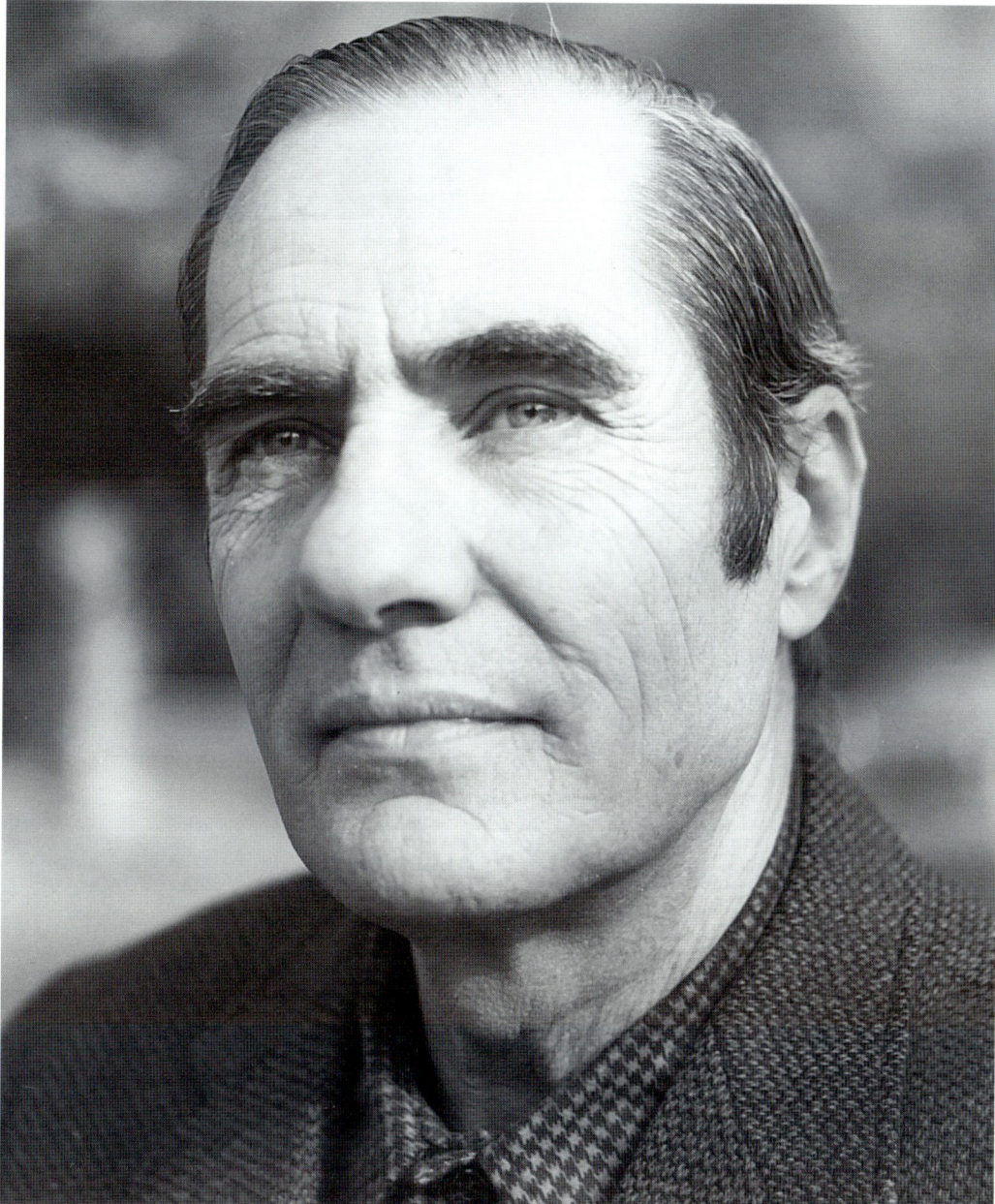

Edgar Pete Leaycraft

Born in 1918, Pete Leaycraft was raised in both New York and Woodstock. He earned a degree from Harvard and a master's from the New School. Following service in the Army Air Corps, Leaycraft went to work as an engineer for IBM in Kingston, where he was credited with a number of patents. Settling in Woodstock with his wife, Winifred, Leaycraft soon began to involve himself in town affairs. Just prior to the Woodstock Festival, he was appointed to fill an unexpired term as town justice. As a result, as young people made their way to Woodstock, his courtroom presided over a host of issues new to Woodstock. During this time, Leaycraft became actively involved with the town historical society, and when Alf Evers stepped down as town historian, he was appointed to fill the position.

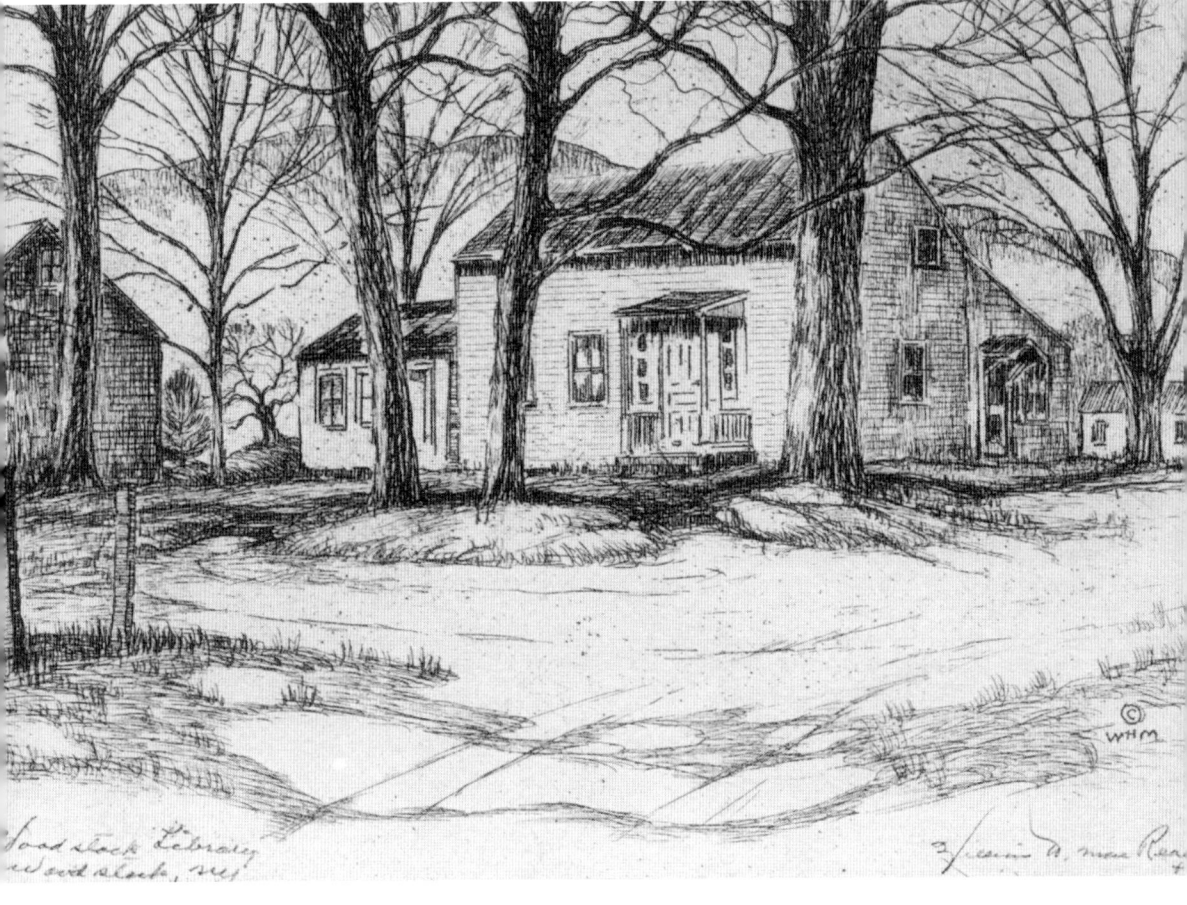

Dr. Larry Hall
During the first half of the 1800s, Dr. Larry Hall was one of four doctors who practiced medicine in Woodstock. Hall's home and office, constructed in 1812, is the current site of the Woodstock Library. He lived there with his wife, an admired Woodstock quilter, until his death in 1836. In her small volume, *From Sunset to Cock's Crow*, published by the Historical Society of Woodstock in 1957, Neva Shultis offers a glimpse at Dr. Hall's daybook, providing a list of the procedures and charges Hall presented to his patients, including $2 for delivery of a baby, 12¢ to have a tooth pulled, $2 to set a bone, and 25¢ to open a boil. In addition to his medical practice, Dr. Hall was also elected to serve as a commissioner and inspector of schools in 1814.

Anita Smith (RIGHT)
Born in 1892, Anita Smith arrived in Woodstock to study at the Arts Student League in 1912. Smith, an impressionist, was soon exhibiting her work at such important institutions as the National Academy of Design and the Art Institute of Chicago. An herbalist and author, she built her home, Stonecrop, at the base of Overlook Mountain in 1934. Stonecrop would later be used as an observation post during World War II, as spotters, with Smith in command, worked around the clock in search of planes intruding on American airspace. Anita Smith went on to write the first true history of Woodstock, *Woodstock History and Hearsay*, chronicling the growth of Woodstock from the days when Native Americans once traversed the slopes of Overlook Mountain to the establishment of art colonies in the 20th century. (Courtesy Weston Blelock.)

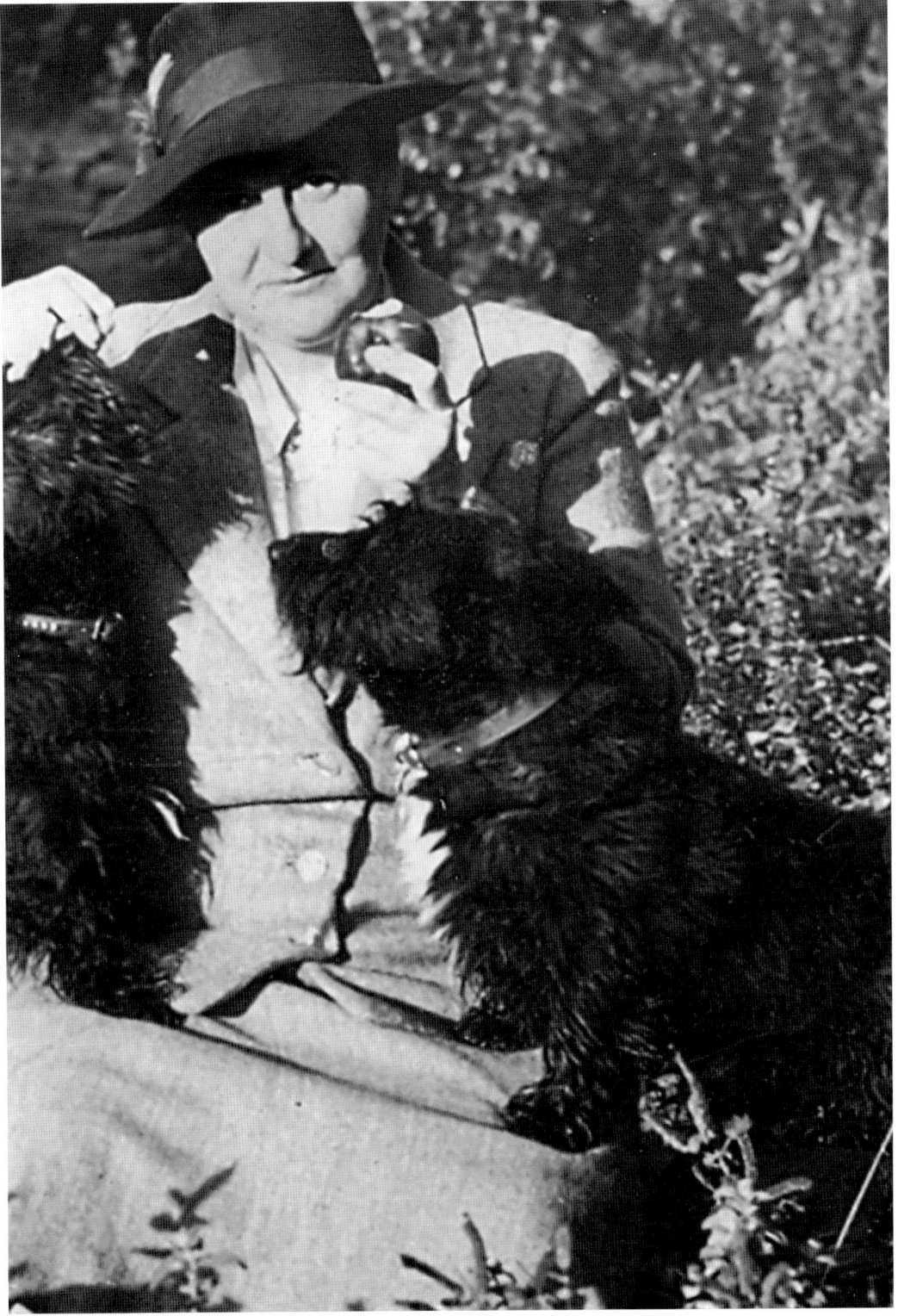

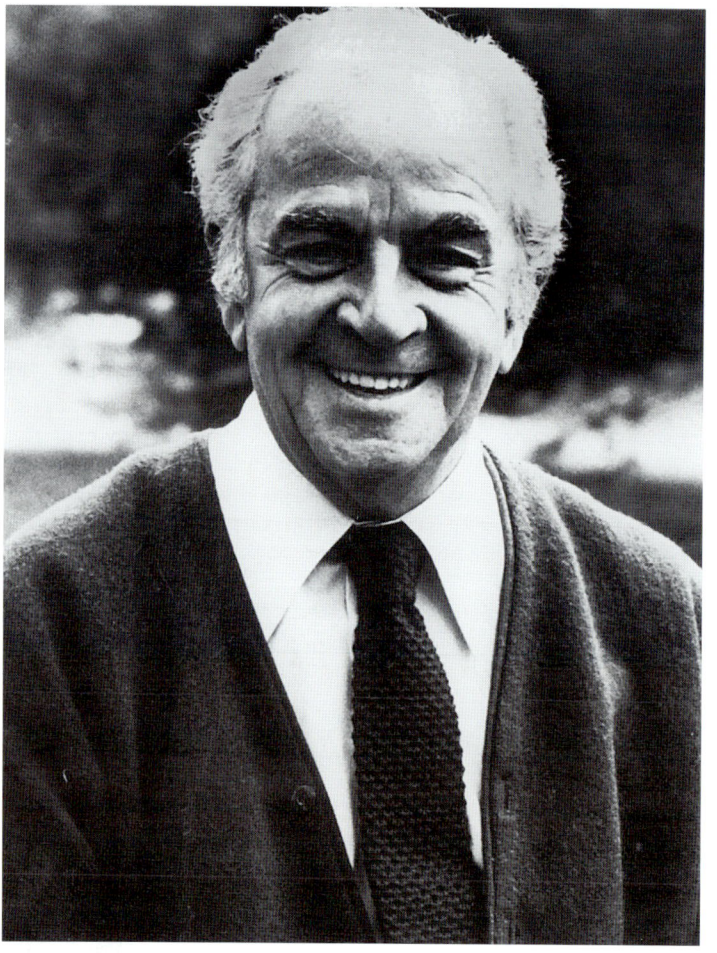

Charlie Tiano
Charlie Tiano is best remembered for the many years he served as sports editor for the *Kingston Daily Freeman*. His commitment to local sports did not stop there, however, as he served as director of the Herdegen Golf Tournament for more than three decades, director of the Ulster County Senior Men's Golf Association Tournament, and onetime director of the Woodstock Open. He also worked tirelessly to bring professional baseball to the area.

Fordyce Herrick (RIGHT)
Fordyce Herrick served as Ralph Whitehead's "boss carpenter" during the construction of Byrdcliffe. Herrick was known as a tough taskmaster, making sure his men worked at full speed. Described as both sturdy and temperamental, Herrick, like many Woodstockers of his day, was also known to love a good story. Fordyce Herrick and his crew were also responsible for much of the cabinetmaking at Byrdcliffe.

Allen "Deanie" Elwyn

Beginning with a small trolley, Deanie Elwyn (left, with longtime bartender Paul Stolpinski) and his family would grow Deanie's restaurant into one of Woodstock's most iconic establishments. His staff, its patrons, and the stories are legendary in Woodstock. Born in 1914, Deanie Elwyn purchased his first restaurant, the Brass Rail, in 1936. Shortly thereafter, he would open the Trolley Car Diner on Mill Hill Road. When World War II came along, Elwyn enlisted in the Navy, and his mother, Eva Ricks Elwyn, took over the task of keeping the diner going. Returning from the war, Deanie Elwyn had bigger ideas. After selling the Brass Rail and closing the diner (legend has it that the trolley remains buried near its original location on Mill Hill Road), Elwyn built the first floor of what would become Deanie's on the corner of Deming Street and Mill Hill Road. Initially serving food only, a mahogany bar was added in 1948, and in 1950, a second floor was constructed. In 1955, however, Deanie Elwyn decided on a career change and, after selling the restaurant, moved to Florida to invest in the shrimp business. It was an investment that did not pan out. Back in Woodstock in 1957, Elwyn went into the construction business, building a number of homes in Bearsville. In 1960, Deanie Elwyn returned to his first love and repurchased his old restaurant. As Woodstock grew, Deanie's became the center of Woodstock's nightlife. There the local plumber, artist, off-duty constable, craftsman, musician, and politician could be found huddled together over one more drink before the piano played them home for the night. In 1974, fire brought an end to the good times on Mill Hill Road. Undaunted, Deanie Elwyn purchased the old Town House Restaurant across from the Woodstock golf course. After extensive renovations, Elwyn was back in the restaurant business. In 1988, after more than 50 years serving Woodstock, Deanie Elwyn died. Though family members had run the restaurant successfully over the last years of Deanie's life, the restaurant would close that same year. More than just a restaurant, Deanie's was where one went to meet friends, family, and neighbors. And while Deanie's was "known from coast to coast," as its motto proclaimed, it truly was the place that Woodstockers called their own. (Courtesy Jon Elwyn.)

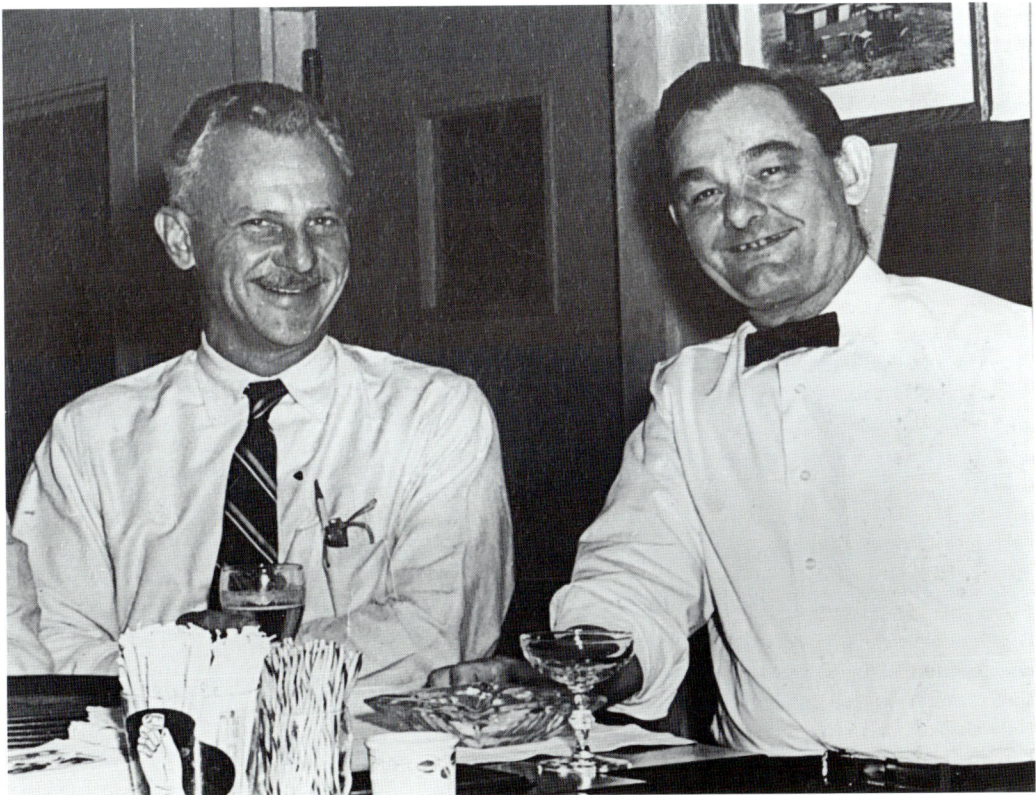

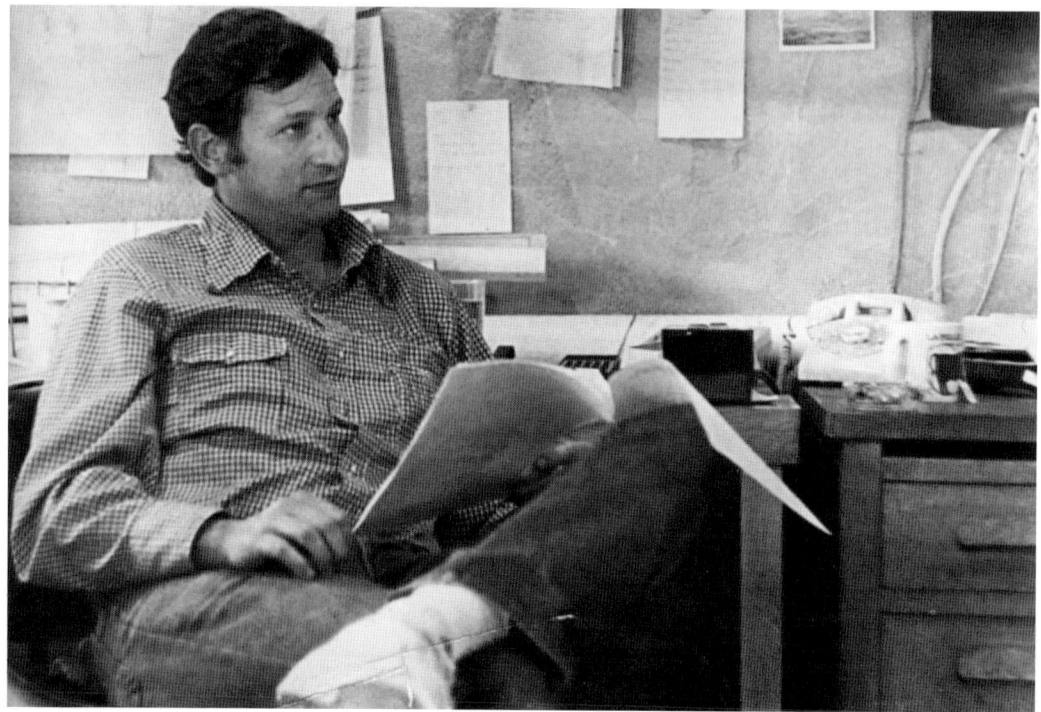

Robert DeLisio

Growing up in Woodstock, Robert "Robin" DeLisio was as at ease with Woodstock's newcomers as he was with descendants of Woodstock's founding families. When the owners of property known as Woodstock Estates proposed building a hotel on the site, DeLisio and others, including Ed Sanders, Murray Prosky, and Bob Haney, formed Friends of Woodstock. Through Robin's countless hours of research and study, the group was able to present to the town why the development of the Woodstock Estates property was environmentally unsound. Unfortunately, where Robin might have gone next in local leadership will remain a mystery. At age 39, Robin was killed when the car he was driving was hit head-on by a drunk driver. His legacy as an advocate for the environment has been carried on by his friends, his wife, and six children. (Courtesy Jill Peacock DeLisio.)

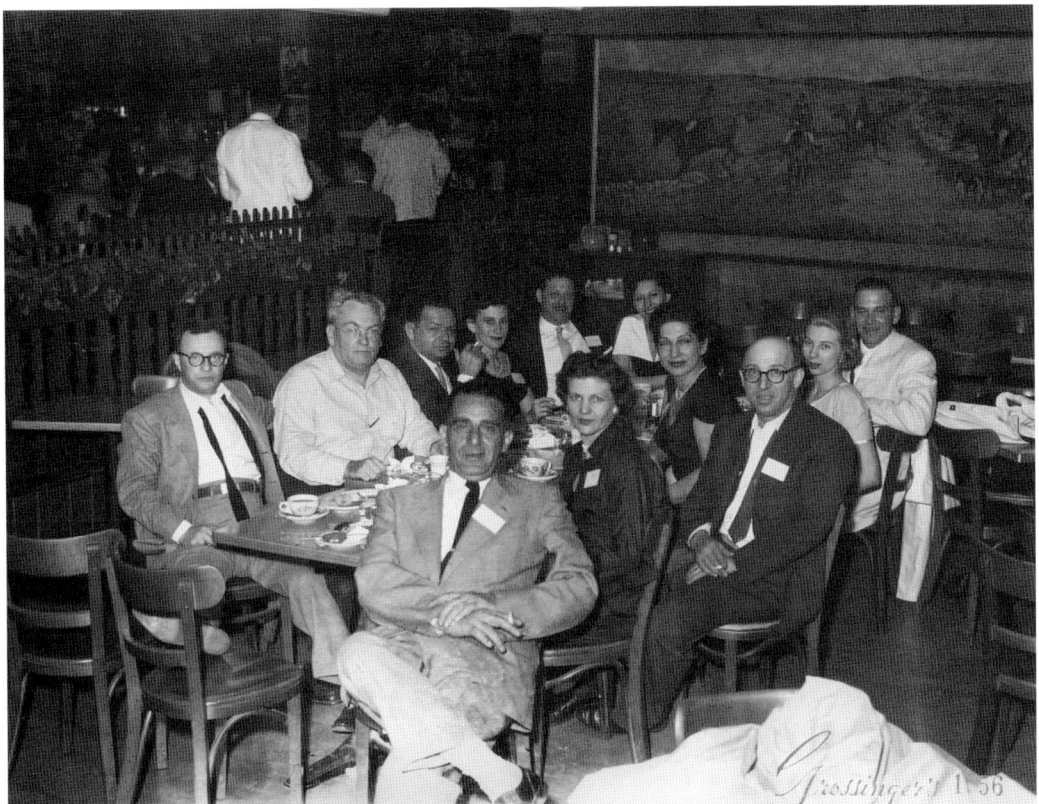

Woodstock Rotarians

Rotary evolved into a very active service organization in Woodstock following World War II. Adhering to Rotary International's principals of networking and building goodwill and friendship between businessmen and professionals, Woodstock Rotary met on a weekly basis at Deanie's Restaurant and, later, Christy's. Locally, Rotarians sponsored scholarships for high school students and funded such projects as providing medical alert devices to Woodstock seniors. In 1989, Rotary International voted to allow women to be members. After much debate, Rose Sheehan Schwarz was admitted as Woodstock's first female Rotarian. Pictured here, Woodstock Rotarians and their wives enjoy a social outing at Grossinger's Hotel. They include, along with a few unidentified guests, Joe and Barbara Forno, Kermit and Betty Schwarz, Carol and Roger Cashdollar, Ed and Audrey Gurland, Walt Van Wagenen, and Al and Vivian Moskowitz. (Courtesy Forno family.)

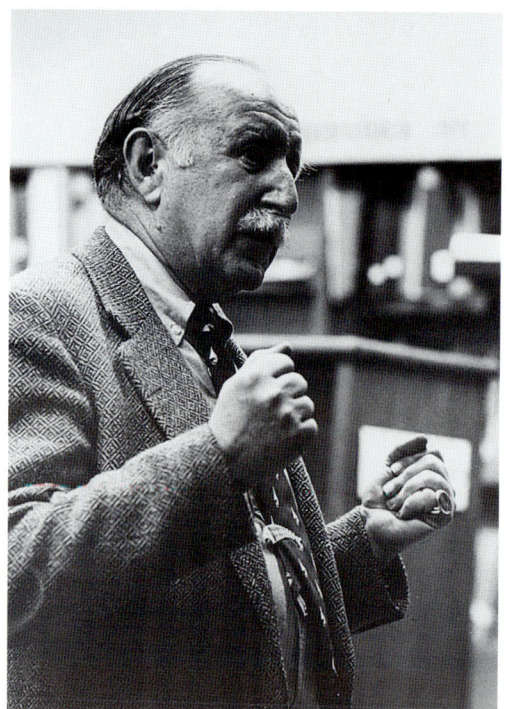

Heywood Hale Broun

Heywood Hale "Woody" Broun arrived in Woodstock in 1948. Throughout the years, he built a career with CBS as a sports commentator. Known for his wisdom and dry wit, he became a fixture at the Kentucky Derby and other sporting events with his handlebar mustache and plaid jackets. Broun was also an author and an actor, publishing three books and appearing in an occasional movie and on television.

Jane Neher Keefe

Born in Woodstock to Gertrude and Clark Neher, Jane is pictured here as Woodstock's May Queen. She would grow up to become owner, operator, and teacher at her County Mouse preschool, giving many Woodstock "Mice" an extraordinary first educational experience through art, music, and the opportunity to explore. Married to Joe Keefe, their home on Glasco Turnpike was filled with music each afternoon as Jane sat to play piano.

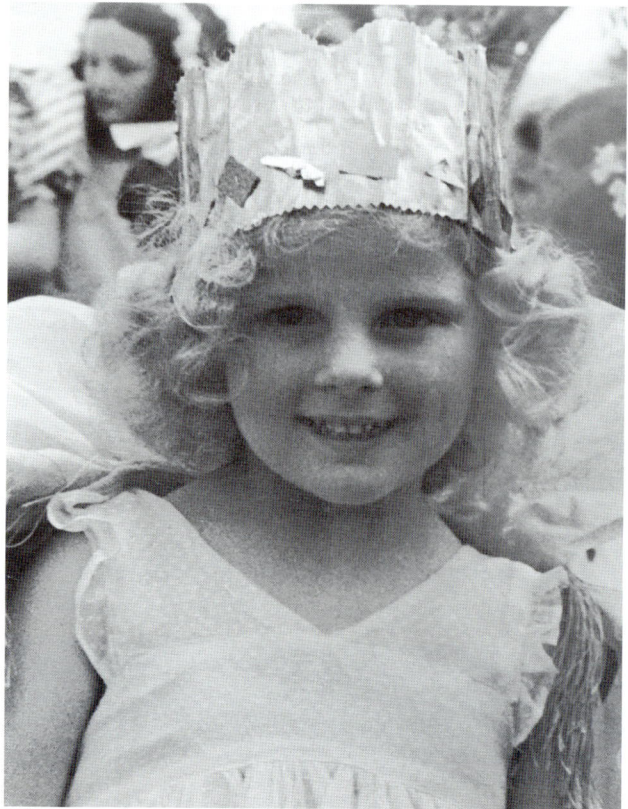

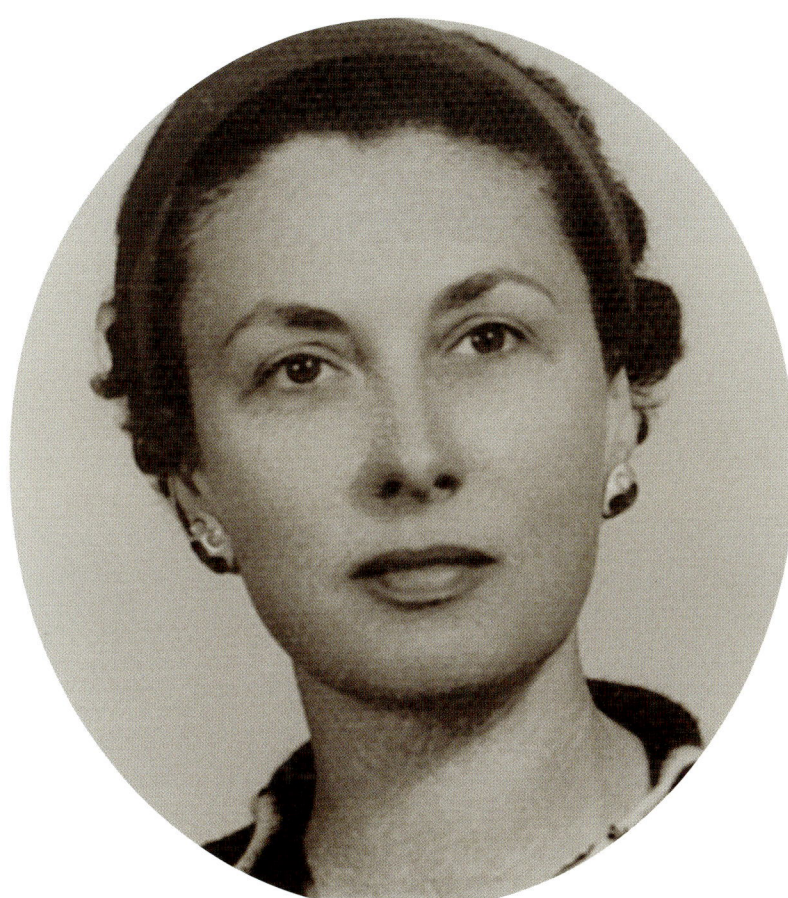

Jane Dow Bromberg
A scholarship student at the Detroit Institute of Arts and Crafts and the Detroit School of Arts, Jane Dow Bromberg, who also studied at the Arts Students League, met Manuel Bromberg in 1940 while attending the Colorado Springs Fine Arts Center. They were married in Woodstock just prior to World War II and his departure for Europe as a war artist in the US Army. Following his return from the war, Manuel Bromberg was hired as a professor of painting at North Carolina State School of Design in Raleigh. Not to be outdone, Jane Bromberg joined him as an instructor of drawing and as one of only two female faculty members at the time. As a resident of the South in the 1950s, Jane Bromberg gave her energies to the emerging civil rights movement. While in Raleigh, she marched for integration and, with her family, became an active member of the United Church of Christ, the first integrated congregation in North Carolina. Returning to Woodstock in 1956, Bromberg became an active member of the community. She cofounded and served as president of the Woodstock Chapter of the League of Women Voters from 1958 to 1960. During the 1960s, she also served as secretary of the Woodstock Library Board of Directors, was cofounder and chair of the American Field Service International Scholarship Program at Onteora High School, and was awarded the PTA's Jenkins Award for her service to students. With her own children grown, she continued to expand her interests. She was a founding sponsor of the Eleanor Roosevelt Center at Val-Kill and became an integral member of the Historical Society of Woodstock. She also served as a dedicated volunteer at the Clermont historic site in Germantown, New York, working in its gardens and creating floral arrangements for the mansion. Jane Bromberg's life was characterized by a deep empathy for all. As one of her friends once remarked, "If you had a visit with Jane, by the time you left, you felt you were a better, kinder person—smarter and more beautiful than when you walked in the door." (Courtesy Tina Bromberg.)

LEGENDARY LOCALS

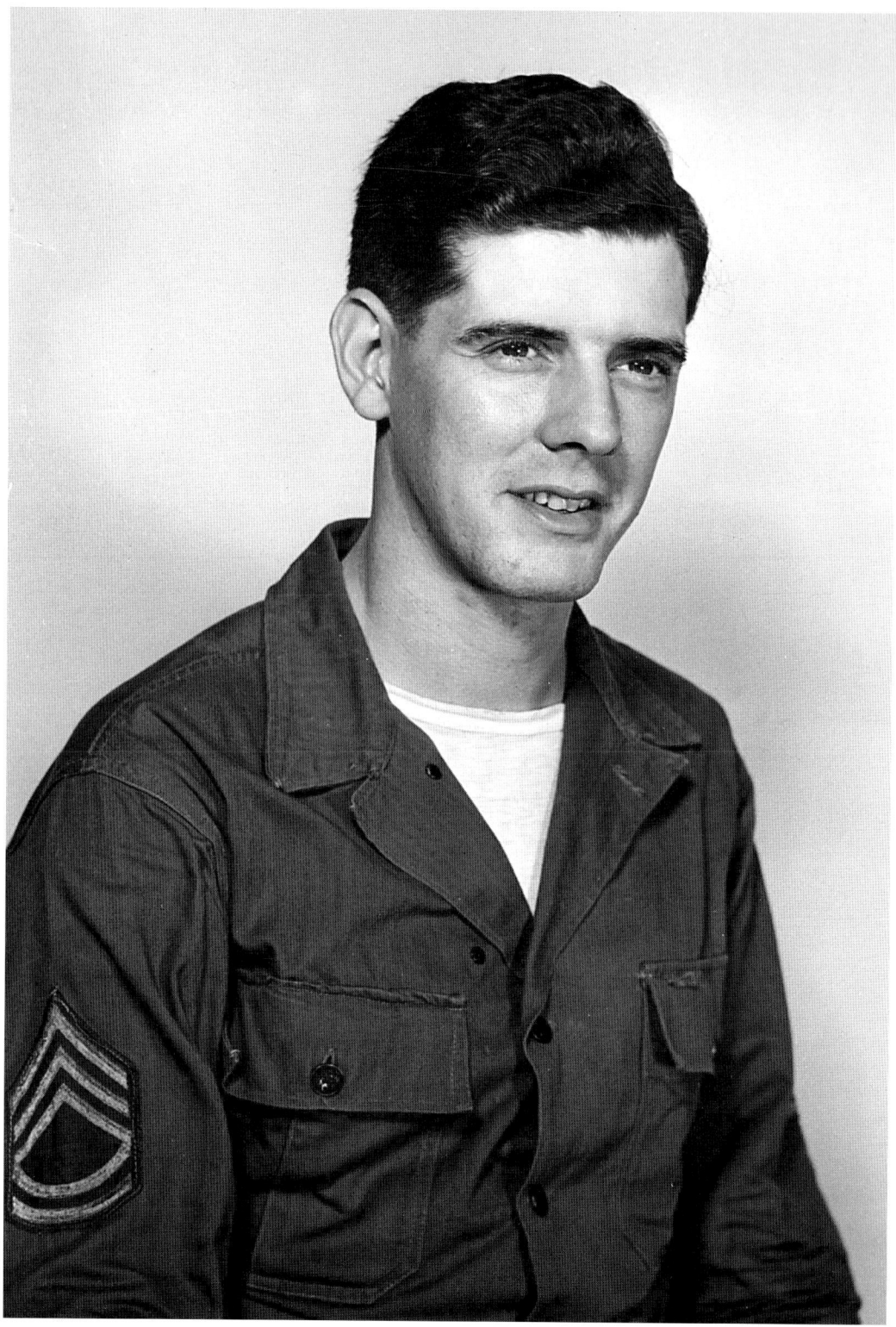

Ludwig Baumgarten (LEFT)
Some people are simply born to serve. Raised in Woodstock, Ludwig "Lud" Baumgarten joined the US Army in 1943 and served in China, India, and Burma. He also served two tours in Korea and later was stationed in Europe and Vietnam. A heavily decorated veteran, he was a life member of the Woodstock American Legion. In 1973, he founded the Catskill Mountain Basha of the China-Burma-India Veterans Association. In 1979, Lud joined the Woodstock Police Department, and he was a member for 10 years. He served 14 years on the Woodstock Rescue Squad as both a member and as president. Baumgarten also served as president of the Woodstock Rotary Club, was elected four times to the Ulster County Legislature and, as chairman of the 911 Task Force, made the first 911 call in Ulster County. (Courtesy Baumgarten family.)

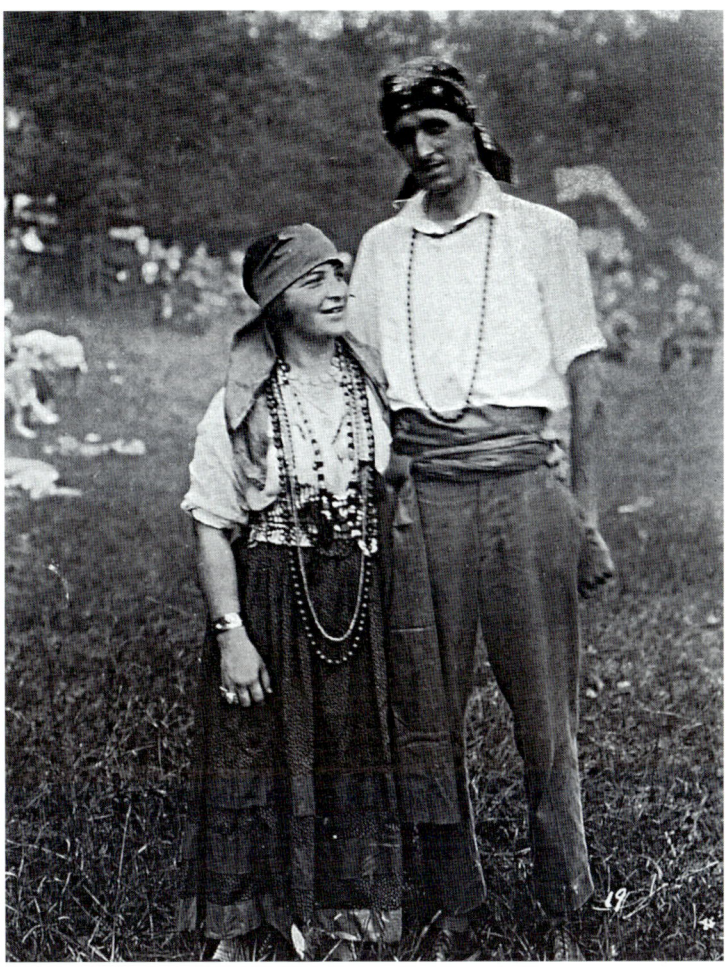

Clarence and Louise Cashdollar Bolton
Pictured here attending the Maverick Festival, Clarence and Louise Bolton left their mark on Woodstock. Arriving in Woodstock in 1917 as yet another young artist, Clarence Bolton took up residence over Wash, Elwyn's garage, at $4 a month. In 1921, he met Louise, and the two decided it would be a wonderful idea to open a soda fountain in Woodstock. With no more than an idea, they converted a barn on Tinker Street (later the site of the Café Espresso), and the Nook was born. In later years, Clarence would publish the *Clatterer*, offering news about Woodstock, while Louise would partner with Winnie Haile in operating the Red Barn antique shop. Louise also claimed another credit in Woodstock history when she became the first female taxi driver in town. (Courtesy Jean White.)

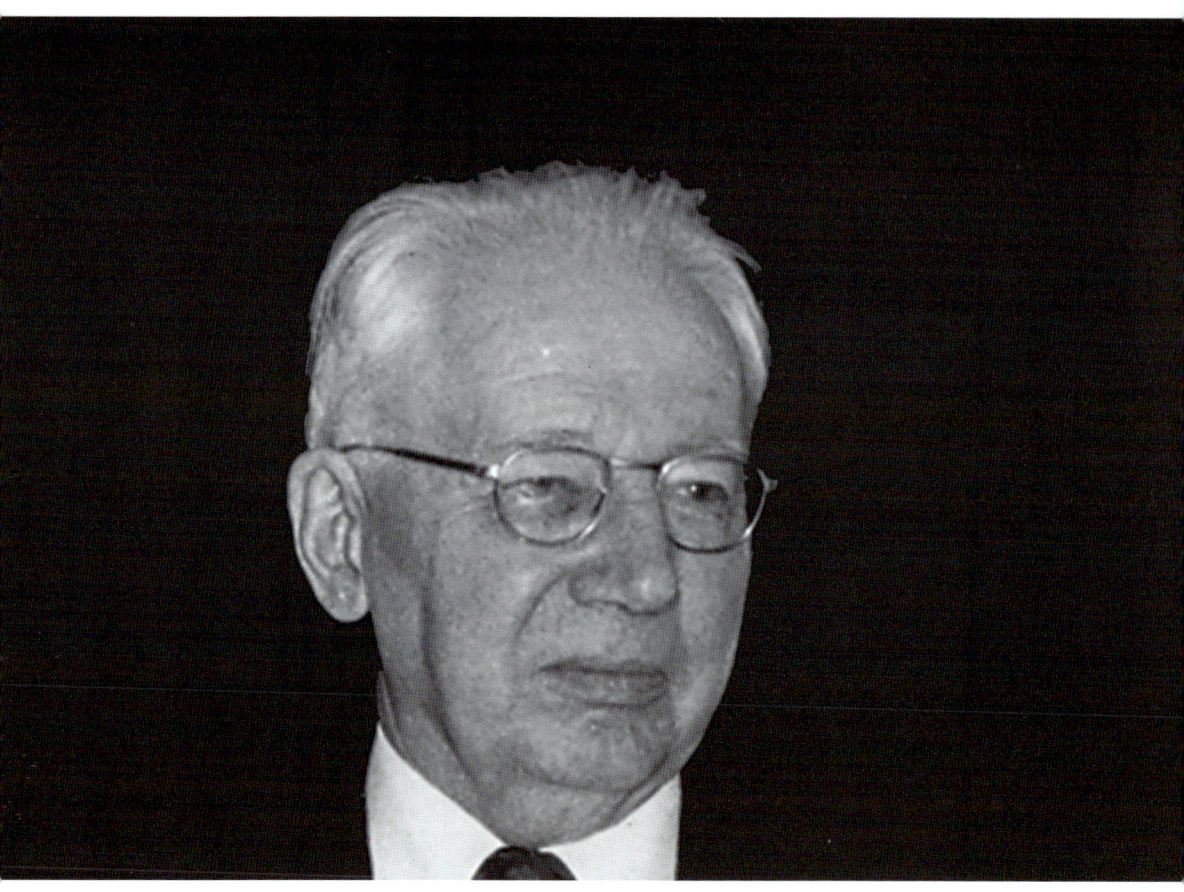

Rev. Harvey Todd

Overlooking Woodstock's village green, the Woodstock Reformed Church has been a major presence in Woodstock for over 200 years. As a result, those who would serve as its minister have an equally important role to play in Woodstock affairs. None, however, match the tenure and significance of Rev. Harvey Todd, who served as minister from 1924 to 1958. Todd, it seemed, could be found at the center of most things happening in Woodstock. As the Depression rolled through Woodstock, for example, Reverend Todd sought to match up those Woodstockers who might have work available with those most in need. During World War II, he was an active part of Woodstock's civil defense efforts, taking on the duties of air raid warden during town blackout exercises. He also served as a member of Company No. 1 of the Woodstock Fire Department. It was during the height of the Maverick Festivals, however, that he garnered the most attention. Serving as a key member of the Gang of 50, Todd was a leading voice expressing the group's concerns over the increased rowdiness that had become part of the annual bacchanal. No longer a celebration of local artists and townspeople, the Maverick Festival had begun to attract a large number of out-of-towers who had little problem shunning their inhibitions. Todd and others, including the Methodist minister, Rev. William Peckham, expressed their concerns directly to Hervey White and urged locals to contact police should they encounter inappropriate behavior such as drunkenness and nude swimming. The Gang of 50 also attempted to pressure local businesses not to support the festival despite the financial loss it could mean. In the end, Todd and his group met with success, though the weight of the Depression also contributed to the eventual end of Hervey White's festivals. Todd would continue as a moral force within the community for many years as he led his church and its members through demanding times. Despite the many challenges, Reverend Todd still found time for young people as an active supporter of the Boy Scouts and, personally, for his enjoyment of music as an amateur musician.

CHAPTER TWO: COMMUNITY LEGENDS: CRAFTING A BETTER WOODSTOCK

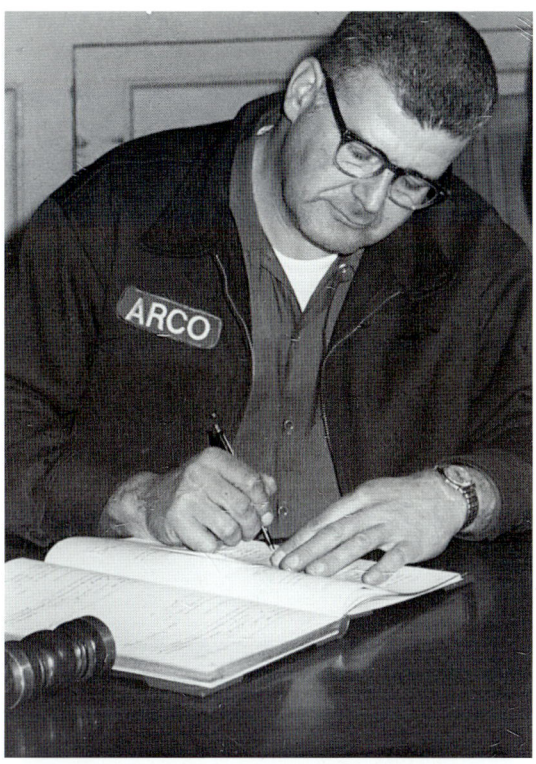

Rudolf "Rudi" Baumgarten
Rudi Baumgarten grew up in the family's 18th-century home on Baumgarten Road with his brother Lud. Married in 1945 to Bessie "Jean" Hoag, Baumgarten worked at the Orange and Ulster Bank in Woodstock before opening Rudi's Service Station on Route 28. He served as town justice for 24 years and, during emergencies, his service station also functioned as the town's courtroom. (Courtesy the Baumgarten family.)

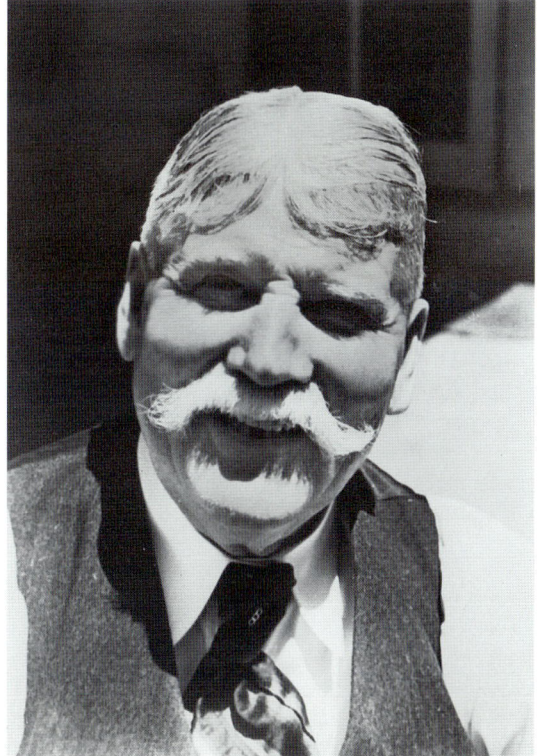

William Reynolds
William Reynolds spent most of his 94 years on Overlook Mountain. Hired by Henry Tupper in 1906, Reynolds took over as manager of the Overlook Mountain House where, at the time, one could stay for $8 a week. Later in life, Reynolds also constructed and operated the Reynolds Boarding House on the mountain for a number of years.

Ruth Simpson

Born to parents who were leaders in the labor movement during the 1930s and 1940s, Ruth Simpson was introduced to activism at a young age. That interest was refueled on the night of the Stonewall raid in 1969. As a natural leader, Simpson soon rose to become president of the New York Daughters of Bilitis, a national lesbian group. Moving to Woodstock in 1976 with her partner, Ellen Povill, she joined the Woodstock Library Board in 1979. Over the course of 28 years, Simpson was elected to every position available on the board, including president, vice president, secretary, and treasurer. During her association with the library, she assisted library director D.J. Stern in waging a successful battle to change the library from a free association to a public library district. In 1982, Simpson began her association with Woodstock Access Television, first as a board member and later as a producer of a weekly Friday night program, *Minority Report*. Beginning with issues relating to the gay community, the program evolved to offer views from the left on national politics. A feisty, courageous, loving, and generous woman, Ruth Simpson excelled as a writer, poet, musician, and baker of wonderful pies. (Courtesy Ellen Povill.)

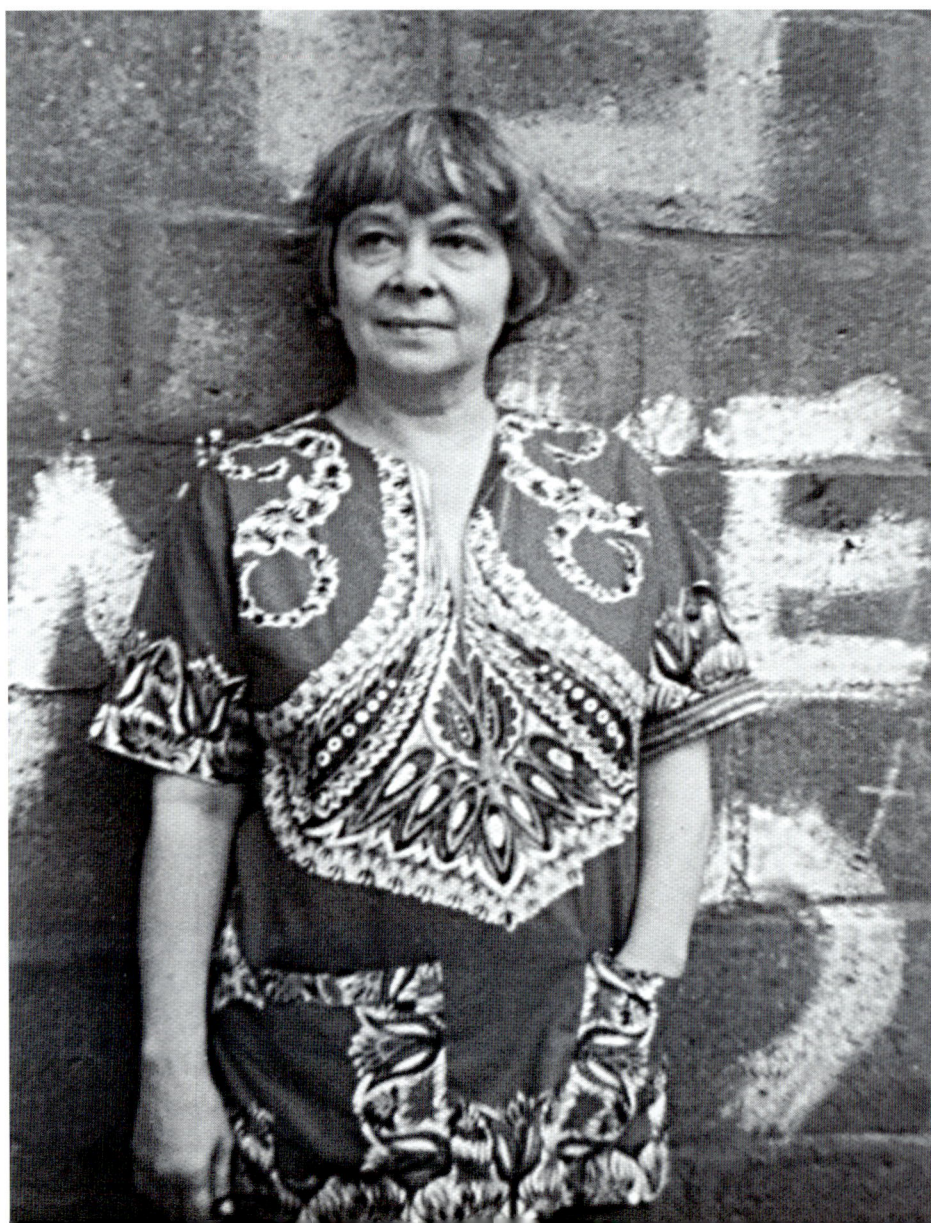

CHAPTER TWO: COMMUNITY LEGENDS: CRAFTING A BETTER WOODSTOCK

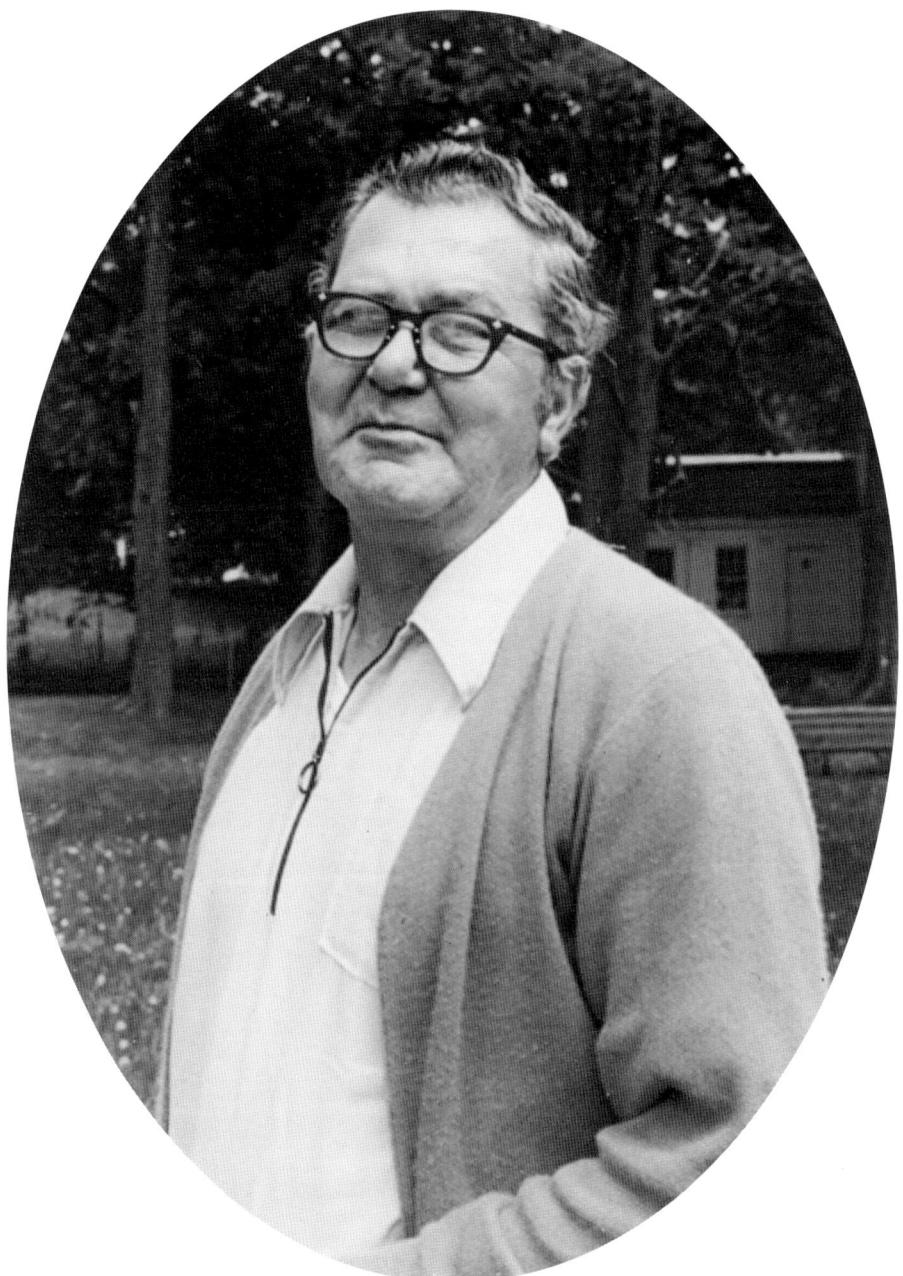

Sam Mercer

Born in 1923, Sam Mercer's family moved from the Boston area to Brooklyn when he was two. Times were not easy for the Mercers, however, and his childhood experiences later shaped his desire to see all children have things better. After serving in Europe during World War II, Sam began work for IBM. In 1956, he purchased a home in Woodstock Gardens in Bearsville. As he worked his way up at IBM, Sam became a tireless advocate for kids, always remarking that "Kids come first." As a result, he won election to the Onteora School Board and served for eight years. He is also fondly remembered as Woodstock Little League's chief umpire for many years. Equally as notable, Sam Mercer took his activist spirit to the airwaves, hosting *Sam's Time*, a local cable show that ran for 25 years.

LEGENDARY LOCALS

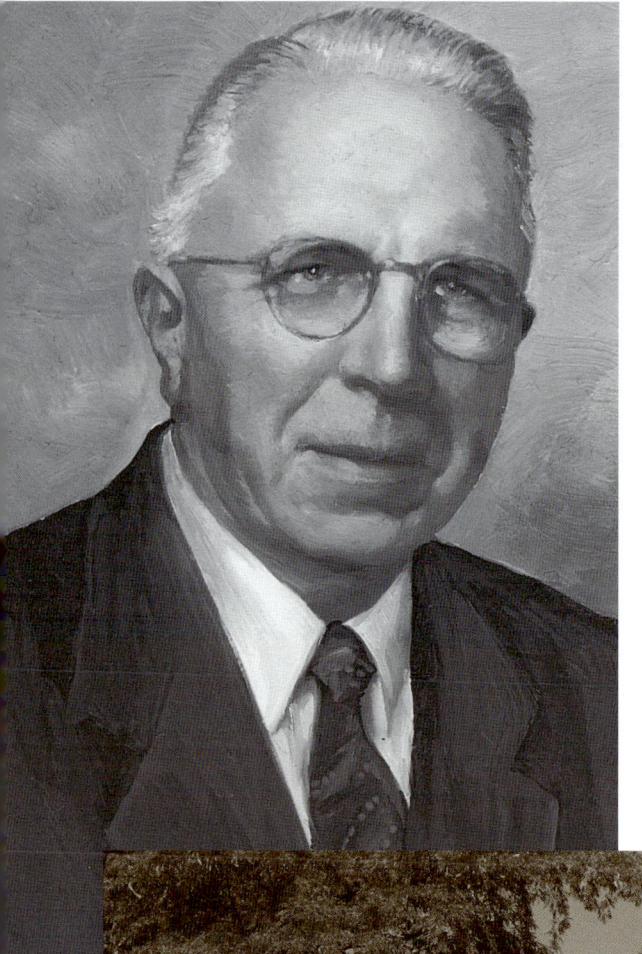

Victor Lasher
The Lasher family arrived in Woodstock just prior to the Civil War. The family home on Tinker Street, which was at the center of a large family farm, was constructed in the 1860s. The family also operated as teamsters, providing teams of horses or oxen to haul freight to or from the train and the river. In the 1880s, the family entered the funeral business. Victor Lasher, born in 1889, took over the operation of the Lasher Funeral Home from his father in 1914 and operated the business for 45 years until his retirement. In addition to his professional obligations, Lasher served as a commissioner of the Woodstock Fire Department and as a member of the Kingston Lodge No. 10 F&AM. Victor Lasher was married to his wife, Edith Risely, for 59 years. (Courtesy Ken Peterson.)

William Riley

In 1937, the town board of Woodstock appointed its first police officer. William Riley, a resident of the Woodstock hamlet of Zena, had served as a member of the New York City police force for 20 years. Despite the Great Depression, Woodstock had begun to attract an increasing number of newcomers. As a result, Riley's primary purpose was to direct traffic on weekends and during special events.

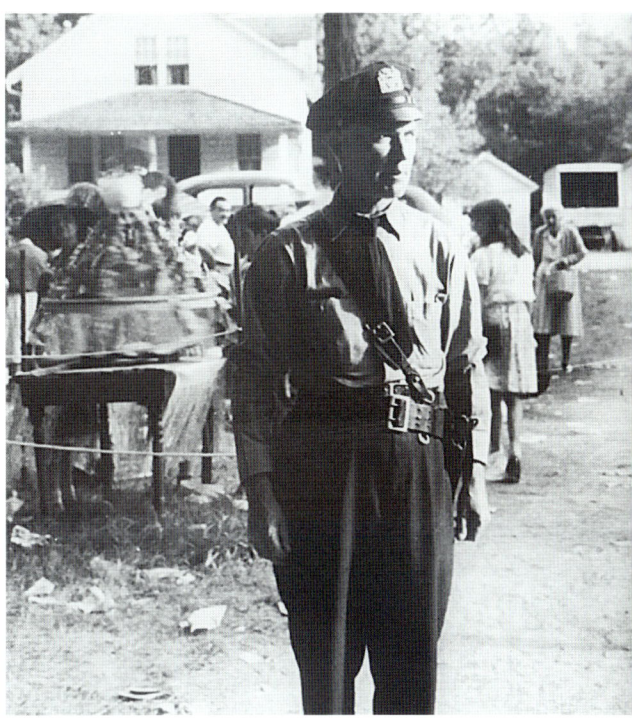

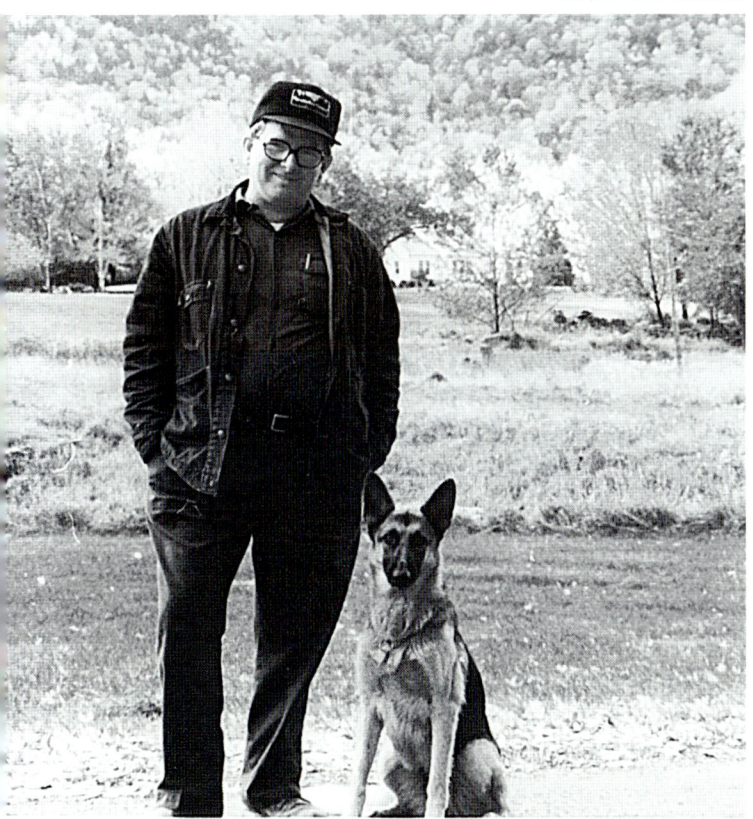

Lester Shultis

Most comfortable in the woods of Wittenberg, Lester Shultis spent most of his life tending to the sawmill and farm that had been in his family for generations. Elected to the 1976 Woodstock Town Board, Shultis found himself in the middle of the changes sweeping Woodstock as the town sought to eliminate the rising costs of home relief generated by an influx of newcomers. (Courtesy Jeanne Shultis.)

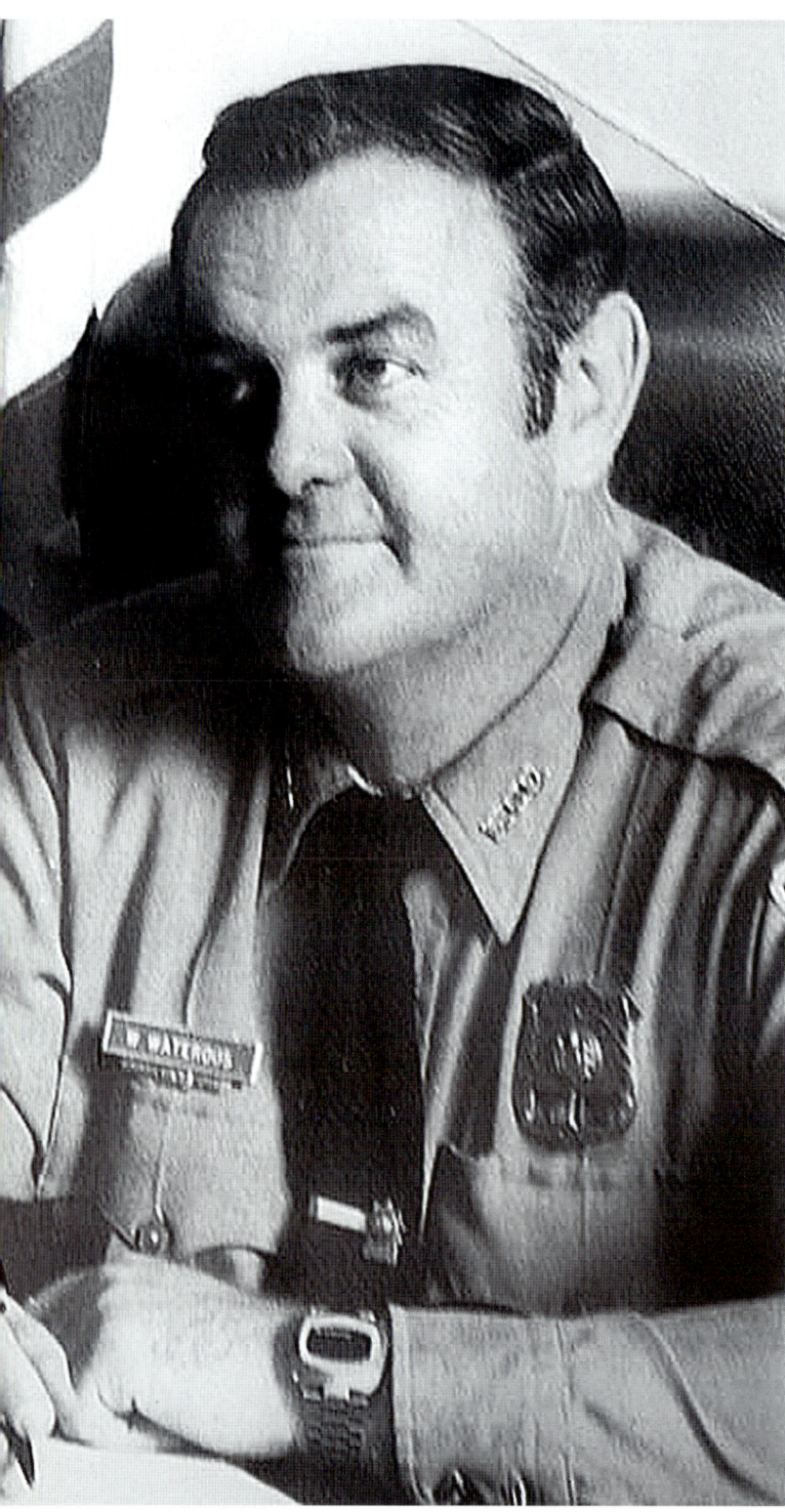

William Waterous

Since its creation in 1931, Bill Waterous holds the distinction as the longest-serving police chief in the history of the Woodstock Police Department. Appointed in the 1960s, he was confronted with the influx of young people into Woodstock following word of Bob Dylan's arrival and later in the aftermath of the Woodstock Festival. As members of Woodstock Nation found their way to town, taxing many of its services, Waterous, in one of more oft-quoted statements of the era, told the local press, "I don't call them hippies, I call them drifters and bums because that's what they are." Serving until 1981, Waterous navigated the small department through challenging times, enhancing its professionalism and earning the respect of the community. Married to Mary Trippico, he was an excellent golfer with three Woodstock Golf Club championships to his credit.

Malcolm Rose

Malcolm Rose, a talented woodworker and local building contractor, was born in Bearsville in the house his father built for his mother. He served in the Army Air Corps, enlisting the day after Pearl Harbor. A long-standing member of Rotary, he was also an advisor and technical assistant for the historical society. Rose served 17 years on the Woodstock Planning Board, a number of them as chair. For a time, he was the only native-born Woodstocker on the board. Often, his philosophy was at odds with members who wanted to make it difficult for new construction to take place. "Everybody wants to be the last one in and then lock the door," he once said. "If we always did it that way I would be the only one in the room." (Courtesy Lorin and Shirley Rose.)

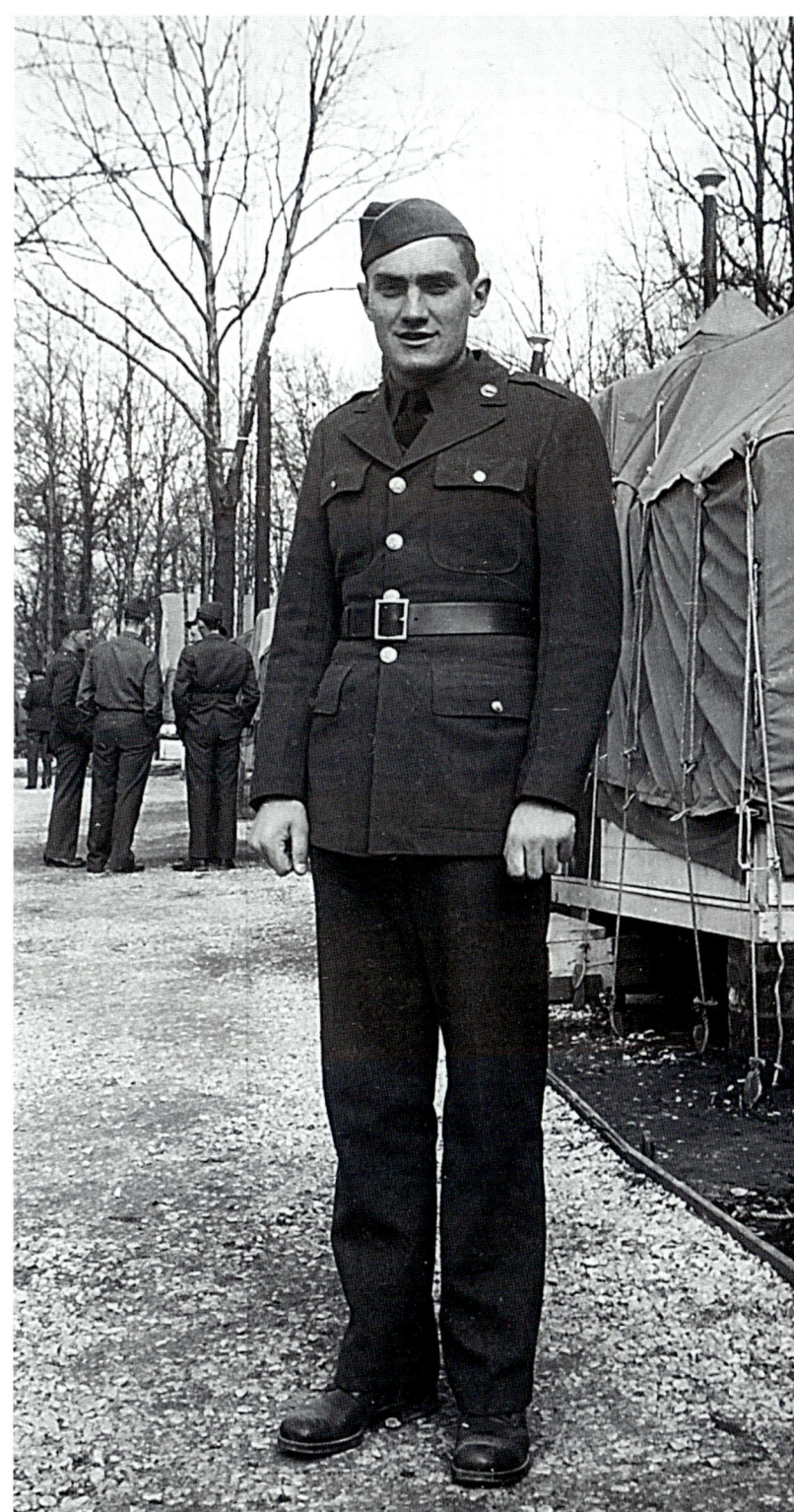

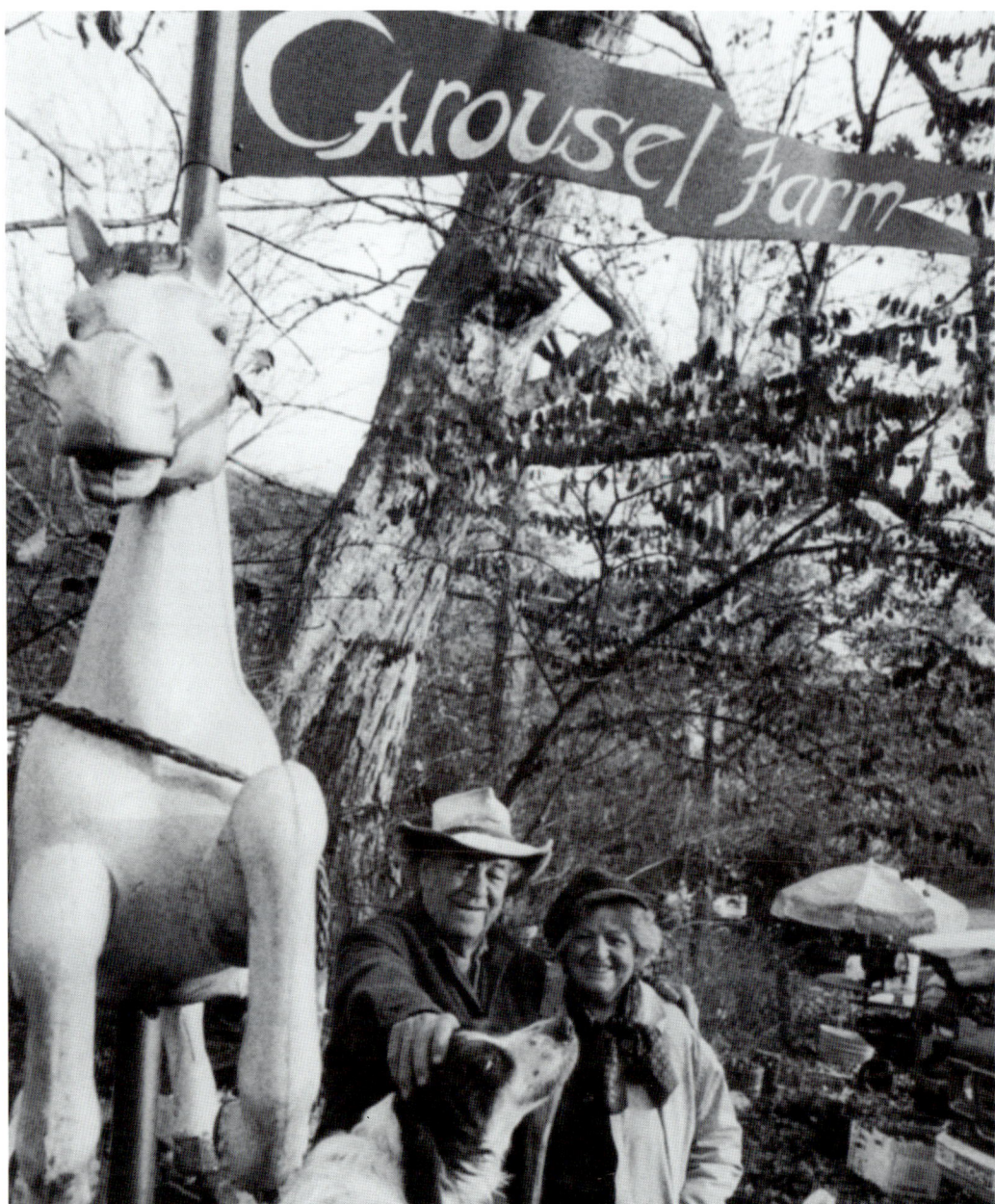

Ed and Margot Balmer
Wanting to relocate to Woodstock in the early 1960s, Ed and Margot Balmer came upon a home in Shady once owned by prominent Woodstocker Stephen Stillwell. Falling in love with the house, the Balmer family soon took up residence. An Army Air Corps veteran and machine shop teacher by trade, Ed developed a love for creating magnificent carousels. Both political and vocal, he would also run (unsuccessfully) for highway superintendent against Ray Van Valkenburg. Many Woodstockers still recall with great fondness the contributions the Balmers made to I Love Woodstock Day. Each year, the Columbus Day celebration included apple cider pressing on the village green, where Ed, in his Colonial-era hat, would readily offer instruction on the finer points of cider and cider pressing. (Courtesy Craig Balmer.)

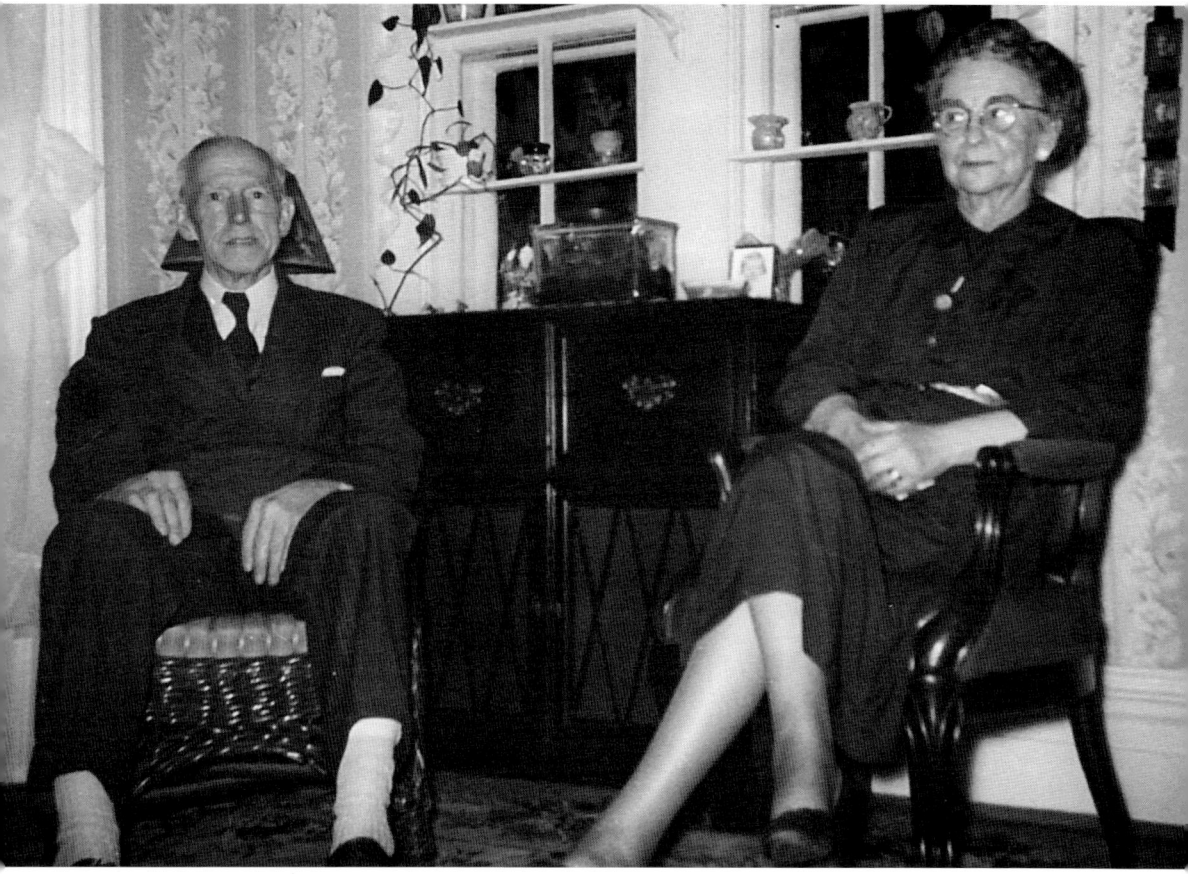

William S. and Bertha Elwyn
William Elwyn, a local businessman specializing in real estate, served at one time as Woodstock postmaster. In 1926, he joined a group of investors in purchasing the Woodstock Lodge (also known as the Woodstock Inn) from Gabriel Newgold. With the building renovated, it reopened under the management of William H. Wilber. Unfortunately, the building would burn to the ground in 1929. His wife, Bertha, was well known as a collector of American glass, including pieces created locally by the 19th-century glass company in Shady. Their home was filled with beautiful pieces, both practical and decorative. In 1929, the Elwyns were part of the founding membership of the Historical Society of Woodstock with Bertha serving as the first elected treasurer. (Courtesy Mary Elwyn.)

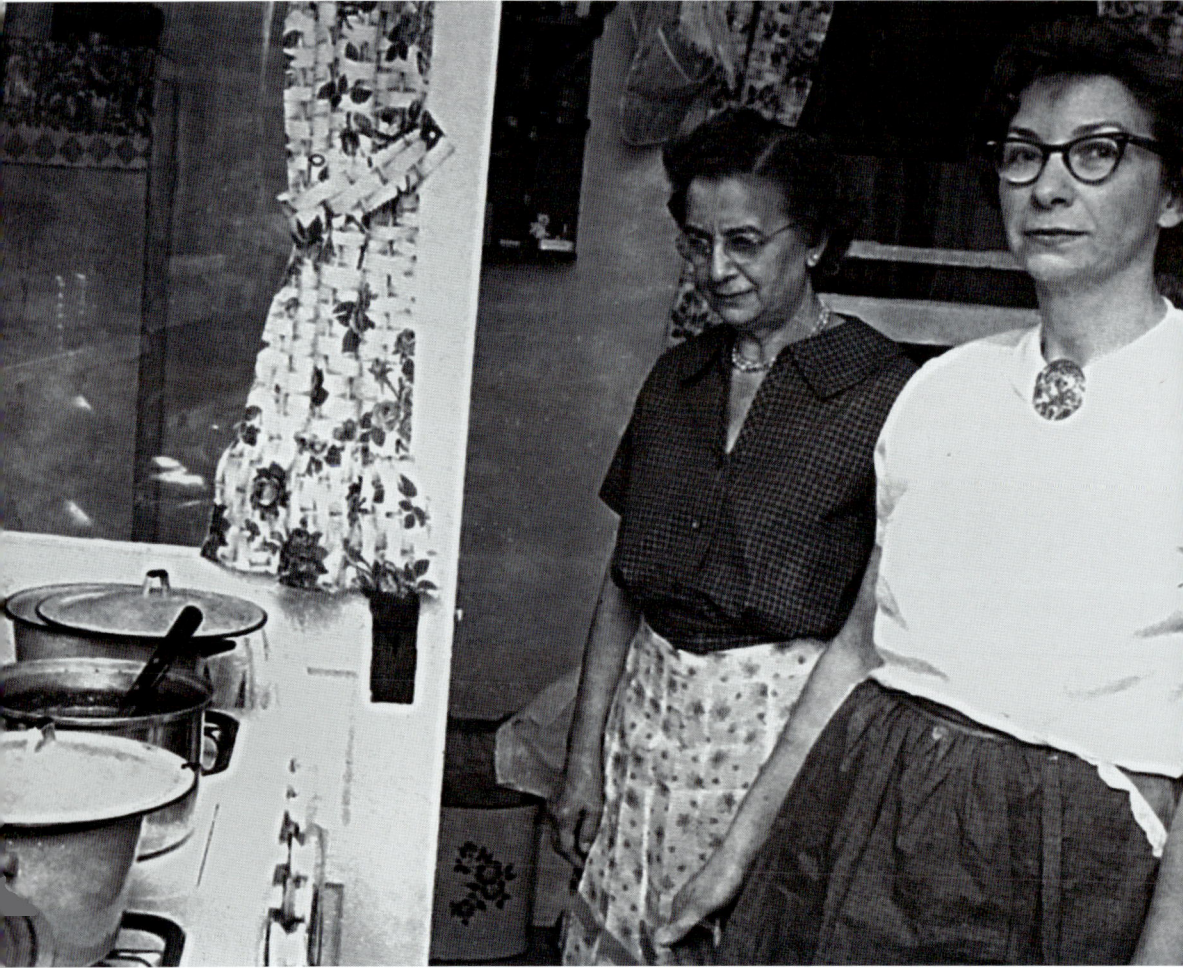

Florence Peper and Marge Peper Harder
Serving as Woodstock town clerk from 1953 to 1978, Marge Harder (right) and her aunt Florence Peper were long-standing members of the Agapae Rebecca Lodge No. 625 in Bearsville. Florence and her brother John lived their entire lives in the family home where Mirabai Books now operates. Their father, Henry Peper, ran the family blacksmith shop next door. "Aunt Florence" was active in Christ's Lutheran Church, serving as treasurer for a period of time. Her greatest gift to Woodstock has been the *Florence Peper Diaries*, detailing town life over a number of years. The blacksmithing operation eventually evolved into Peper's Garage, where Marge Harder acted as bookkeeper for many years. Harder also supported the Ladies Auxiliary of American Legion Post No. 1026 and was very active in the Woodstock Republican Party. (Courtesy Bill Harder Sr.)

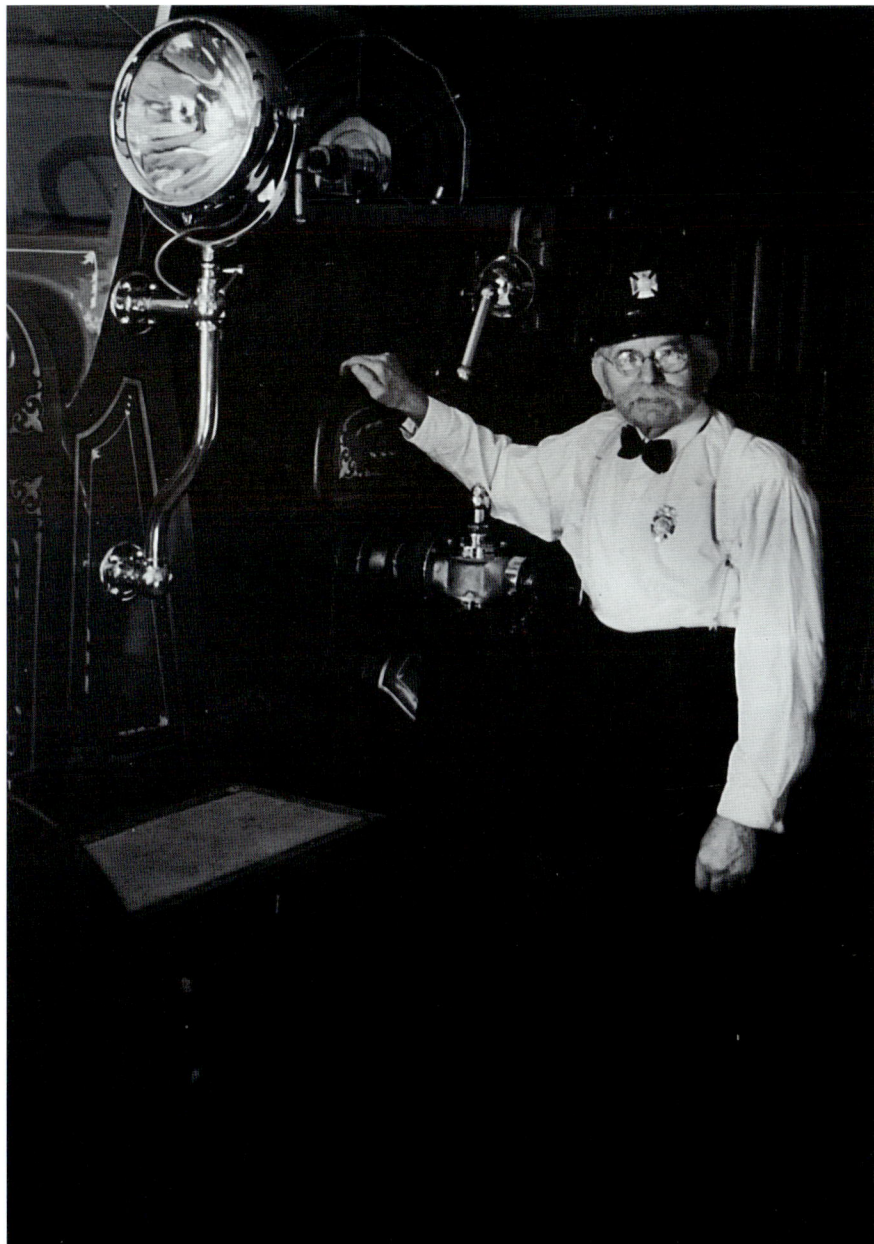

Henry Peper
Henry Peper was Woodstock's blacksmith. But he was more. Working from his shop on Mill Hill Road, Peper was a craftsman. His work found its way into such places as the Overlook Mountain House and Morris Newgold's Colony Hotel on Rock City Road, where his handcrafted window boxes and interior trim were featured. Born in 1859, Peper was a devoted Lutheran. In 1913, he joined other Woodstockers to form the Woodstock Club, an organization begun by the Whiteheads, Lindins, Downers, and Weyls for the purpose of forming a nursing service, a library, and other community programs. In 1918, when the influenza epidemic swept through Woodstock, Peper's son Will would succumb to the disease despite the nursing efforts of Hervey White. (Courtesy Bill Harder Sr.)

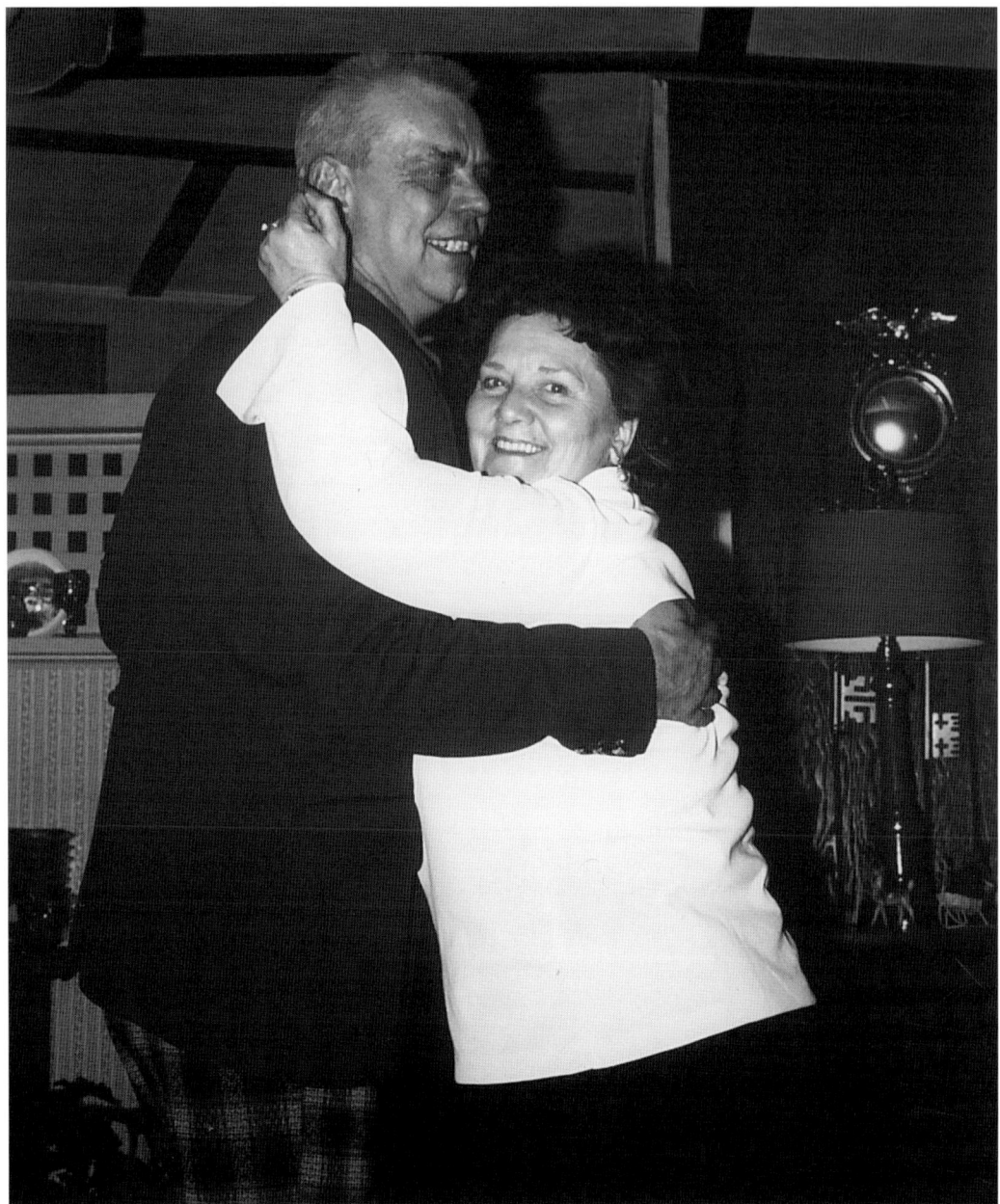

Ken and Dodie Maclary Reynolds
In 1960, Ken and Dodie Reynolds opened Ken's Esso (later Exxon) on Mill Hill Road. Loved by the community, Ken was known to curse foreign cars but would never hesitate to go out on a wintry morning to jump-start them. Ken, who grew up in the farmhouse built by his grandfather Harford Reynolds, met Dodie when he was a driver for Needs Express. A volunteer with the fire company, he also served on the board of the Woodstock Cemetery Association. For many years, he worked seven days a week, though eventually finding time to pursue his passion for photography. Dodie, a member of the Ladies Fire Auxiliary and the Overlook Methodist Church, also served as a regular driver for Meals on Wheels. (Courtesy Gary and Sharon Reynolds.)

Stanley Brinkerhoff Longyear

Pictured here with his wife, Emily, and daughter, Janet, Stanley Brinkerhoff Longyear was one Woodstocker one did not want to cross. Raised in the house built by William Brinkerhoff, "S.B." Longyear served as a page in the New York State Senate. Later, he oversaw a large farm in the center of what is now the Woodstock business district. Managing a livery stable as well, Longyear provided coach rides from the train station in West Hurley to Woodstock. As transportation evolved, he would later offer taxi and bus service between Kingston and Woodstock. A shrewd businessman, Longyear constructed an apartment building on Rock City Road and, following the destruction of the Brinkerhoff Hotel by fire, built the current Longyear Building on the corner of Mill Hill Road and Rock City Road. (Illustration by Earle B. Winslow; both, courtesy Kathy Longyear.)

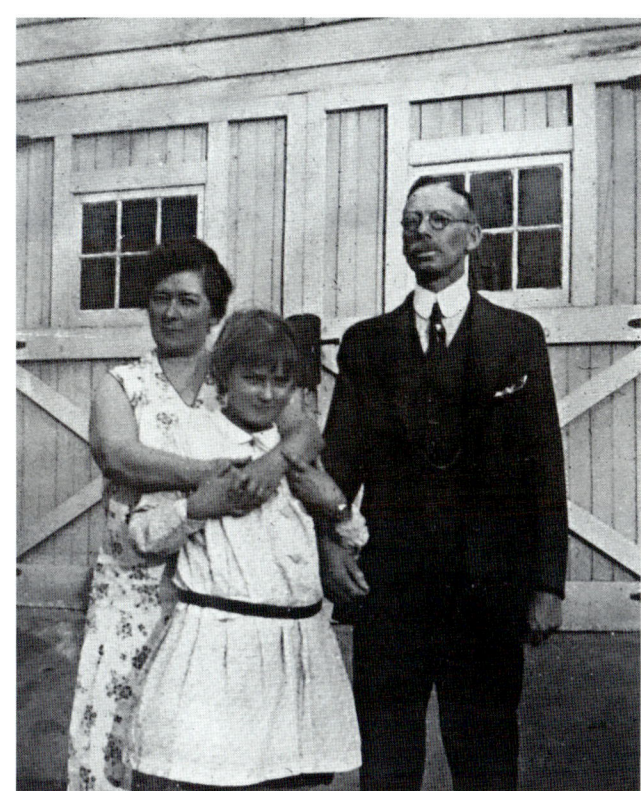

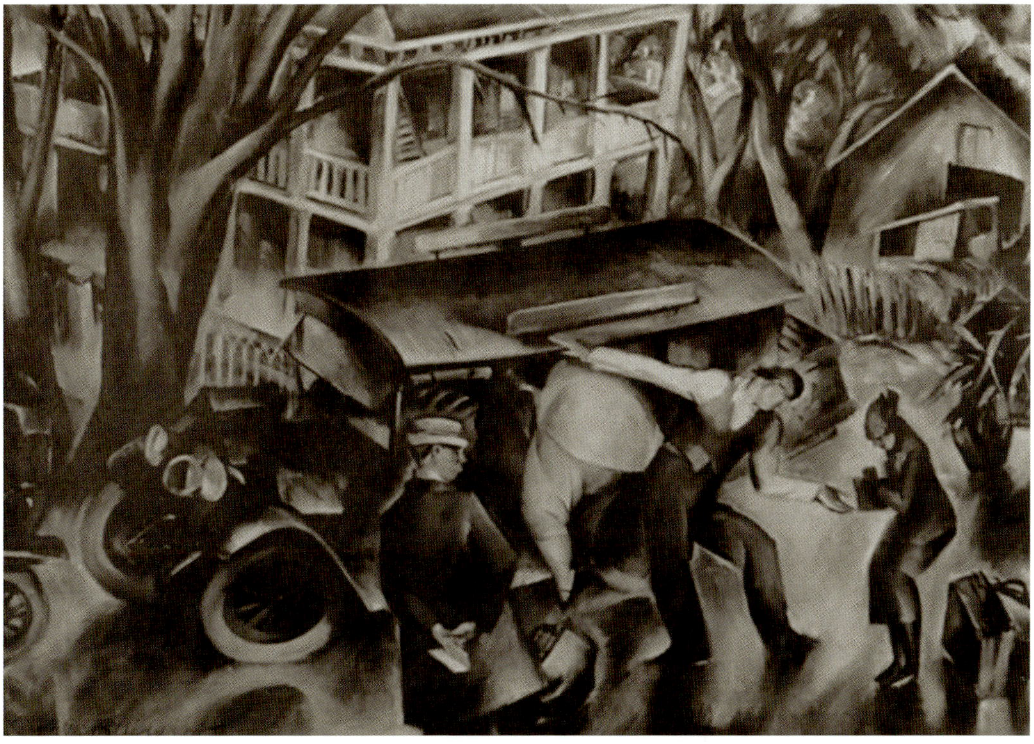

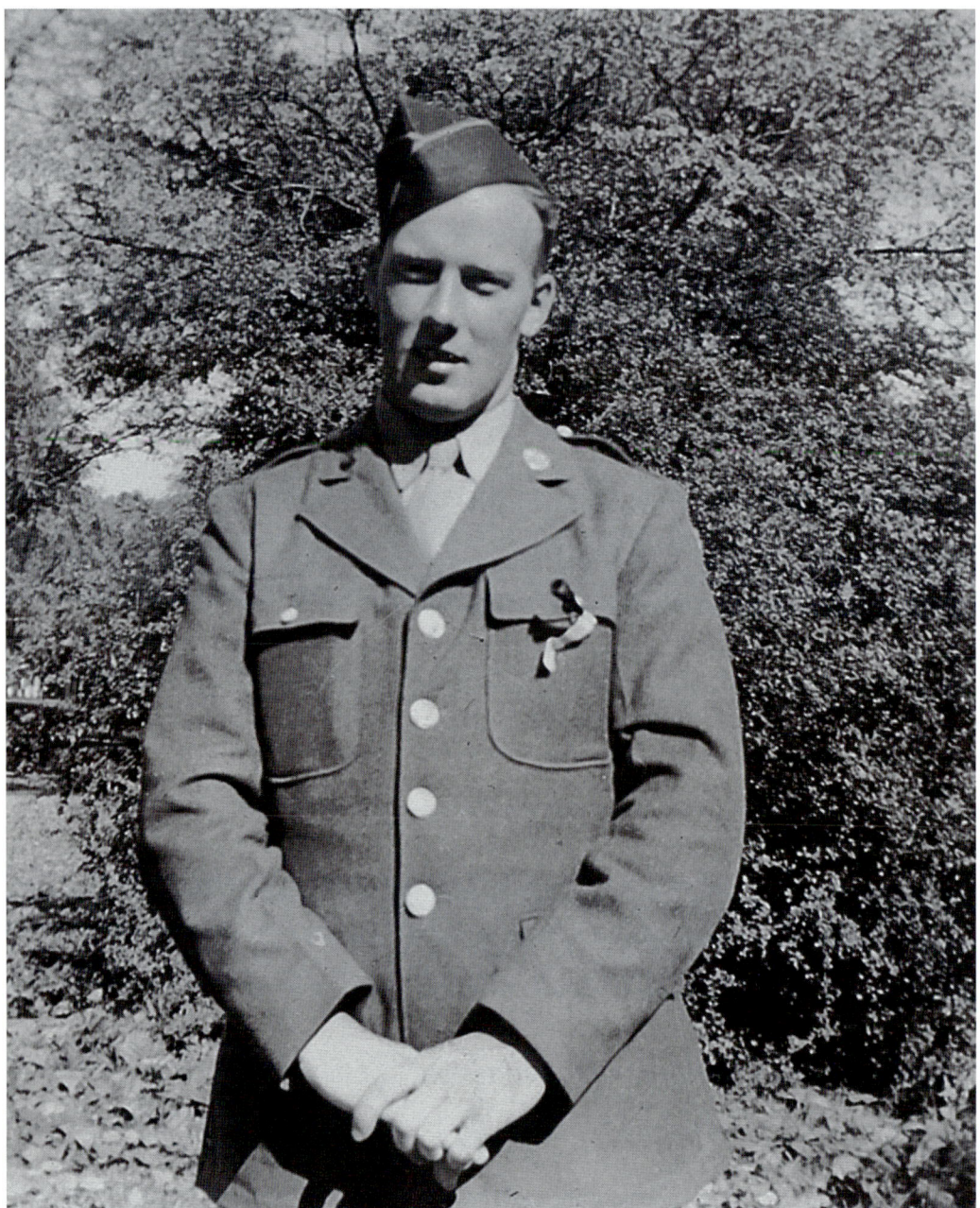

Stanley "Sonny" Longyear
Sonny Longyear was raised in the center of Woodstock in the same grand old house on Rock City Road that his father, Stanley Brinkerhoff Longyear, was raised in. Serving in the Pacific theater during World War II, he was awarded the Air Medal for courageous acts during aerial flight. Upon his return to Woodstock in 1944, Longyear made the decision to leave the center of town and purchase a rundown farm on Schoonmaker Lane. Over the years, his efforts were the genesis of Long-Year Farm. A tireless worker, Sonny Longyear operated the Woodstock Garage on Mill Hill Road with his half-brother Lew Wilson before opening his own service station in West Hurley. (Courtesy Kathy Longyear.)

Stan Longyear

Remembered as a passionate outdoorsman and environmentalist, Stan Longyear possessed an intimate knowledge of the trails and mountains of Woodstock and neighboring environs. Following graduation from Onteora High School, Longyear went on to receive a bachelor's of science in electrical engineering from Norwich College and a master's of business administration from the State University of New York at Albany. After two years in the US Army, mustering out as a first lieutenant in 1975, Longyear returned to the family farm on Schoonmaker Lane with his wife, Kathy. While working with his father, Sonny, at the family's West Hurley service station, he took on the task of building and shaping the family farm into his vision of sustainability. In 2003, he would decide to mix town politics with raising Texas longhorns and launched a successful bid for town highway superintendent. During his tenure, he would oversee the building of a new town highway garage. After his untimely death in 2005, his family continues to carry on his dedication to land conservation and sustainable farming. In 2009, the Woodstock Town Board voted to name a portion of the town-owned Comeau Property the Stan Longyear Meadow. (Courtesy Kathy Longyear.)

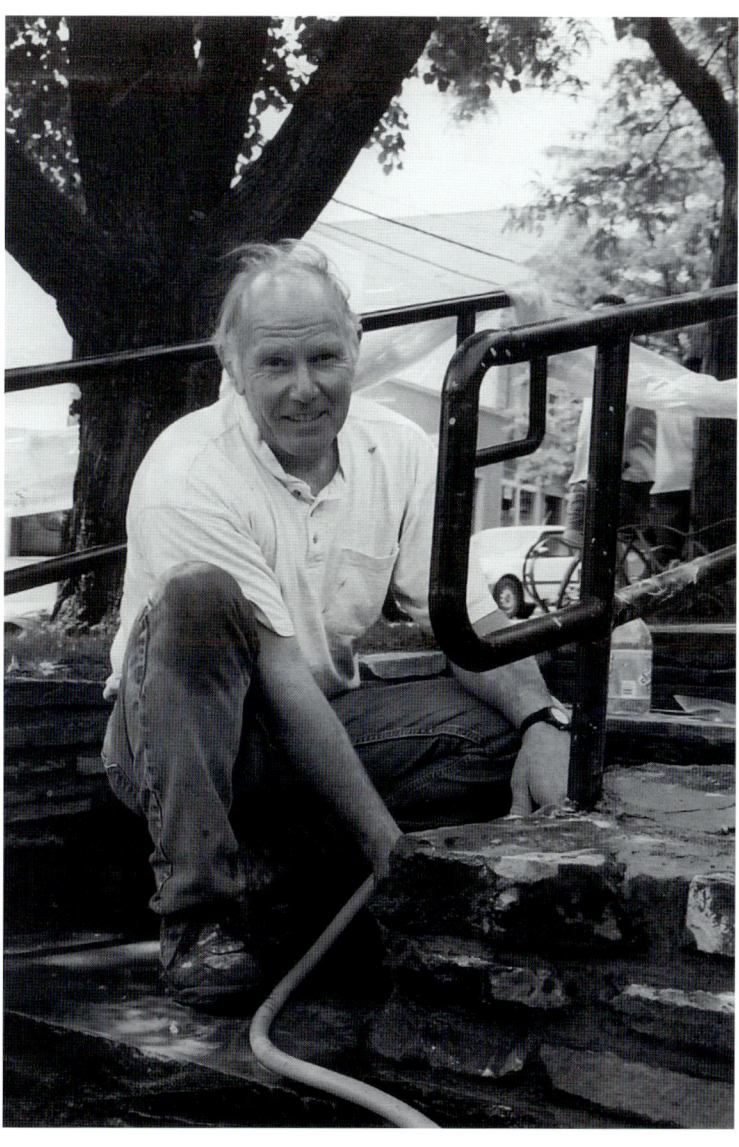

Levon Helm

Levon Helm loved Woodstock, and Woodstock gladly returned the favor. First arriving in Woodstock in the shadow of Bob Dylan, Helm would later emerge as a member of the Band, making the Woodstock area home. As classics albums such as *Music from Big Pink* (nearby) and songs such as "Up on Cripple Creek" took them to the pinnacle of rock, Helm continued to keep the Woodstock community close. Yet, despite the heights the Band would reach and the success an entry into film would bring, times and opportunity would change for Levon. Fire would destroy his home. Bankruptcy would follow, and cancer would threaten to take it all. But Helm would not quit. Battling back from cancer, with the help of family, friends, and community, he would return to music. Writing a new chapter and inching his way back to the top, he began the Midnight Ramble at his home in Woodstock. Initially seen as a way to pay the rent, the Ramble prospered and, at the same time, returned music to Woodstock in ways the town had not seen in years. Helm was back, and more Grammys would follow. Equally important, he also returned to Woodstock the support and love he had received over the years. Benefits for the community became a part of his schedule as he lent his voice and his music to aid the art and music programs of local schools, families in need, the local food pantry, a free concert for a local farm, flood victims, troops, and many more. So it was, following Helm's death in April 2012, that Woodstock turned out to honor the passing of its adopted son. Busloads of friends and admirers made their way from points in town to Helm's barn where the Rambles were held to pay their respects. Hundreds more lined the streets on the day of his funeral as the procession made its way to the Woodstock Cemetery, where, as music carried through the air and over the town, Levon Helm was laid to rest next to fellow Band member Rick Danko. (Courtesy Dion Ogust.)

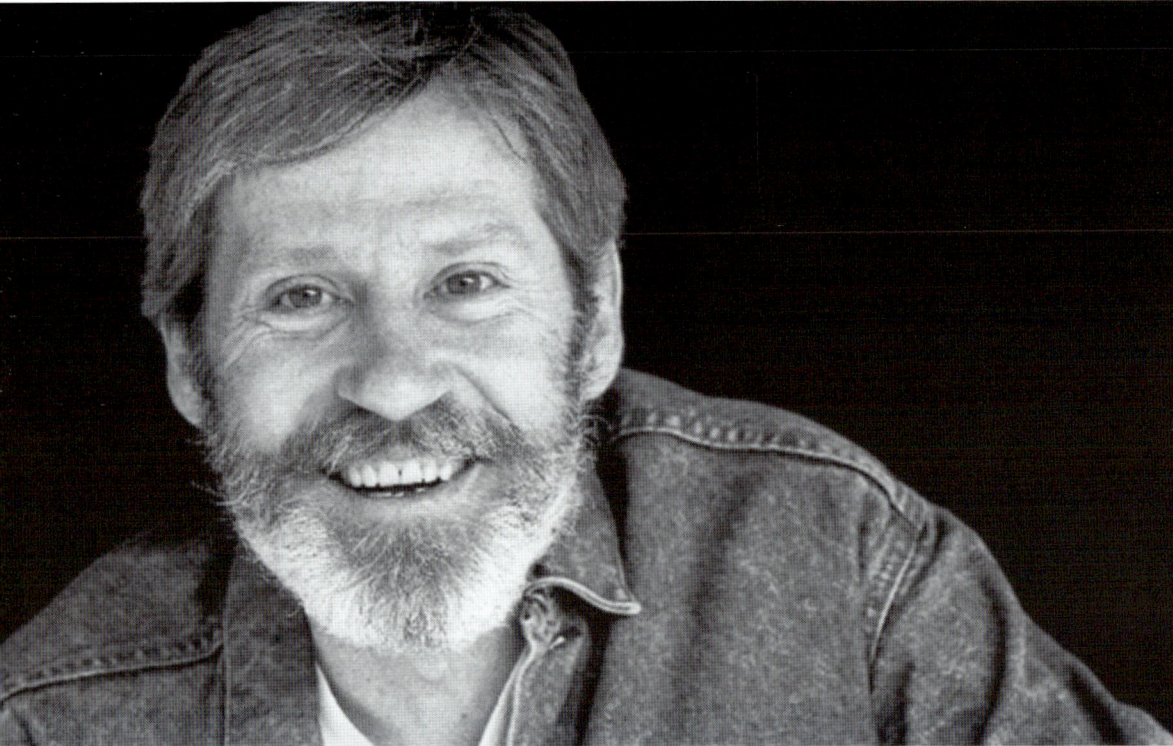

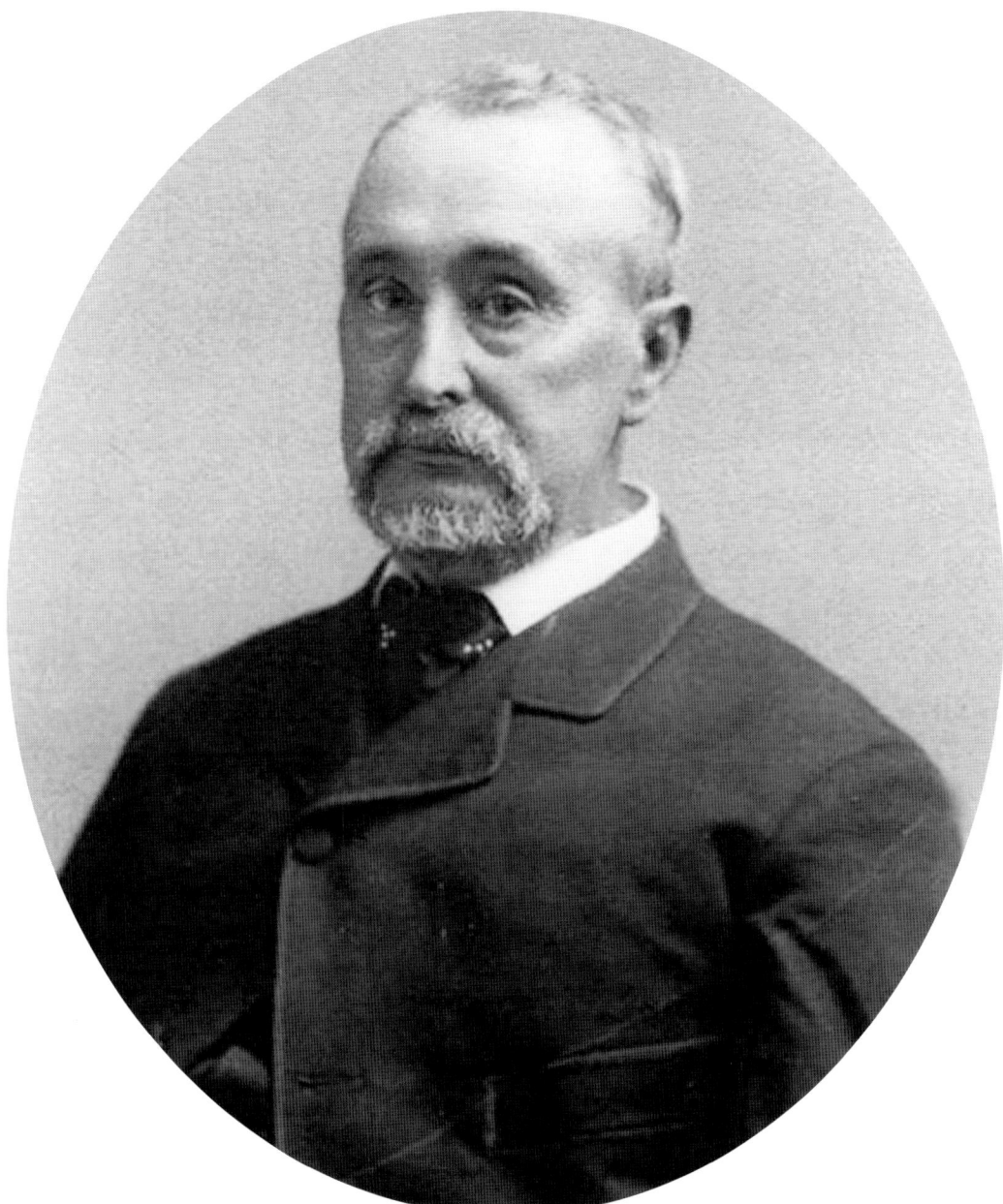

Alexander Elwyn
Like his grandfather John M. Elwyn, Alexander Elwyn was a well-known innkeeper in 19th-century Woodstock. Moving from New England to Woodstock in the late 1700s, the Elwyn family acquired the land that lies between Library Lane and Orchard Lane. Their holdings also included what is now referred to as the Comeau Property. Legend has it that the accommodations and food at Elwyn's establishment were highly recommended by travelers throughout the region. As leadership at the time was often drawn from men in the business community, Elwyn served as town clerk for Woodstock in 1859, 1862, and 1865. After a brief hiatus from political life, he returned to politics and was elected town supervisor, serving one term beginning in 1877. (Courtesy Jon Elwyn.)

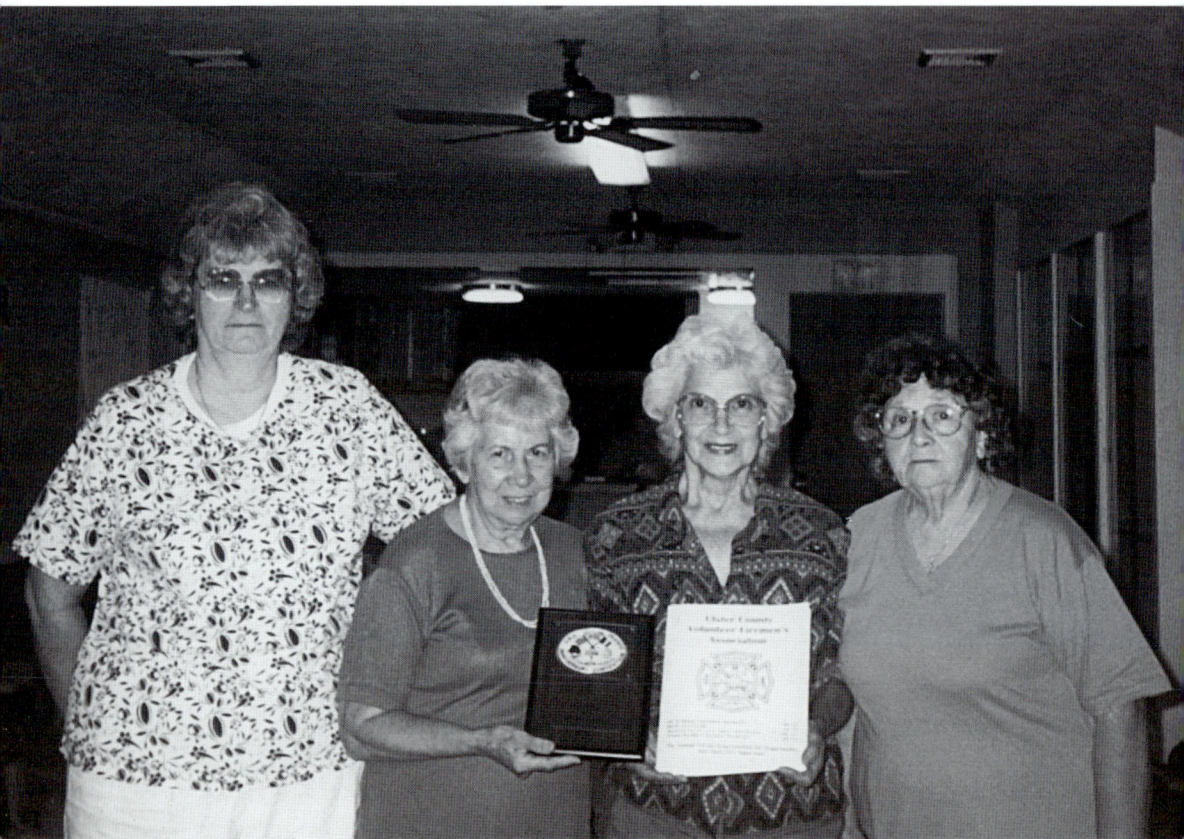

Ladies Auxiliary Fire Company No. 1
Commemorating the 40th anniversary of the Fire Company No. 1 Ladies Auxiliary were (from left to right) Priscilla Hastie Koehn, Anne Mower, Ann Park, and Dodie Reynolds. Both Mower and Koehn were charter members of the organization, founded in 1961. Typically, the Ladies Auxiliary held three or four fundraisers for Fire Company No. 1 yearly, including bake sales, a Christmas fair, and penny socials. Perhaps the most memorable weekend of the year for all was the "wash down breakfast" held each Memorial Day weekend. On the Sunday prior to Memorial Day, Ladies Auxiliary members gathered at the firehouse before dawn to prepare a breakfast of bacon, eggs, and French toast for the dozens of volunteer firemen who would spend the morning hosing down Woodstock's streets prior to the Memorial Day parade.

CHAPTER TWO: COMMUNITY LEGENDS: CRAFTING A BETTER WOODSTOCK

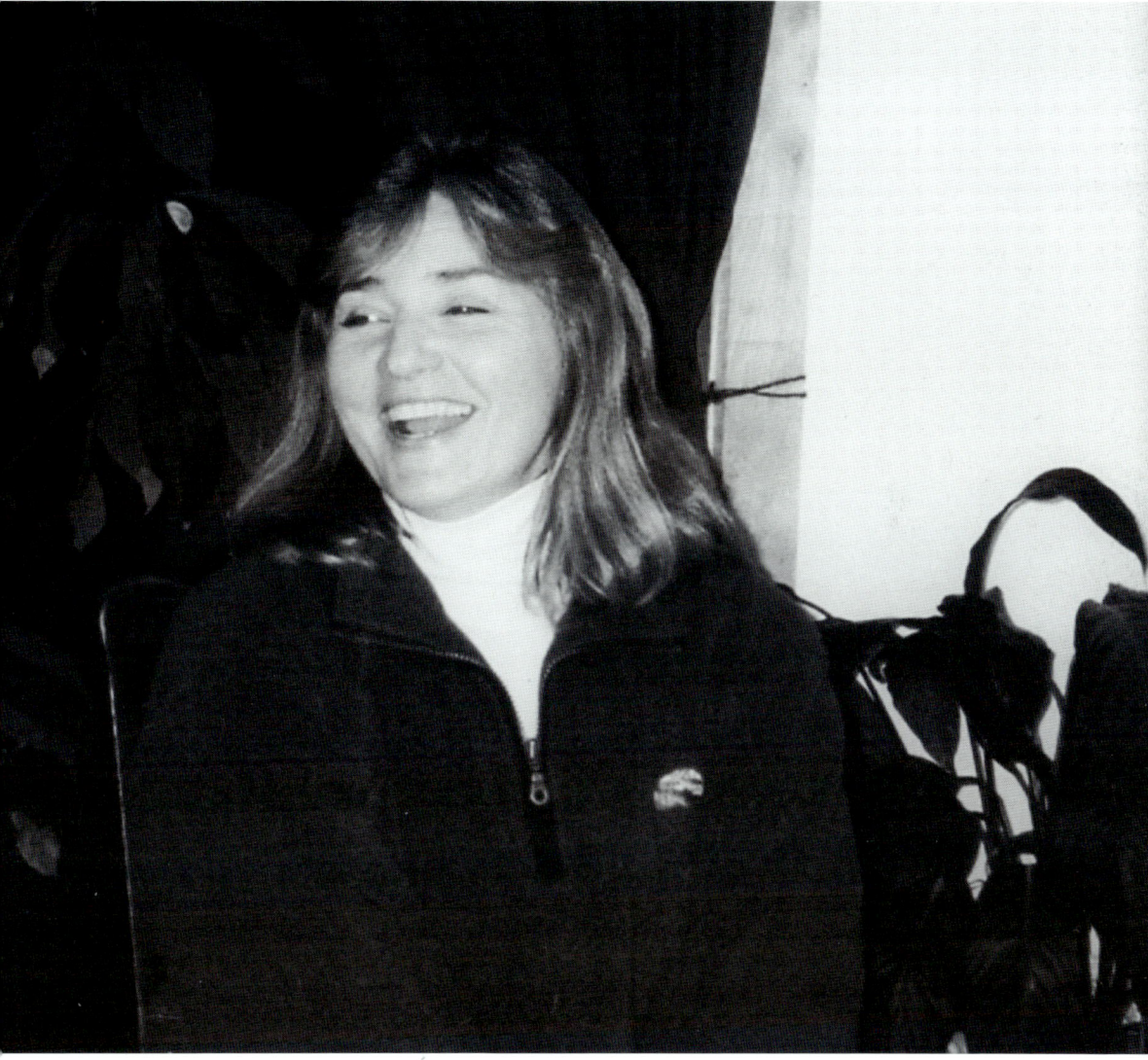

Elizabeth "Liz" DeLisio Spinelli
Liz learned early to love the Woodstock Golf Club. Her father, Tony DeLisio, joined the club in 1943 and served as president in the 1940s and 1950s. Her mother, Wiggy, was a well-known champion golfer. Liz became general manager of the club following the untimely death of her husband, Phil Spinelli, in 1992. Her ability to make everyone feel welcome and at ease was a tremendous asset to an organization that faced many challenges in the latter part of 20th century. Her passion for the club and its members, her community involvement, and love of family remains etched in the memories of many. It was with grace and a commitment to life that she faced the challenge of cancer right up to the time of her passing in 2010.

Betty MacDonald

What did Betty MacDonald mean to Woodstock? To know, one only needed to have witnessed her friends singing her home as they gathered outside her house during her final days or to view the people who assembled on Woodstock's village green to do the same. Betty MacDonald was central to Woodstock music and community. A multitalented force, MacDonald impacted Woodstock through her music as a jazz artist, a teacher, a radio personality and a friend who gave back to Woodstock whenever called upon to do so. Musically, she seemed to perform with everyone, including Warren Bernhardt, Jack DeJonette, and Dave Holland. Most memorable for Woodstockers, however, were the many nights she spent on stage with Marc Black and Michael Esposito and, equally as important, the countless performances she gave to benefit a family or a Woodstock cause.

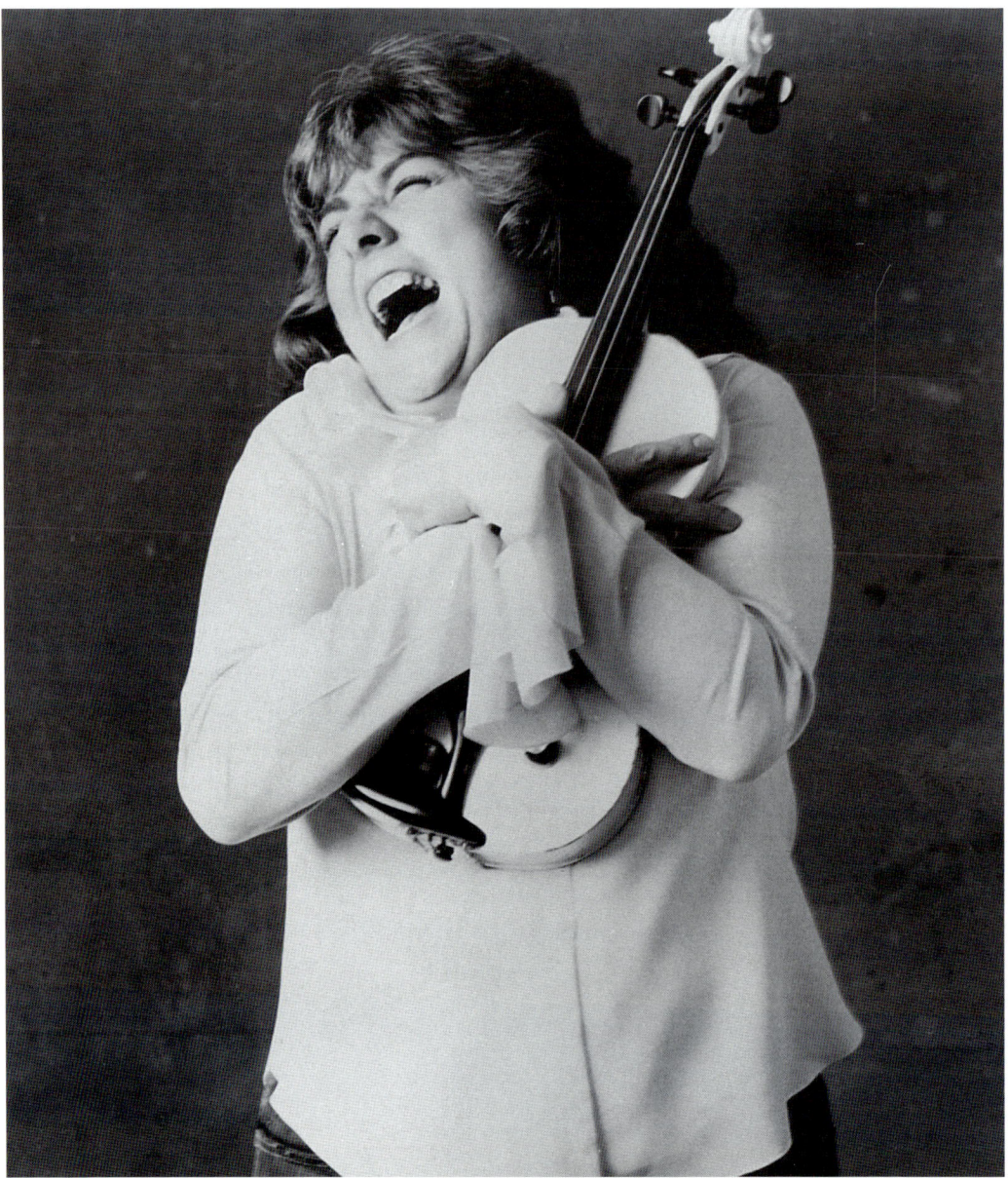

Larry Elwyn

Larry Elwyn's barbershop, located at the corner of Tannery Brook Road and Tinker Street, was the center for politics, gossip, and storytelling. But Elwyn was a man of many interests. Once a quarryman, he was also a housepainter, builder, foxhunter, and fisherman. When the artists came to town, Elwyn was a busy man. As Will Rose recalled in *The Vanishing Village*, published by Twines' Catskill Bookshop: "In the old Woodstock you had to watch for him [Elwyn] because he might be painting a house somewhere, or butchering a pig in the fall, or even out hunting foxes with his hound. But now he is in the barber shop all the time because of so many people in Woodstock, although some of the artists don't pay much attention to their hair." (Courtesy Jon Elwyn.)

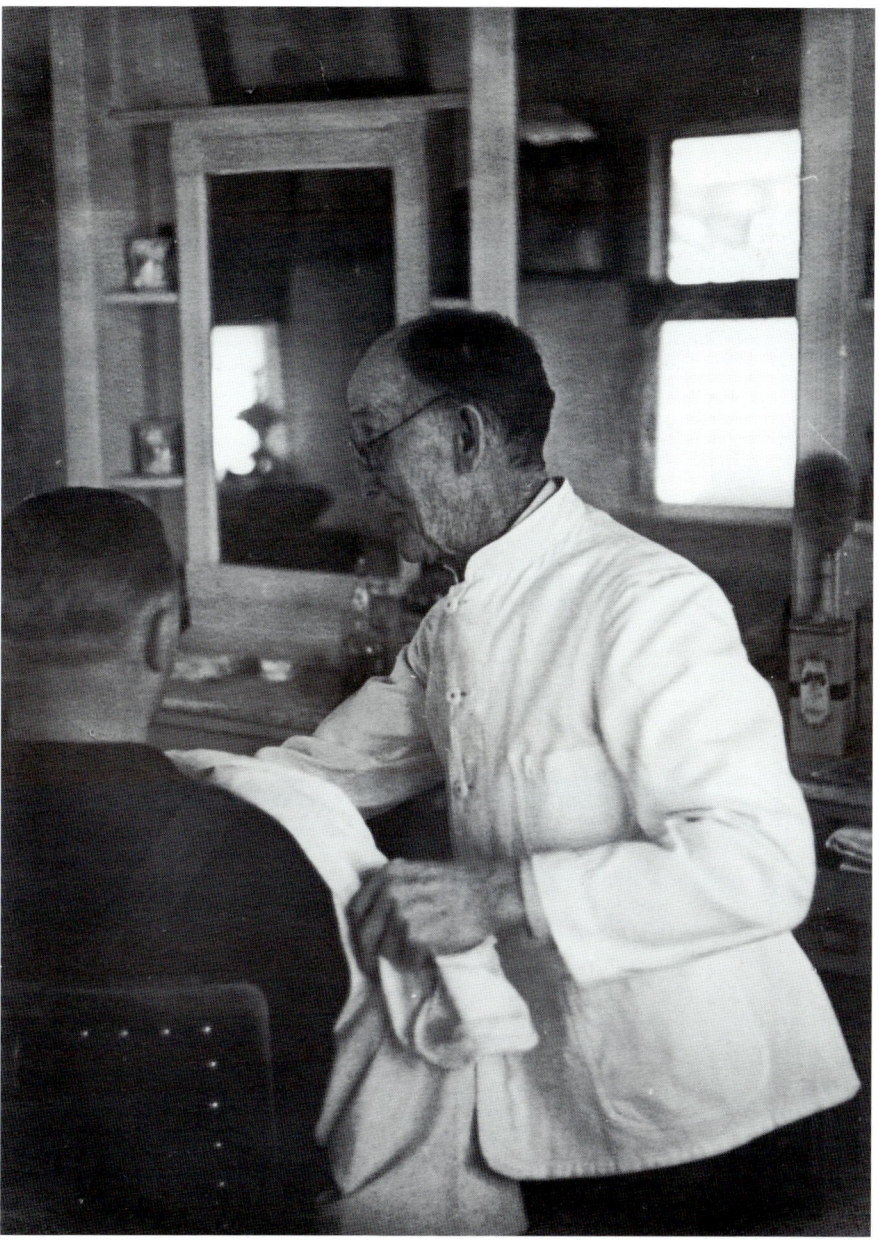

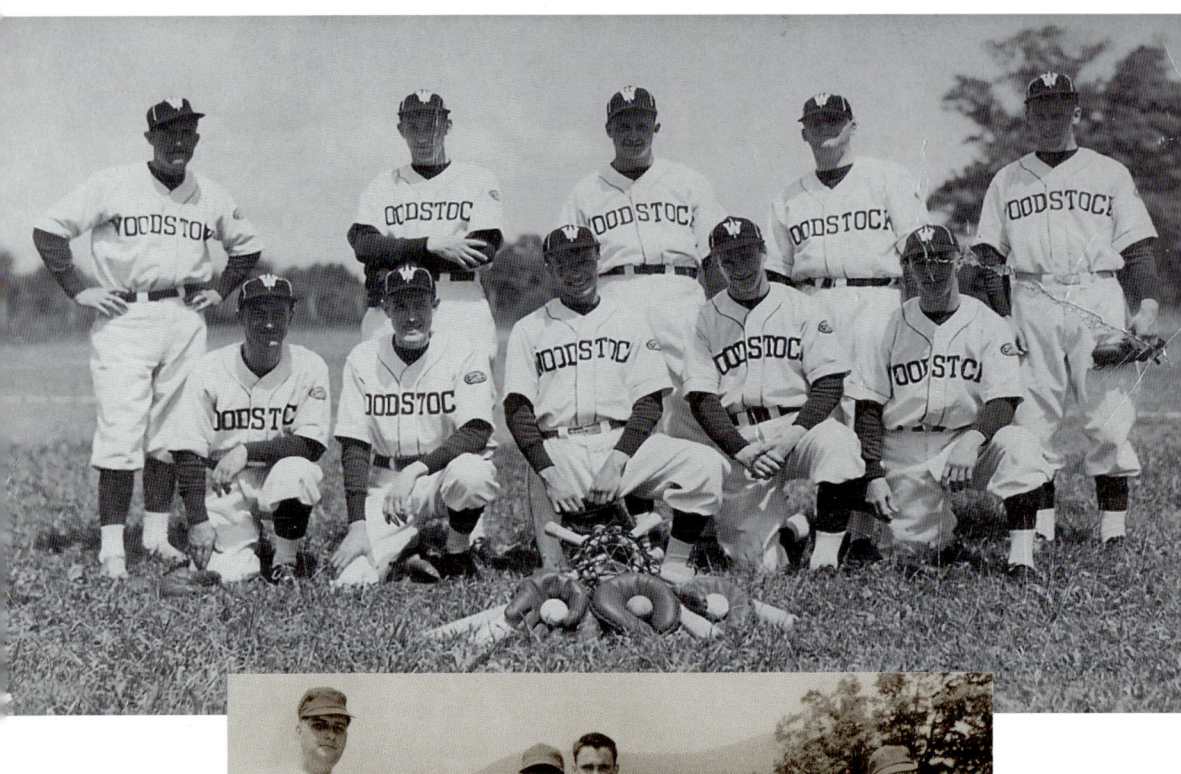

Woodstock Baseball

Prior to World War II, and shortly thereafter, local adult baseball teams barnstormed throughout the Catskills. Woodstock was no exception, playing Sunday games against teams from towns such as Oneonta, Kingston, Catskill, and Saugerties. Generally recognized as the best player Woodstock produced, Clayton Harder (first row, second from the right) played shortstop for the 1936 team pictured here. In the 1950s, adult baseball in Woodstock gave way to younger players and the arrival of little league baseball. The idea of introducing youth baseball was first discussed in 1956 and, by the following year, teams like the 1957 Dodgers had taken the field. More than half a century later, at Rick Volz field, little league baseball continues to be an integral part of the Woodstock community.

CHAPTER TWO: COMMUNITY LEGENDS: CRAFTING A BETTER WOODSTOCK

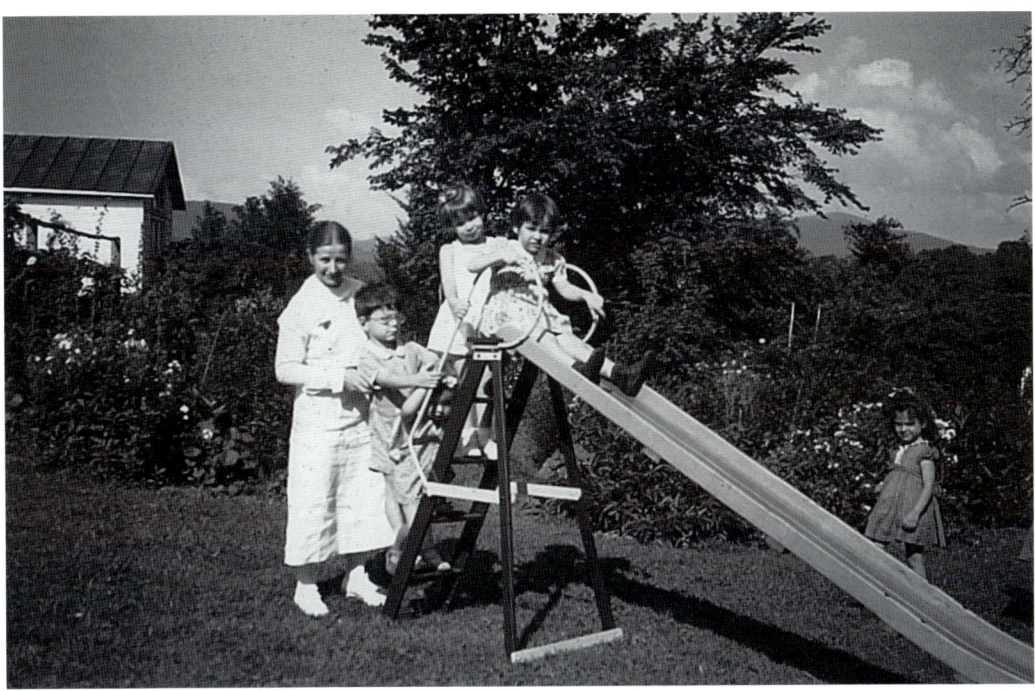

Neva Shultis
Neva Shultis was Woodstock's school nurse. Shown here at Gretchen Smith's nursery school, Shultis would visit the school once a week. In addition, she would also visit the one-room school in the village, where Olive Toms was the teacher. In her day, Shultis would maintain records of student growth and development and act as a resource for nutritional guidance, common childhood illnesses, and possible home remedies. As an herbalist, she would share her remedies with the community for common maladies, rheumatism, corns, bunions, or coughs. Neva Shultis was also an author. In 1957, she penned *From Sunset to Cock's Crow*, a collection of folktales gathered while making her rounds as a midwife. Many of her interesting stories centered on witches who were said to have inhabited the hills and valleys of Woodstock. (Above, courtesy Judson Smith.)

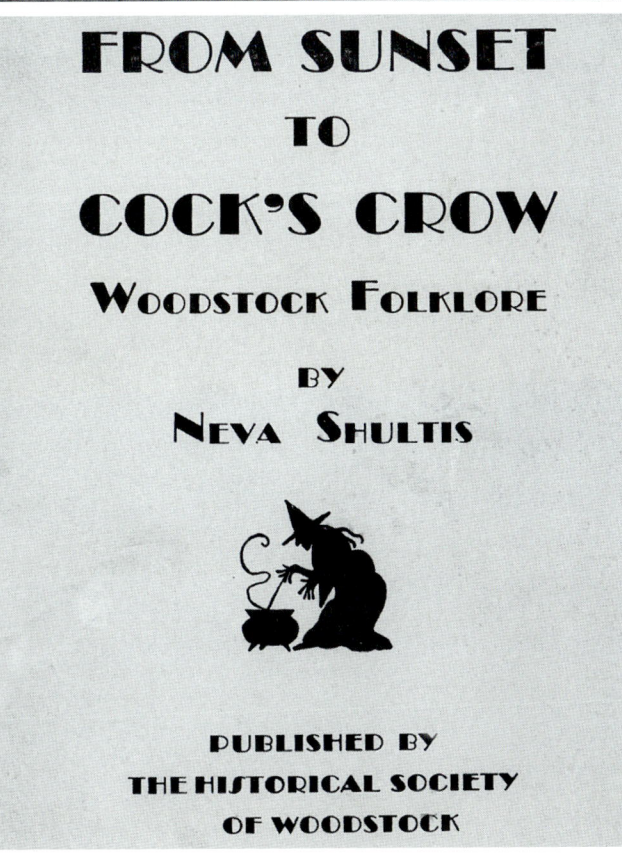

FROM SUNSET TO COCK'S CROW

WOODSTOCK FOLKLORE

BY

NEVA SHULTIS

PUBLISHED BY
THE HISTORICAL SOCIETY
OF WOODSTOCK

81

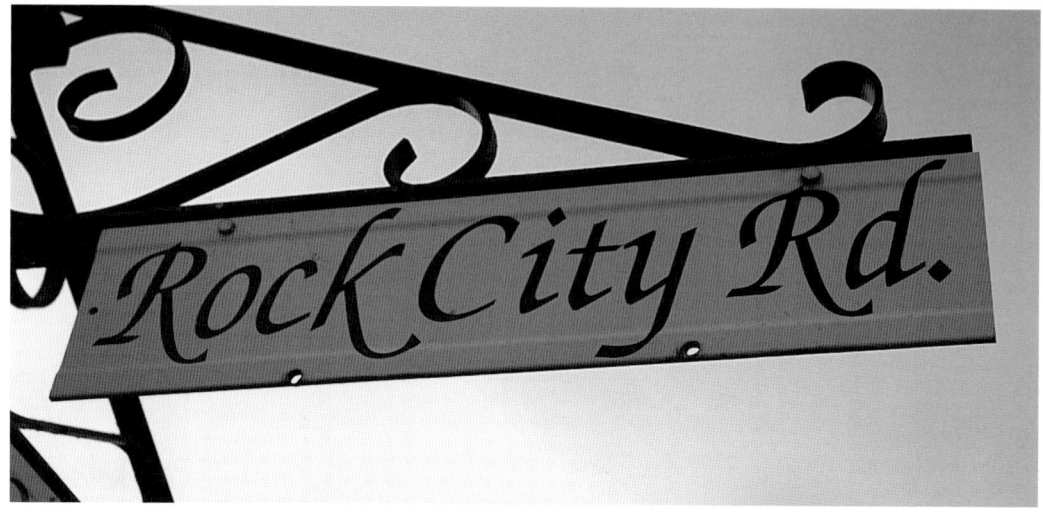

Rock City and Rosie Magee
In the early 1900s, Woodstock knew her as Rosie Magee. To the young art students familiar with Rock City Road and the nearby falls she became "Mother Magee." Married to a quarryman who found less and less work as the demand for bluestone declined, Rosie Magee opened their home on the corner of Rock City Road to boarders. As art students began to arrive, seeking lodging in her home or in the barns along Rock City Road, the Magee kitchen became a center of activity for what became known as the "Rock City group." A remarkable cook who fed those artists fortunate enough to find her table, Rosie Magee also demonstrated compassion, kindness, and a sense of humor when it came to caring for her young guests, traits not all Woodstockers possessed when encountering the newcomers.

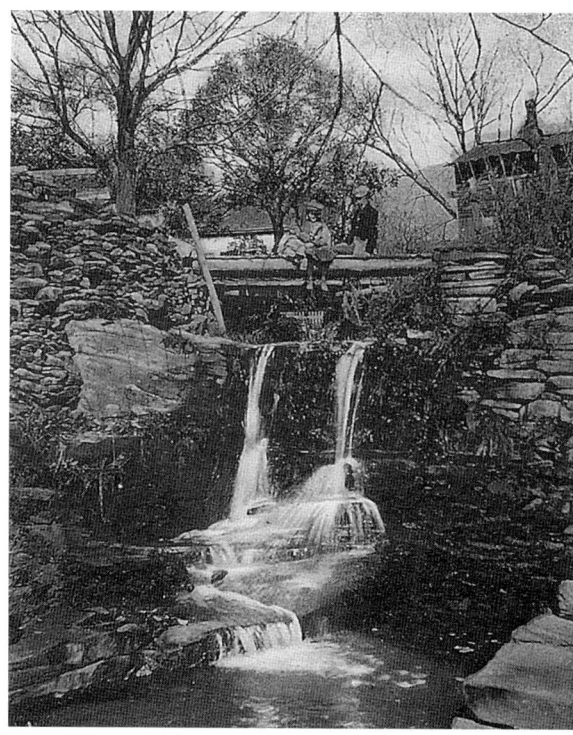

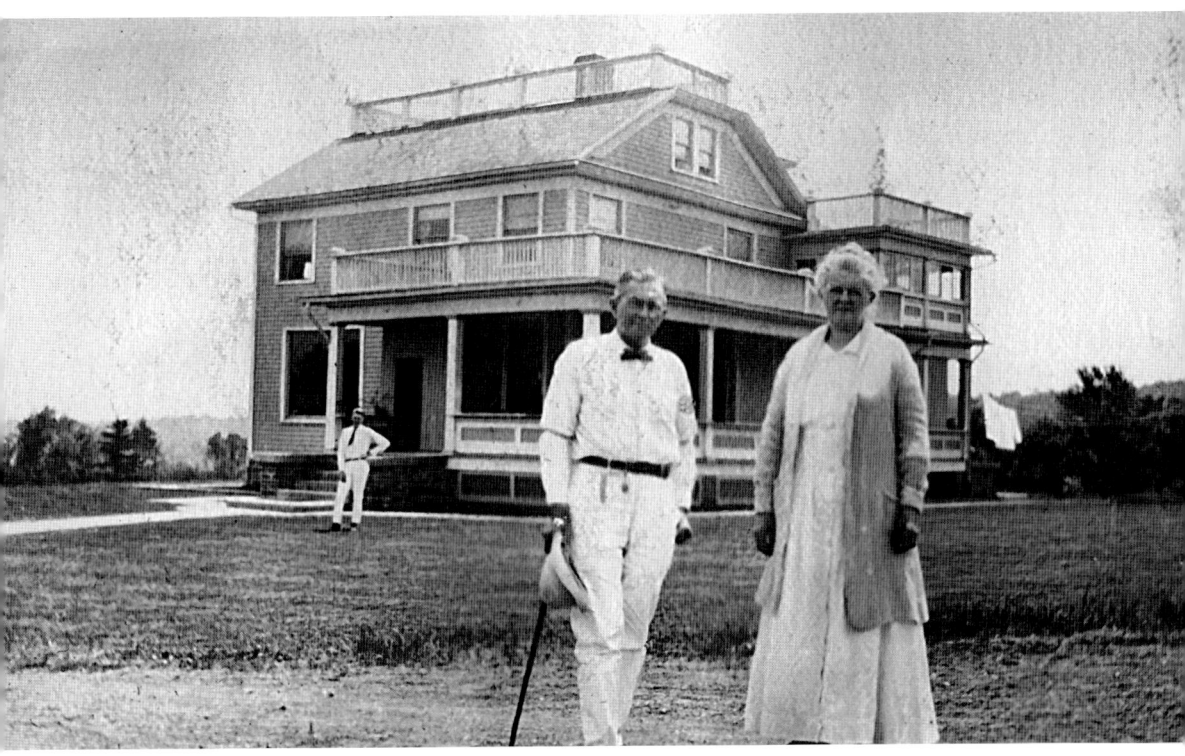

Willard Allen
Standing before the home he built in Woodstock (now the site of the American Legion), Willard Allen arrived in Woodstock in 1913 following a career in publishing and as an entrepreneur. A partner in the Chicago-based Cram-Allen Publishing Company and an appointee to the International Irrigation Congress in 1893, Allen went on to create the Morning Daily News Company of Los Angeles. Later, he headed the Allen Manufacturing Company in Toledo, Ohio. Ill health and an acquaintance with Birge Harrison eventually provided the reasons for his move to Woodstock. A well-known landscape painter, Allen also built Allencrest Hotel next to his home where some early classes of the National Youth Administration Craft Center, a Works Progress Administration program, were held. His wife, Augusta Allen, was the creator of the Woodstock Dress, which she sold to help provide additional income for the family.

Olive Burgher Toms

Before the construction of the Woodstock Elementary School, Woodstock children attended one of seven one-room schoolhouses based on where they lived in the township. They were Woodstock village, Bearsville, Wittenberg, Shady, Lake Hill, Zena, and the Daisy School near the Saugerties line. Over the years, many of the students who attended school in Woodstock recalled their teacher, Olive Burgher Toms, with great fondness. Shown here with one of her classes, Toms was married to Frederick Wellington Gifford Toms, a well-known carpenter and handyman in Woodstock who built the couple's home on Ohayo Mountain Road in the early 1950s. Following the death of her husband, Olive would live to the age of 102, cared for by her daughter Mescal Hornbeck. (Courtesy Kathy Longyear.)

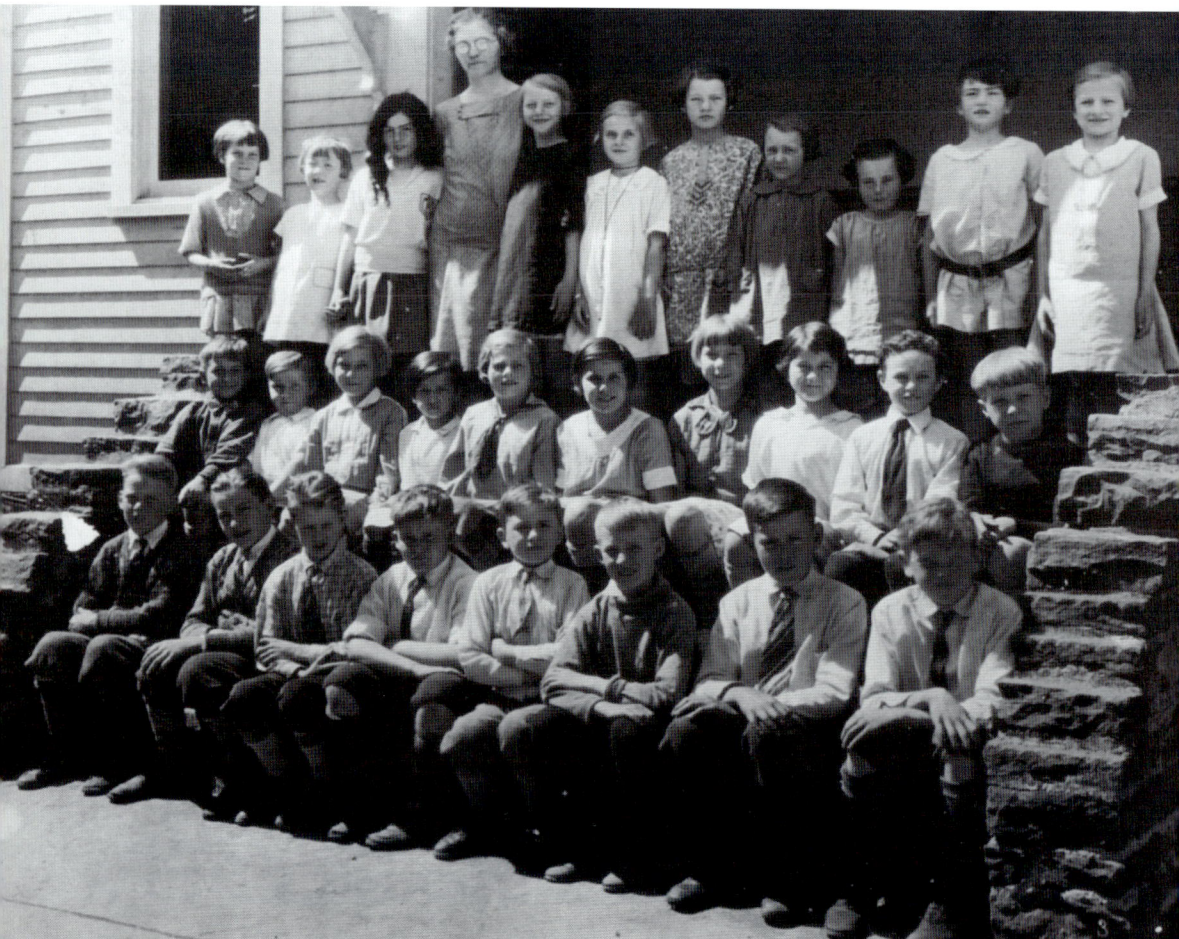

CHAPTER THREE

Legends Recalled: Tales and Stories that Remain

Collective memory not only shapes a community's sense of history but provides common points around which the community identifies its shared way of life. At its basic form, these are the memories that are offered when people gather together and ask each other, "Do you remember?" This section of *Legendary Locals of Woodstock* offers a look at those individuals and institutions that are often the subject of that very question.

By their very nature, such stories are sometimes funny and, at times, sad. They may be offered in words of admiration or disbelief. They might be simple things, a kindness given, or a silly act performed. As are all such remembrances, of course, they are also subject to the accuracy of memories. Often related in conversation, they are told and retold with old facts altered or new ones added. They evolve, much like the community. Yet despite their potential for change, they remain integral as a distinguishing element of the community.

Such memories recall individuals like Sarah MacDaniel Cashdollar, who as a young girl hauled milk each morning up Overlook Mountain in a buckboard. They include Johtje and Aart Vos, who came to Woodstock from the Netherlands following World War II, contributing their time and energy to the Woodstock Reformed Church; few knew of the heroic acts the two had undertaken during the war. This chapter also includes answers to common questions asked by many unfamiliar with the details of Woodstock history such as, "Why are our recreation fields named after Rick Volz and Andy Lee?" While their stories are both sad and tragic, that their memories are kept alive in Woodstock is testament to a town that understands what is important. More happily, this chapter also remembers the oompah music of Holley Cantine, groceries delivered by John Wolven, and Christmas Eve with Joe Holdridge on the village green. Along the way, Woodstock's lost watering holes will also be remembered.

The individual selections that follow are not meant to be the definitive collection of Woodstock tales; they are but a glimpse at those individuals and places whose presence in town has left an impact in one form or another. Nor are they meant to hold one individual over another. Woodstockers are stubbornly proud of all that has shaped the town and, on a good day, will even admit to a stranger, "Yeah, we're a little different." But that's Woodstock, a town carved out of wilderness, settled and built by independent and long-standing families who witnessed and eventually came to appreciate the waves of immigration by artists, musicians, hippies, and second-home owners.

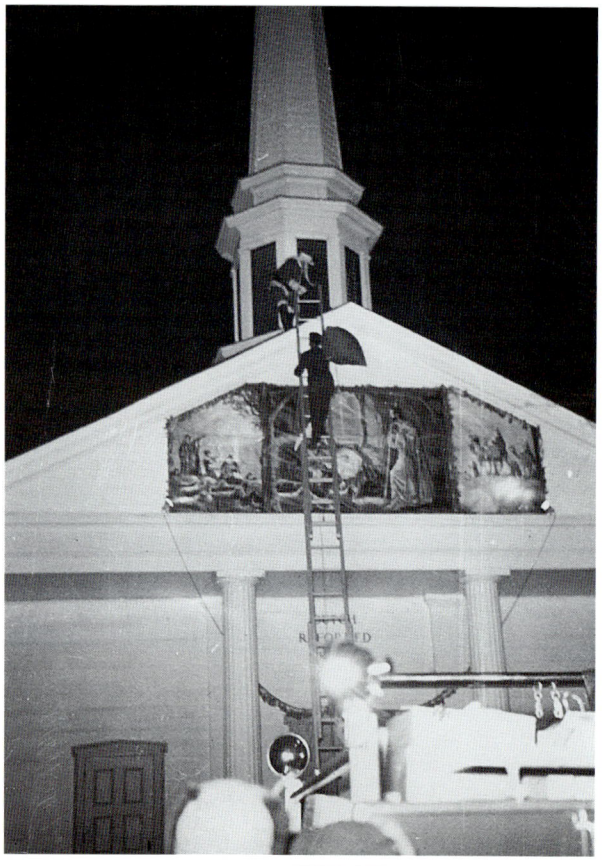

Joe Holdridge Sr.

Most Woodstockers knew Joe Holdridge Sr. as a painting contractor. Most Woodstock children knew him only as Santa Claus, as Woodstock's annual Christmas Eve celebration on the village green climaxed with his arrival. For 14 years, Joe Holdridge was at the center of Woodstock's most popular tradition. Each year, Holdridge would amaze those gathered on the green with a new and exciting way for Santa to appear. One legendary Christmas Eve saw him sliding down a guide wire from the steeple of the Woodstock Reformed Church. On another, he burst into view on the roof of the Longyear Building with live reindeer. In many ways Joe Holdridge was also the "real" Santa, bringing stockings on Christmas morning to children too ill to attend the previous night's program. (Both, courtesy Leslie Koehn Fertel.)

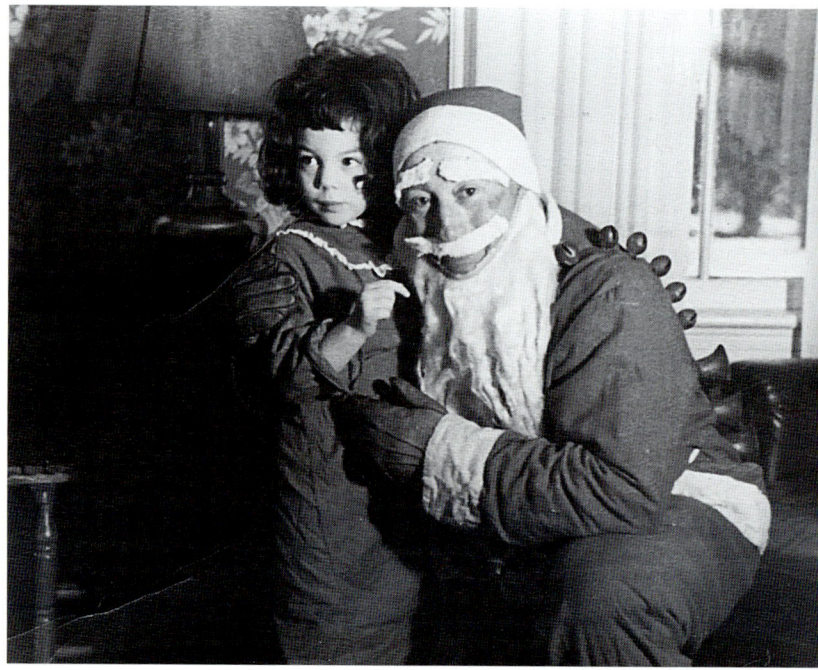

CHAPTER THREE: LEGENDS RECALLED: TALES AND STORIES THAT REMAIN

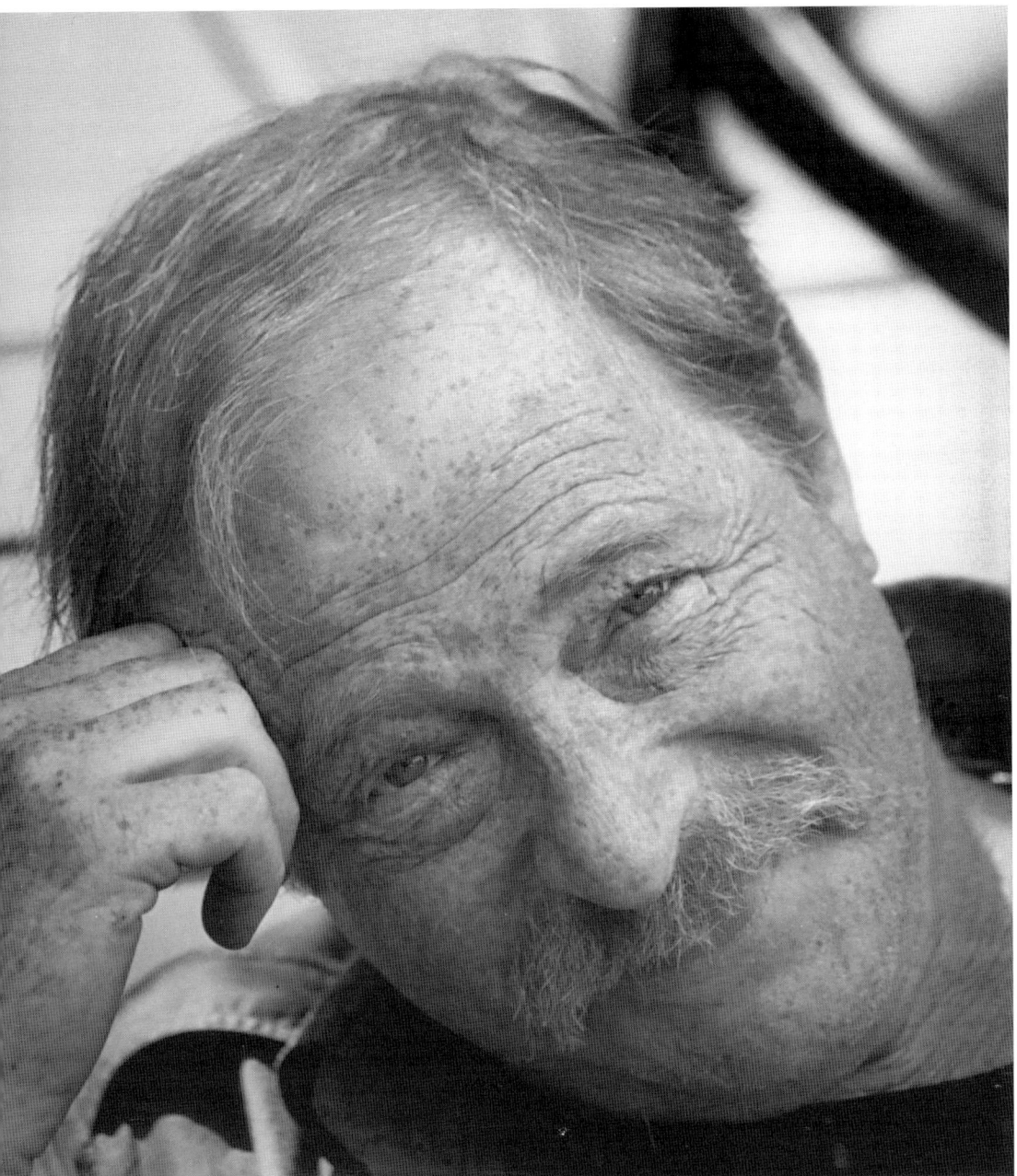

Bill Lubinsky
For many, it takes just one weekend trip from New York City to come under the spell of Woodstock. Leaving a job at the Playboy Club, Bill Lubinsky soon became part of the music scene in Woodstock as part owner of a club called the Elephant, former home of the Seahorse. In 1969, Lubinsky became acquainted with festival promoter Michael Lang and worked on site at the Woodstock Festival. Following the event, Bill and his wife designed a T-shirt to commemorate the 1969 festival and began selling them. As a result, he became a much sought-after festival storyteller and T-shirt vendor at Mower's Fleamarket and the original festival site. (Courtesy Marcia Weiss.)

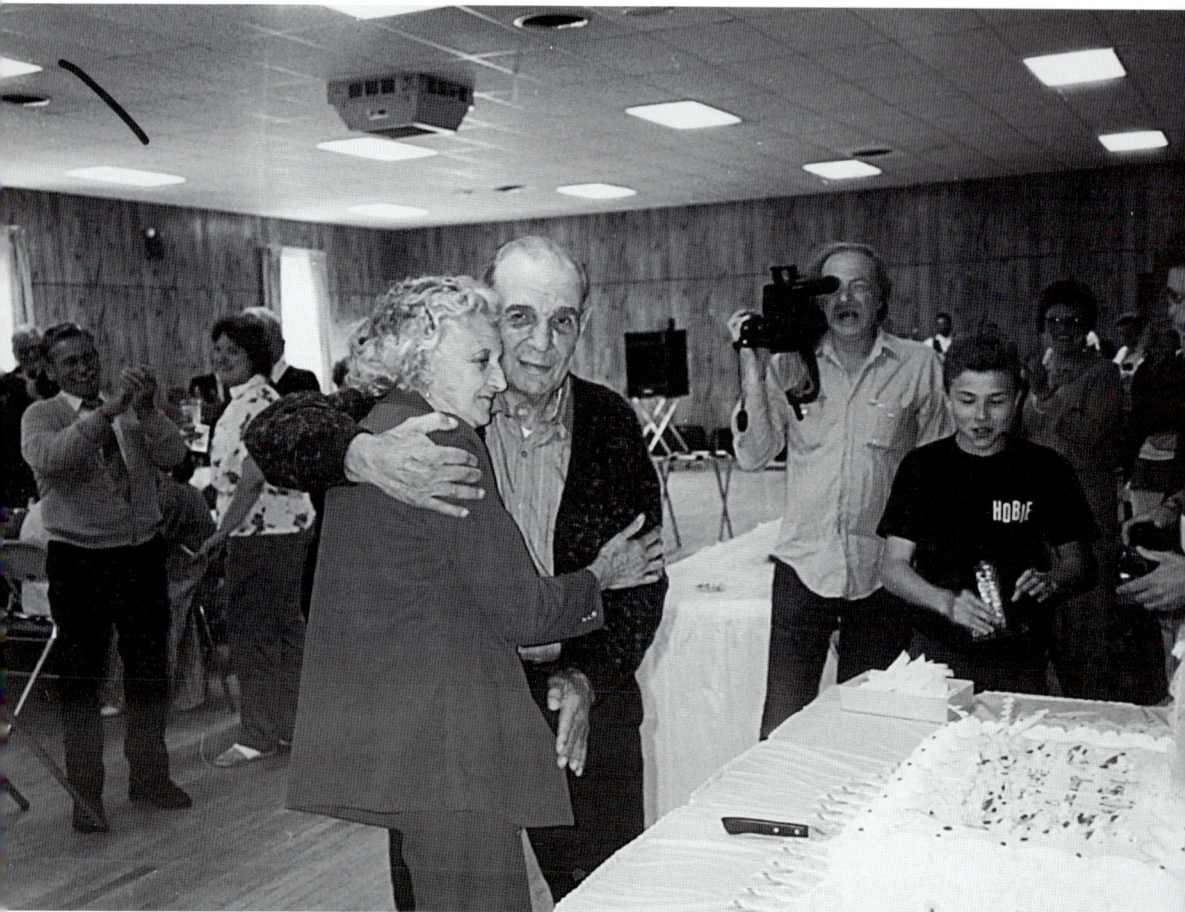

Bert and Clara Van Kleeck
As Bert Van Kleeck and Clara Reynolds Van Kleeck celebrated their 50th wedding anniversary, they could look back at a life well lived. Married in 1940, the couple moved to Byrdcliffe in June 1951. For 49 years, they lived in the caretaker's house at Byrdcliffe as Bert evolved into an extraordinary handyman. His love and respect for what Byrdcliffe represented was evident in his dedication to making sure that pipes did not freeze, the heat was working, the roads were plowed, and cars were rescued from snow-filled ditches—all accomplished with an unassuming manner and a warm smile. (Courtesy the Van Kleeck family.)

Catherine Van Debogart

The horrible death of Catherine Van Debogart and her unborn child—and the subsequent miracle that would follow—is one Woodstock's oldest and most enduring legends. First told by R. Lionel DeLisser in *Picturesque Ulster* in 1897 and later retold by Neva Shultis in her work on Woodstock folklore, *From Sunset to Cock's Crow*, in 1957, it is a story of rage and redemption. Early in the 19th century, 17-year-old Catherine married the middle-aged John Van Debogart, a man possessed with a suspicious mind and a great capacity for jealousy. So it was, in the summer of 1821, that a pregnant Catherine was visiting a sick neighbor and was greatly delayed in her return home. Arriving home from work, her husband found an empty house and no dinner waiting. When Catherine still had not arrived home by midnight, the increasingly angered husband went outside to cut a hefty stick from an elm tree and waited for her return. As she made her way home, Catherine feared what awaited her. Upon entrance to the house, her husband immediately began to beat her with the stick he had cut. Despite her screams, the beating continued until she fell unconscious. Neighbors, aroused by the commotion, arrived and placed her lifeless body on the bed. Though she would regain consciousness a bit later, giving birth to a lifeless child, Catherine knew that death was upon her as well. While she would not make any complaint against her husband, she asked that she be buried with the elm stick and prayed that it would grow from her heart into a mighty elm, serving as a symbol of caution to others. Catherine died that night and was buried with her infant child and the elm stick in the Woodstock cemetery. As Neva Shultis would later write, "Then the miracle happened. A few years later, a sturdy young elm grew on the grave, so closely to the stone that the stone was dislodged and had to be reset. And it grew into a towering tree." While the elm would later be lost during a storm, Catherine's stone remains as a reminder of the plight and status of many women in the country's early history.

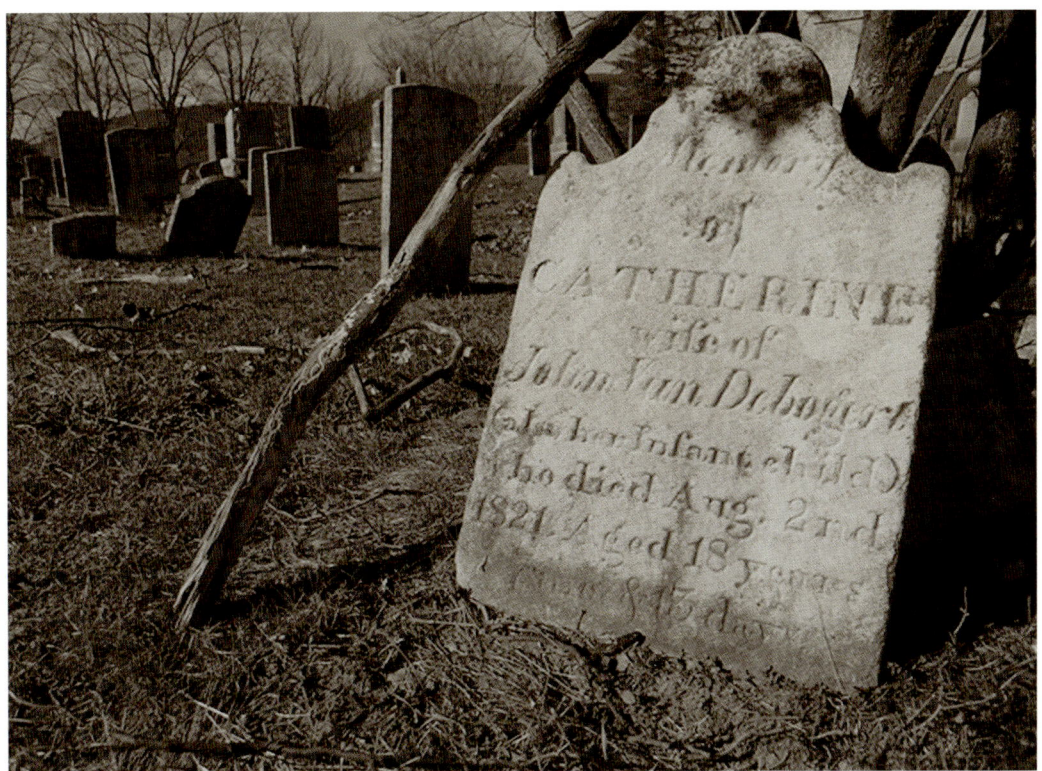

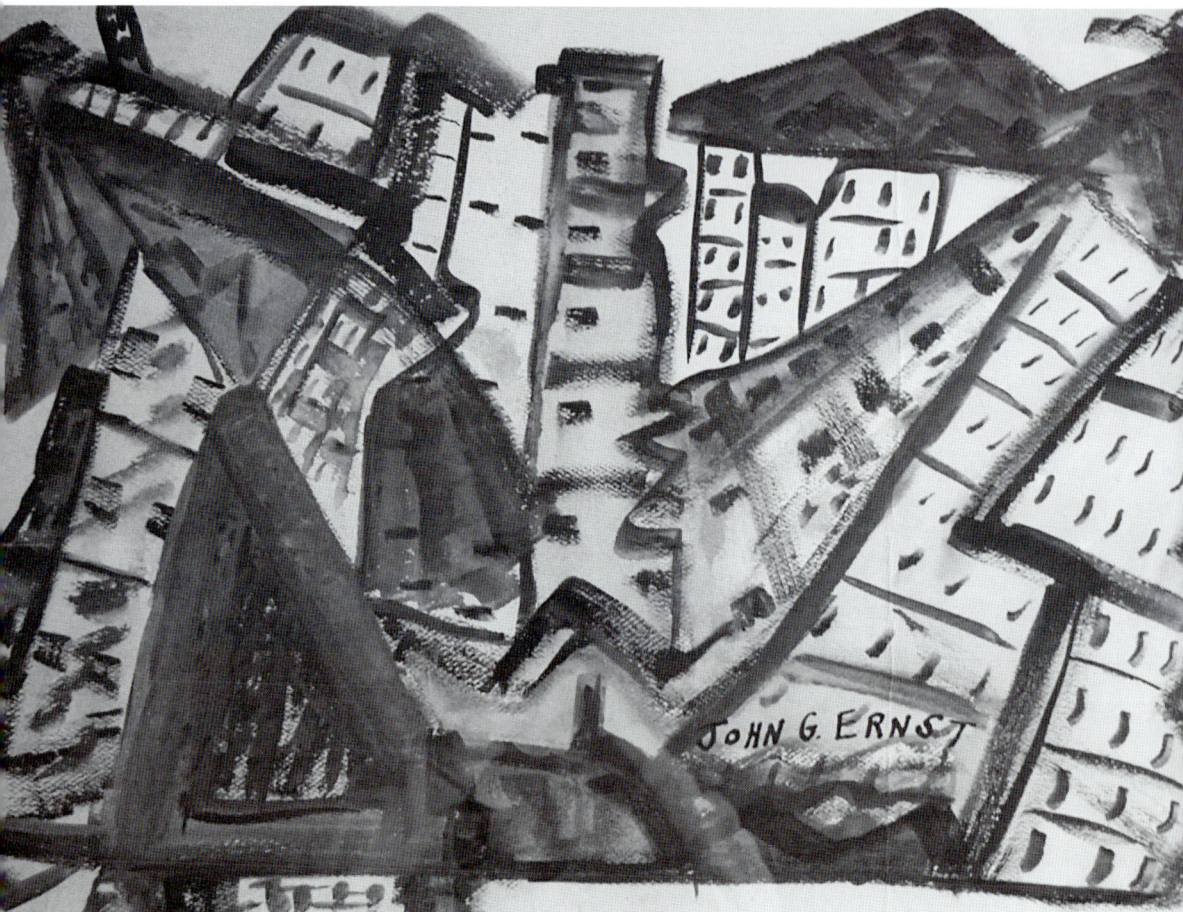

John Ernst
While there are few photographs of John Ernst, the fact that there are hundreds of his paintings stored in closets around Woodstock offers indication as to the sadness behind his story. Arriving in Woodstock in 1947 to study at the Art Students League, the former circus performer's artwork would be well received by his contemporaries. Fueled by alcoholism, however, Ernst's life would take a series of tragic turns. The death of his daughter by suicide, illness, periodic stays in jail and psychiatric wards, and a fire that destroyed his home reduced Ernst to exchanging hastily produced art for cigarettes and alcohol on the streets of Woodstock. While many would attempt to provide help, John Ernst would die in obscurity in a nursing home on Cape Cod in 1995. (Courtesy Donald Allen.)

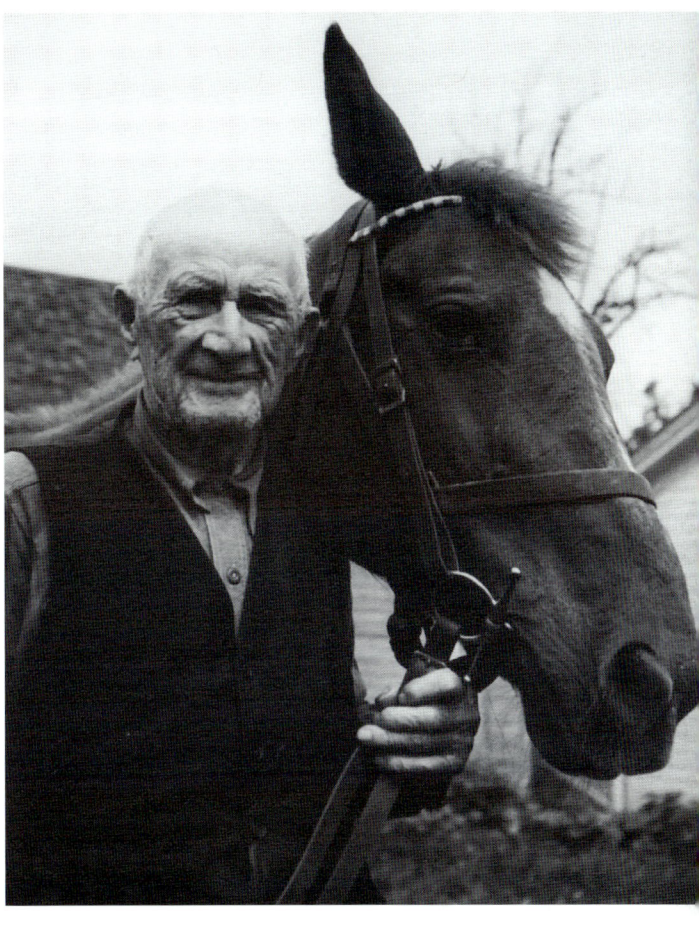

Jim Twaddell

The following anonymous poem, "Jim," is about Woodstock resident Jim Twaddell: "We love to see him set his hoss / In his own careless way, / He fears no man, he knows no boss / Sept he who hears him pray." In a small town that has produced its share of wonderful characters, Jim Twaddell ranks at the top of the list. Known for his legendary tales, Twaddell was a fixture on the Woodstock scene for many years. Perhaps his most favorite story centered around Pres. Ulysses S. Grant's visit to Woodstock in 1873 and Grant's stay at the Overlook Mountain House. As Twaddell would recall—to anyone willing to listen—he encountered Grant one morning in the stable of the mountain house. Grant told Twaddell that he admired his horse Scott very much. Not wishing to be rude to the president, he saddled Scott up for Grant, and off they went along the trails of Overlook. Within a short period of time, Twaddell noticed, due to the magic of the Overlook Mountain air, Grant was physically turning younger before his very eyes. Recognizing the effect, Grant panicked, yelling to Twaddell that if he were to become any younger he would not meet the 35-year-old age requirement of the Constitution and would be impeached. Thinking quickly, Twaddell and Scott reversed course and quickly guided the president back to the mountain house. Upon reaching the stable in short order, Grant, it seems, had returned to the proper age of 51. Twaddell and Scott were known to leave their mark elsewhere on Woodstock memory, as they could be found in later years leading off the annual Memorial Day parade. In 1927, when the City of Kingston wanted to force a cleanup of the Sawkill Creek, which fed its reservoir, Twaddell was offered a replacement for his broken-down, poorly functioning privy. He refused. Even his age was the subject of a Twaddell tale. Claiming to be the oldest-living Woodstocker—over 100—it was discovered upon his death in 1939 that he was a "mere" 90. It is said that he buried his horse Scott on the spot in the road leading to Overlook where he first encountered Grant. For many years, old-timers referred to the abrupt incline as Scott Hill.

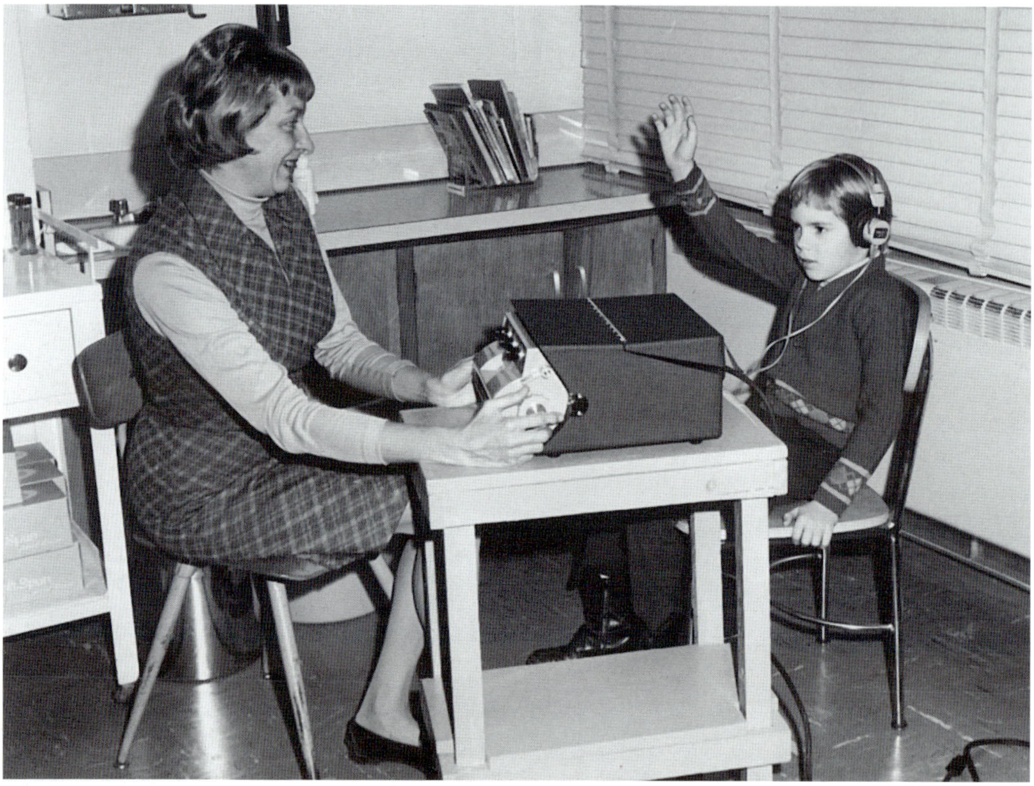

LEGENDARY LOCALS

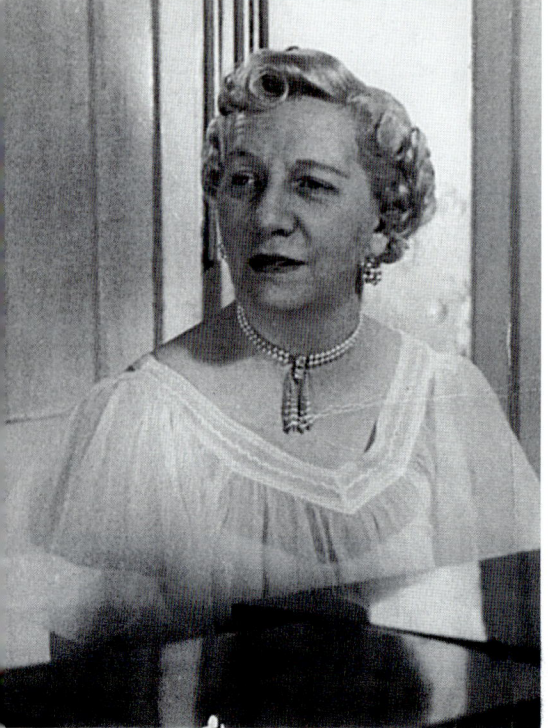

Elizabeth Busch Rose
"Betty" Rose loved her job as nurse at the Woodstock Elementary School. A graduate of the Russell Sage School of Nursing during World War II, Rose came to Woodstock when her father was diagnosed with tuberculosis and sought out the mountain air. Dedicated to the children of Woodstock, she also served as a volunteer at the Woodstock Library. (Courtesy David Rose.)

"Flo" Odell Scism
An accomplished and gifted pianist, Flo entertained the patrons of Woodstock's most famous restaurant, Deanie's, for many, many years. First hired by Deanie Elwyn in 1936 to entertain at the Brass Rail on Rock City Road, Flo's music brought Woodstockers together for over 40 years. From her tiny house on Orchard Lane, neighbors and passersby could hear her practicing Broadway tunes most any time of the day.

CHAPTER THREE: LEGENDS RECALLED: TALES AND STORIES THAT REMAIN

Clarence Schmidt

Born in 1897, Clarence Schmidt can perhaps be best described as an environmental sculptor. In 1920, he inherited five acres on Ohayo Mountain and built his first home, Journey's End, from railroad ties. Schmidt then embarked on his life's work, a seven-story, multi-room complex. Utilizing recovered and recycled objects such as discarded pieces of metal, plastic, appliances, and chrome from automobiles, Schmidt worked tirelessly as he crafted his new home. Featured in *Life* magazine, Schmidt was hailed as a pop art genius and denigrated as crazy. Construction continued until 1968, when fire destroyed his work. Soon after, he constructed a new home, a tree house of sorts with branches wrapped in aluminum foil. It too would catch fire. Badly burned in the blaze, Schmidt never fully recovered. Clarence Schmidt died in a nursing home in 1978.

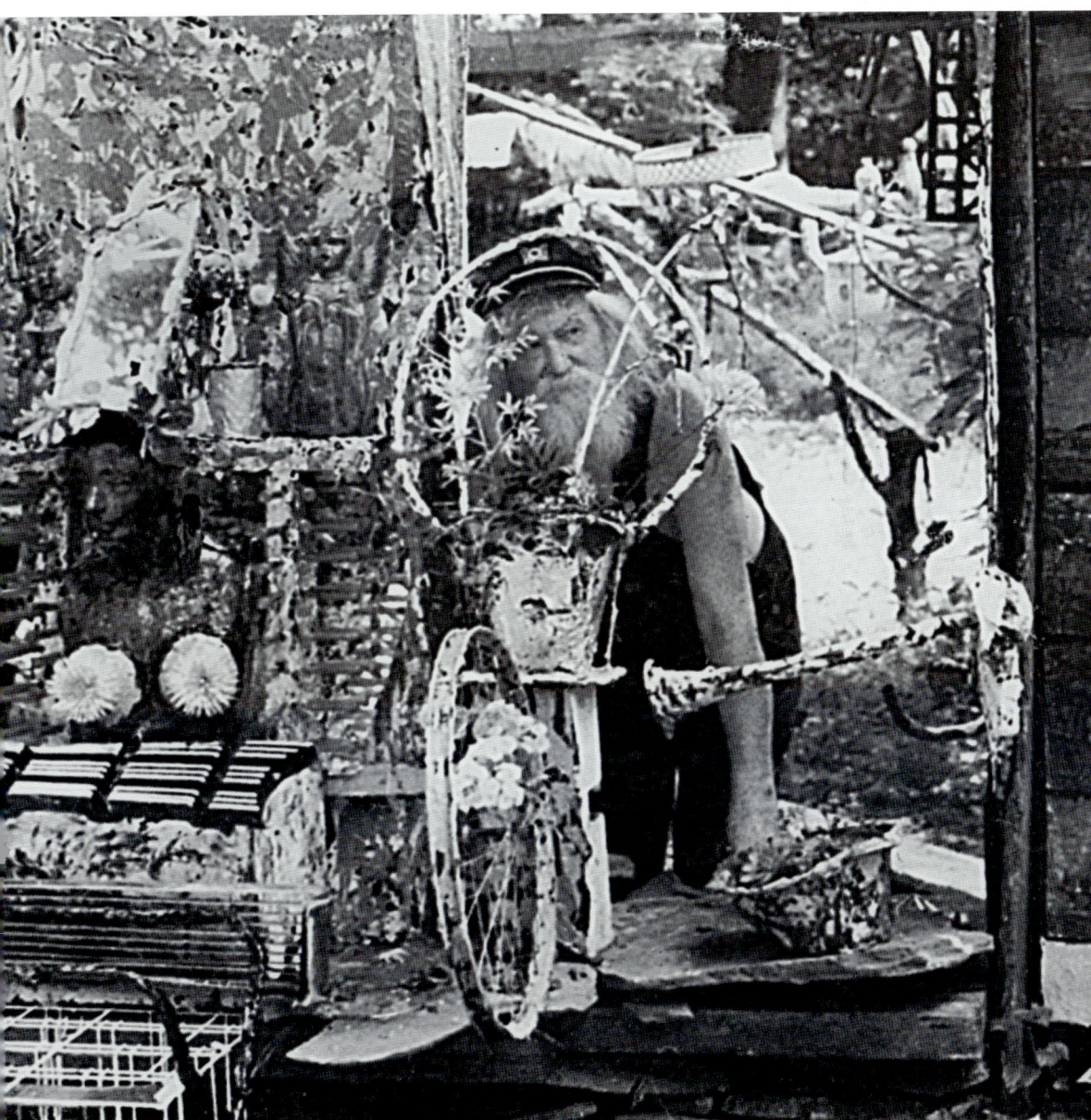

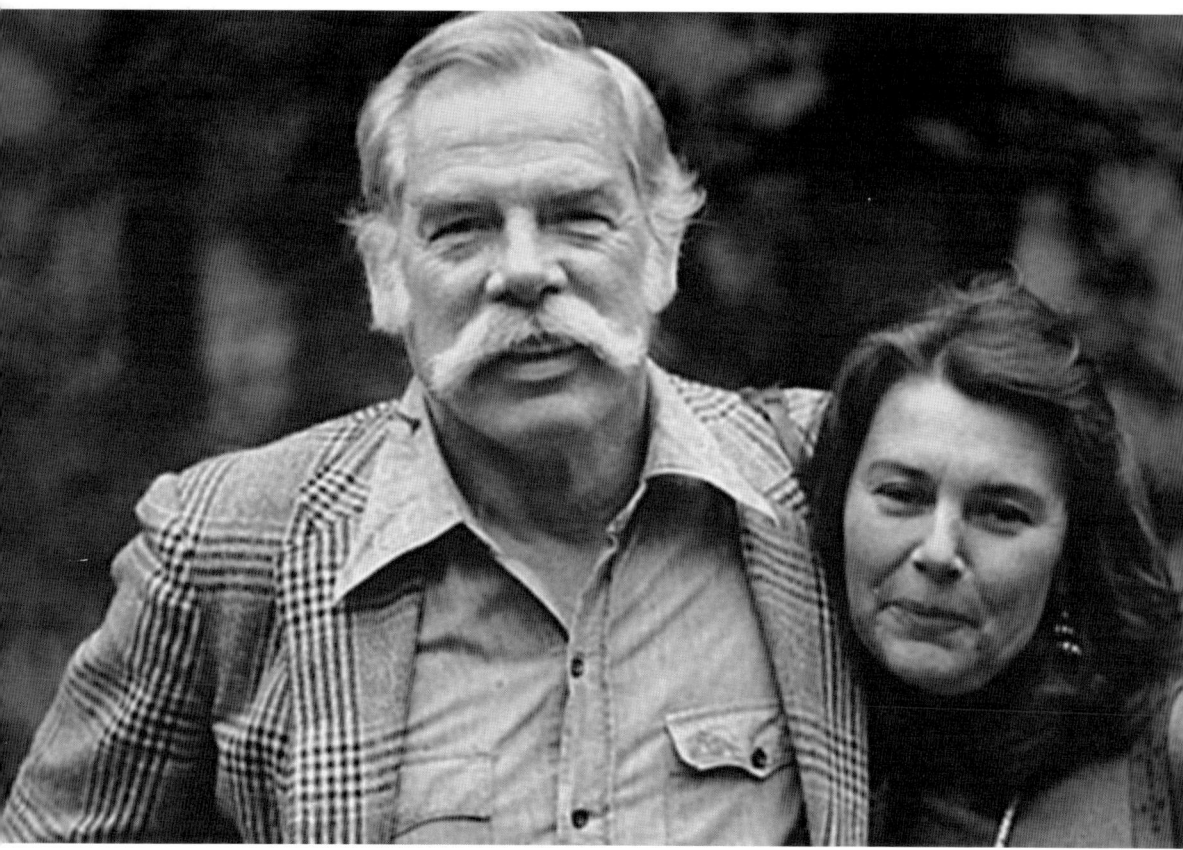

Lee Marvin

As a child, Lee Marvin had some issues. Born in New York City—his father worked in advertising, and his mother was a fashion writer—the future Hollywood legend ran away from home at age four and, as the years progressed, would find himself tossed out of most schools he attended. When World War II broke out, he joined the Marines and was wounded while fighting in the Pacific. Coming under fire by a Japanese sniper, a bullet severed a nerve in his back. Receiving a medical discharge, Marvin made his way to Woodstock, where his parents had a home, and found work as a plumber's helper with Heckeroth Plumbing. As the now-legendary tale is told, Lee Marvin's acting career was launched while performing plumbing work at the Maverick Theater. (Some say he was repairing a toilet on that fateful day.) Asked to fill in for an ailing actor, Marvin found himself at home on the stage. The rest, as they say, was history. The actor who would earn an Oscar for his roles in *Cat Ballou* in 1965 would go on to perform on Broadway, act in numerous television programs, and star in more than 60 films. A return to Woodstock in 1970 to be with his ailing father would lead to renewing a relationship with Pamela Feeley (also pictured). When they first met in 1945, following Marvin's arrival in Woodstock, she was 15 and he 21. Married 25 years after their first meeting, Marvin and his new bride made Tucson, Arizona, their primary home. Occasional trips to Woodstock would follow, however, where, on certain evenings, the now-famous actor could be found talking with old friends around the bar at Deanie's. The legendary star—who spoke his first lines on a small Woodstock stage—died of a heart attack in 1987. (Courtesy Jay Peterson.)

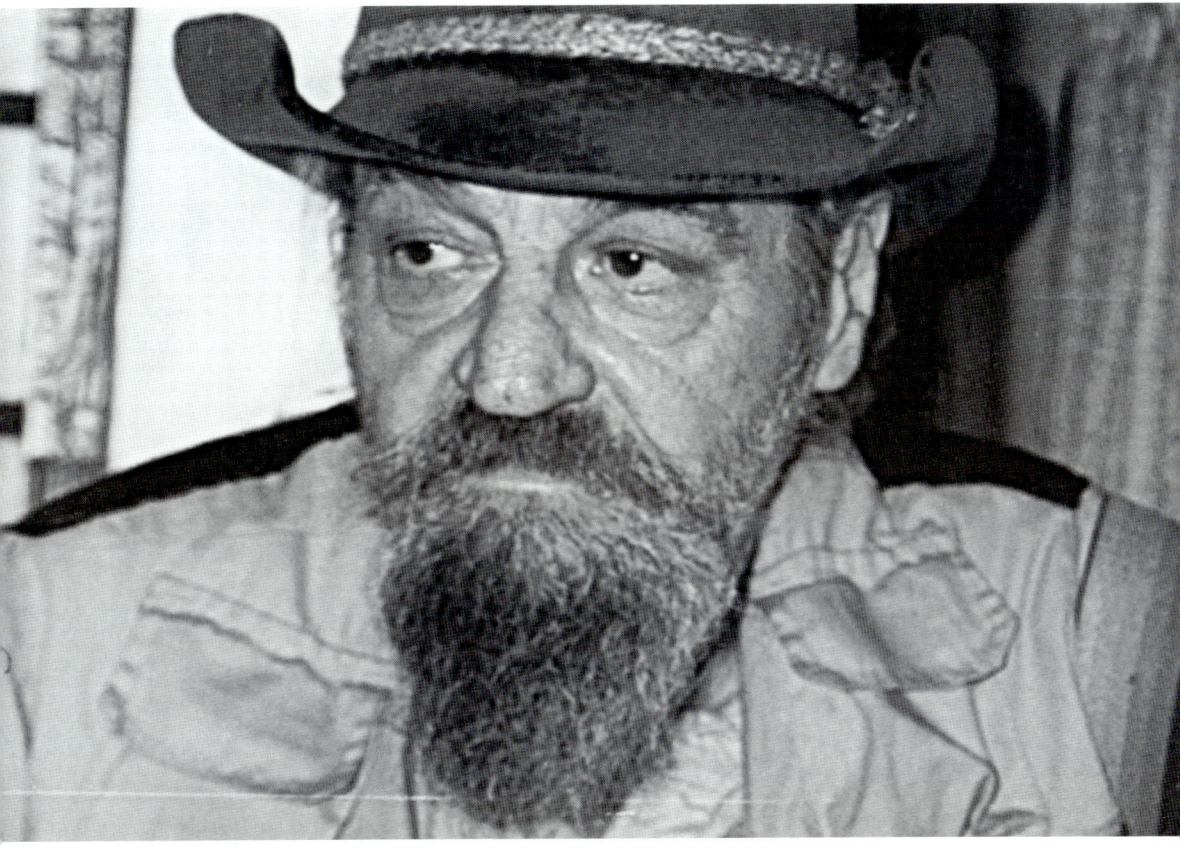

Luke Klementis
Luke Klementis grew up in Zena and is remembered by many as a good father, brother, and uncle. In addition, his friendships were many. It was no surprise, therefore, when Luke received a call from his good friend Jim Matteson wondering if Luke could meet him in Oklahoma to go on a treasure hunt. Luke was agreeable and, after meeting up, they set out in Luke's Winnebago. Unfortunately, Jim was a man of poor health and died during their trip. Believing that his friend would be best cared for by Lasher's Funeral Home back in Woodstock, Luke made the long drive back to Woodstock with Jim's lifeless body still in the Winnebago. The astonished undertaker respectfully accepted Jim's remains, and the legend of Luke Klementis as a friend grew a little larger. (Courtesy Esther Baldwin.)

Charles Pierpoint

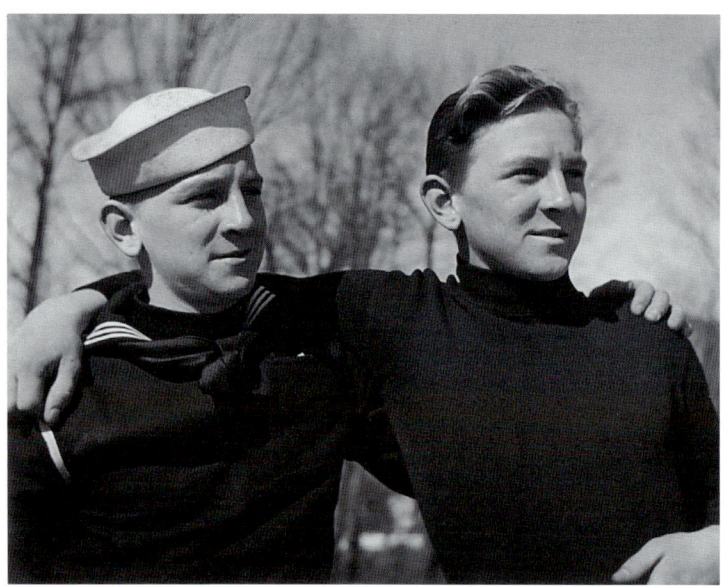

With the outbreak of World War II, Charles Pierpoint (left) and his twin brother, Bill, enlisted in the US Navy on the same day. Sadly, Charles would become the first of 12 men Woodstock would lose during the war. Pierpoint was killed when, attempting to deliver supplies to Guadalcanal, his ship, the *Meredith*, was bombed by Japanese planes. (Courtesy the Pierpoint family.)

Clementine Nessel

Pianist and accordionist Clementine Nessel entertained many townspeople in post–World War II Woodstock. She could often be found playing music with artists John Pike, Dave Huffine, and John Striebel. Equally as important for Woodstock's children, Clementine was an excellent music teacher. Her outgoing and generous personality made her a charming and much loved member of the Woodstock community.

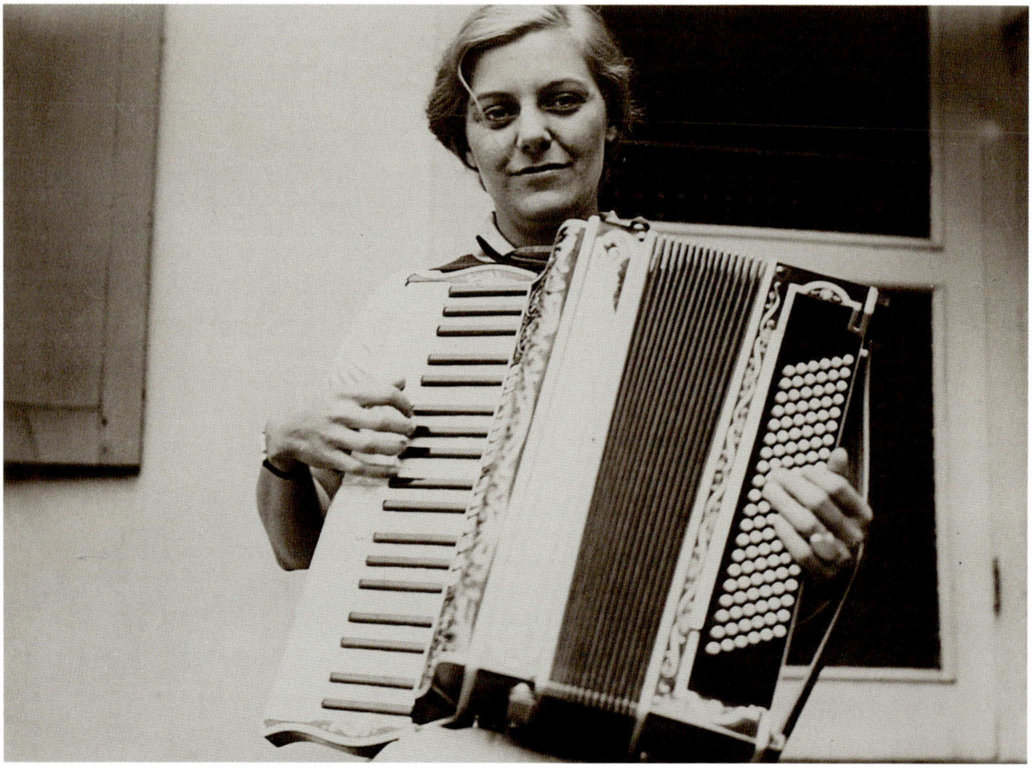

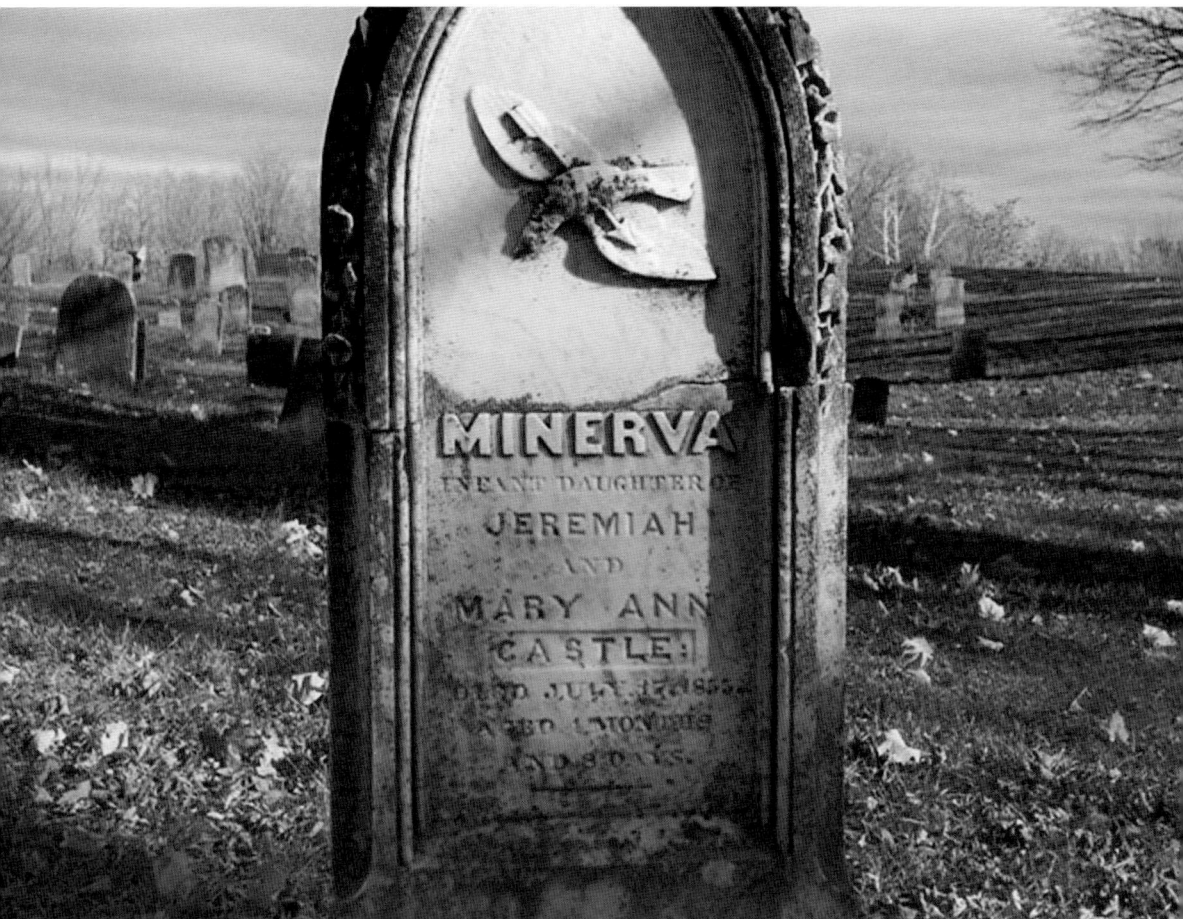

Minerva Castle

Minerva Castle was five months old at the time of her tragic death. Gathered in Kingston on a July afternoon in 1855, a large crowd looked on as members of the 7th New York Militia offered a musket demonstration using blank cartridges. Mistakenly, one soldier placed a live round in his musket. His next shot struck Minerva, who was being held by her mother. While she would linger for a few days, the shot proved fatal. Minerva Castle is buried in the Woodstock Cemetery. The Castle family was one of the earliest to settle in Woodstock. As a tenant on lands owned by Robert Livingston in the latter half of the 18th century, William Castle worked alongside fellow tenants and slaves building the road that traveled through Lake Hill and Mink Hollow, eventually reaching Greene County.

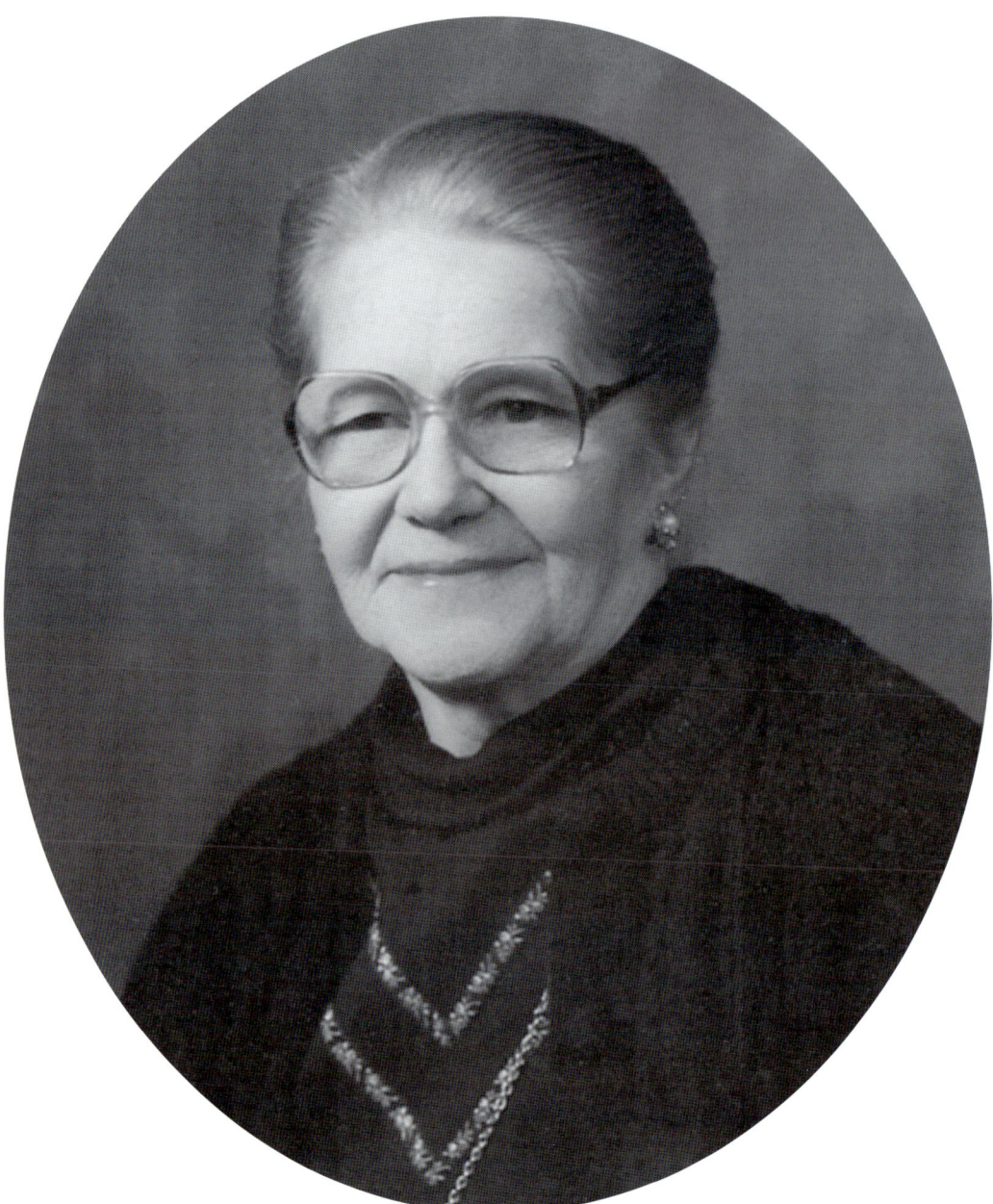

Pauline Lane Baldwin
A resident of Willow, Pauline Baldwin was, in the 1950s, the proprietress of the Wildwood Rest Home, located on Route 212. Ironically, the home would later become Jolene's, a favorite area watering hole. Residents of Wildwood, mostly local seniors unable to live alone, were treated as guests. Attendants lived in their own quarters and assisted Baldwin in the day-to-day tasks of caring for the residents. Three meals a day were served in a common area and, on occasion, Baldwin's children would help serve the meals. Her philosophy was to keep a watchful eye over the residents but give them the freedom to be themselves. In the years before Medicare and Medicaid, Pauline Baldwin offered Woodstock seniors excellent care in a safe and pleasant atmosphere. (Courtesy Esther Baldwin.)

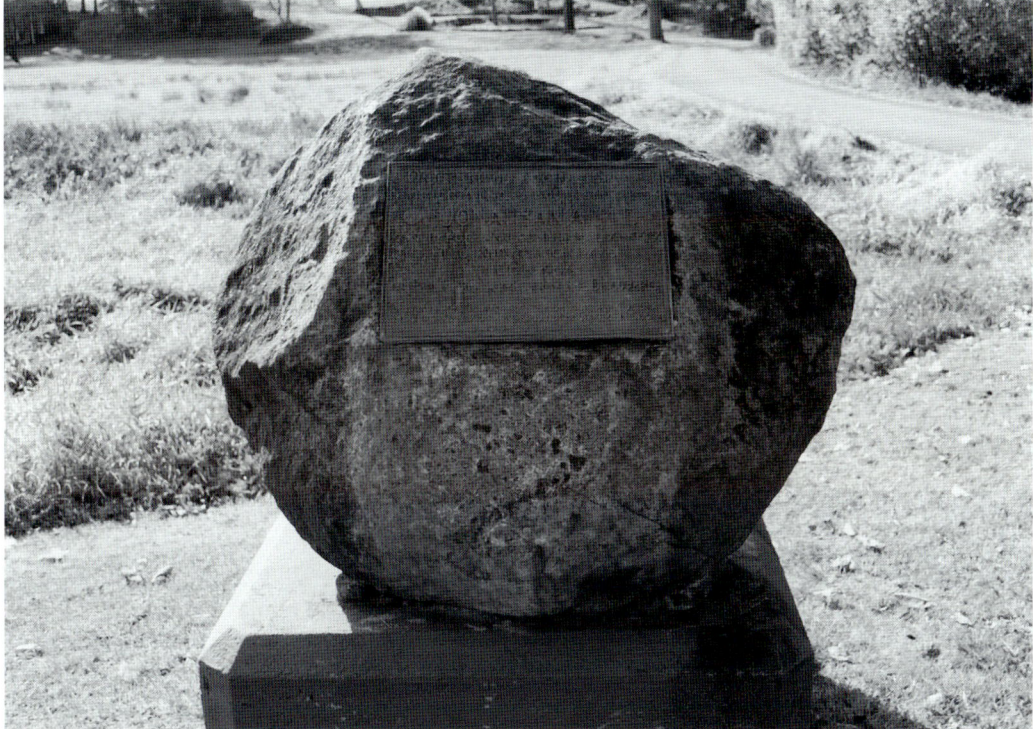

Philip Rick

Heading away from the center of Woodstock towards Bearsville, a large boulder monument is on the left side of the road. The monument, installed in 1927, commemorates the work of Philip Rick, Woodstock farmer and developer of the Jonathan apple. Though theories on the Jonathan's origin and even the source of the apple's name have been a source of debate, Woodstockers hold firm to the belief that it was on his farm in Bearsville that Philip Rick nurtured the Jonathan apple (also known as the Rickey or the King Philip) from the seed of the Esopus Spitzenberg. Originally leased from Madame Livingston in 1792, Rick's farm consisted of 86 acres, part of which now comprises the town-owned Comeau Property. The property—where Philip Rick lived with his wife, Ami, and eventually their eight children—was one of the few prosperous farms in Woodstock. Following the death of both Philip and Ami in 1828, their son Jonathan Rick continued to work the land in Bearsville until his death in 1872. Today, the importance of what occurred on Rick's farm two centuries ago is marked only by a large stone on a country road. Though seemingly minimized by time and history, historian Alf Evers underscored the impact of Philip Rick's work when he offered in *Woodstock—History of an American Town* that, "No event in Woodstock history has affected the people of the world more than the apple they know as the Jonathan."

Philip Buttrick (RIGHT)
Philip Buttrick was perhaps as unlikely a soldier as ever called Woodstock home. A graduate of Yale and an expert on cork forests, he was stationed in France as a member of the Red Cross in 1917. Eager to join the fight on behalf of France in World War I, he became increasingly dissatisfied with his work overseeing the construction of barracks. That desire—and a fear that the war would pass him by—would eventually lead to a position as an officer in the French army. So it was, after fighting on the side of the French for more than a year, Philip Buttrick found himself near the Meuse River on November 11, 1918. At precisely 11:00 a.m. that morning, as he later wrote home, the words "Cessez le feu!" (Cease Fire!) filled the air, and the guns of World War I fell silent. For his service in the French army, Buttrick was awarded the Croix de Guerre for acts of bravery in the face of the enemy. Buttrick, who would later reside on Rock City Road with his wife, Helen (of Byrdcliffe note), during World War II continued his support for the French. According to local historian Anita Smith in *Woodstock History and Hearsay*, published by WoodstockArts in 2006, Buttrick was instrumental in the organization of the Woodstock chapter of France Forever, the first such chapter ever begun "by Americans rather than by exiled French nationals."

Woodstock Farmers
Today, when people speak of Woodstock's past, there is a tendency to romanticize the old farms that once were a central part of the town. Truth is, farming in Woodstock was difficult. From the earliest days, when the land first had to be cleared, to the rocky soil found, to the occasional flooding of the Sawkill Valley, being a Woodstock farmer was no easy proposition. Crops were used to sustain the family, to sell what could be sold, and for the earliest tenant farmers, to the pay rent. Following the Civil War, approximately 150 farms were located in Woodstock, including the Peter Ricks farm, pictured here. As land value rose and building expanded, farming faded from Woodstock's landscape. (Courtesy Jon Elwyn.)

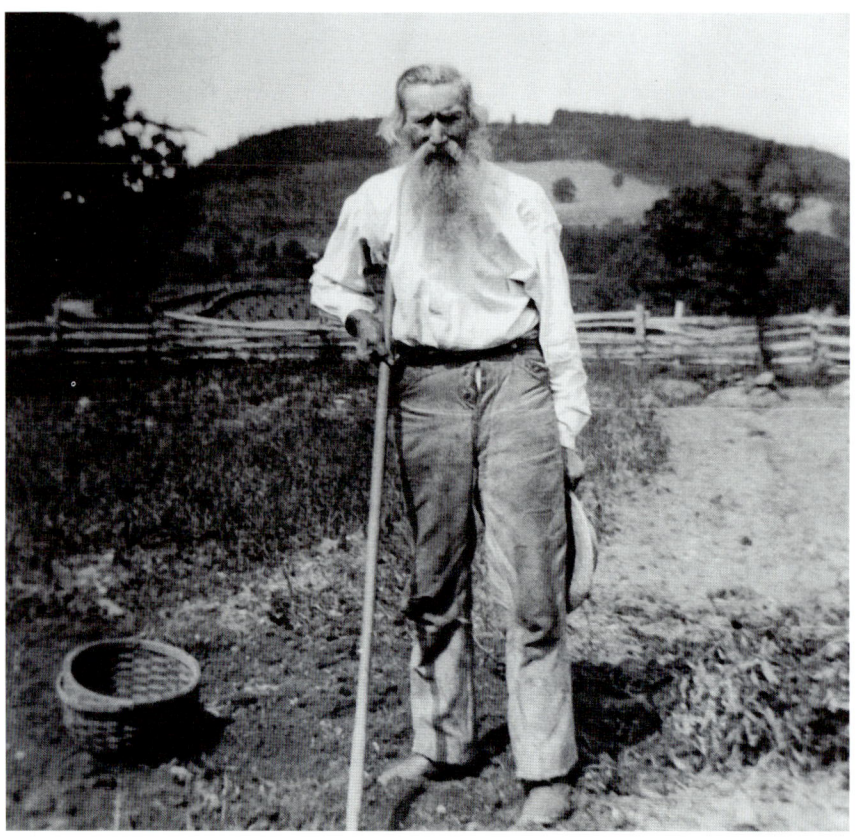

CHAPTER THREE: LEGENDS RECALLED: TALES AND STORIES THAT REMAIN

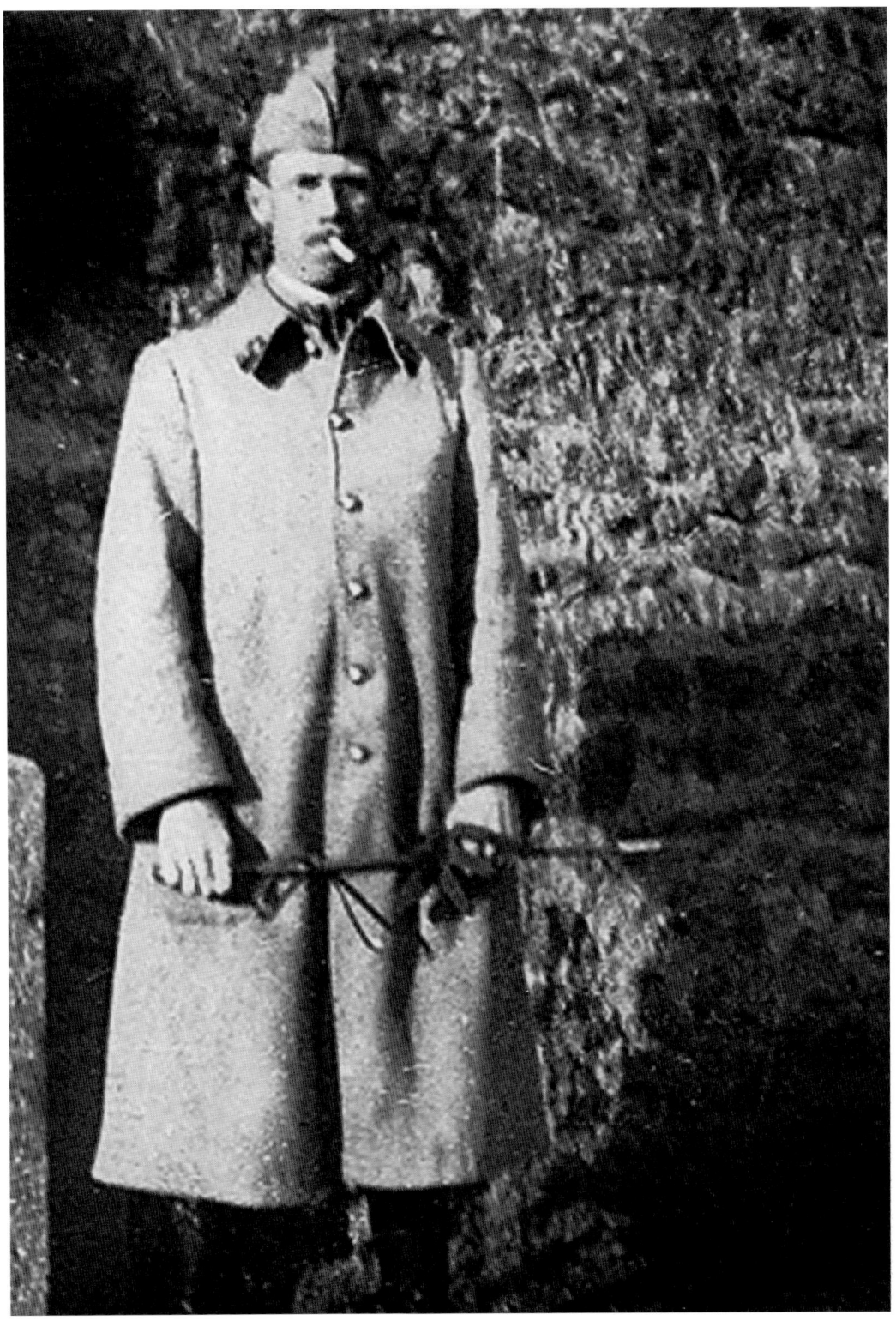

LEGENDARY LOCALS

Quarrymen

Bluestone became an important industry in Woodstock during the mid-1800s. The quarries, particularly along the base of Overlook Mountain, were often worked by Irish immigrants, many of whom migrated towards stone cutting and quarrying after leaving Ireland in wake of the devastation caused by the Famine. These immigrants and their families formed what became known as the "Irish Village" in the Lewis Hollow area of Woodstock. Through hard, dirty, and often dangerous work, the stone was excavated, rough cut, and brought down the mountain where, ultimately, it was transported on sledges to shipping docks in Saugerties and Kingston. When cement began to replace bluestone for use in sidewalks and curbs in metropolitan areas, many of the larger quarries closed, and the quarrymen moved on, many to help in the construction of the Ashokan Reservoir.

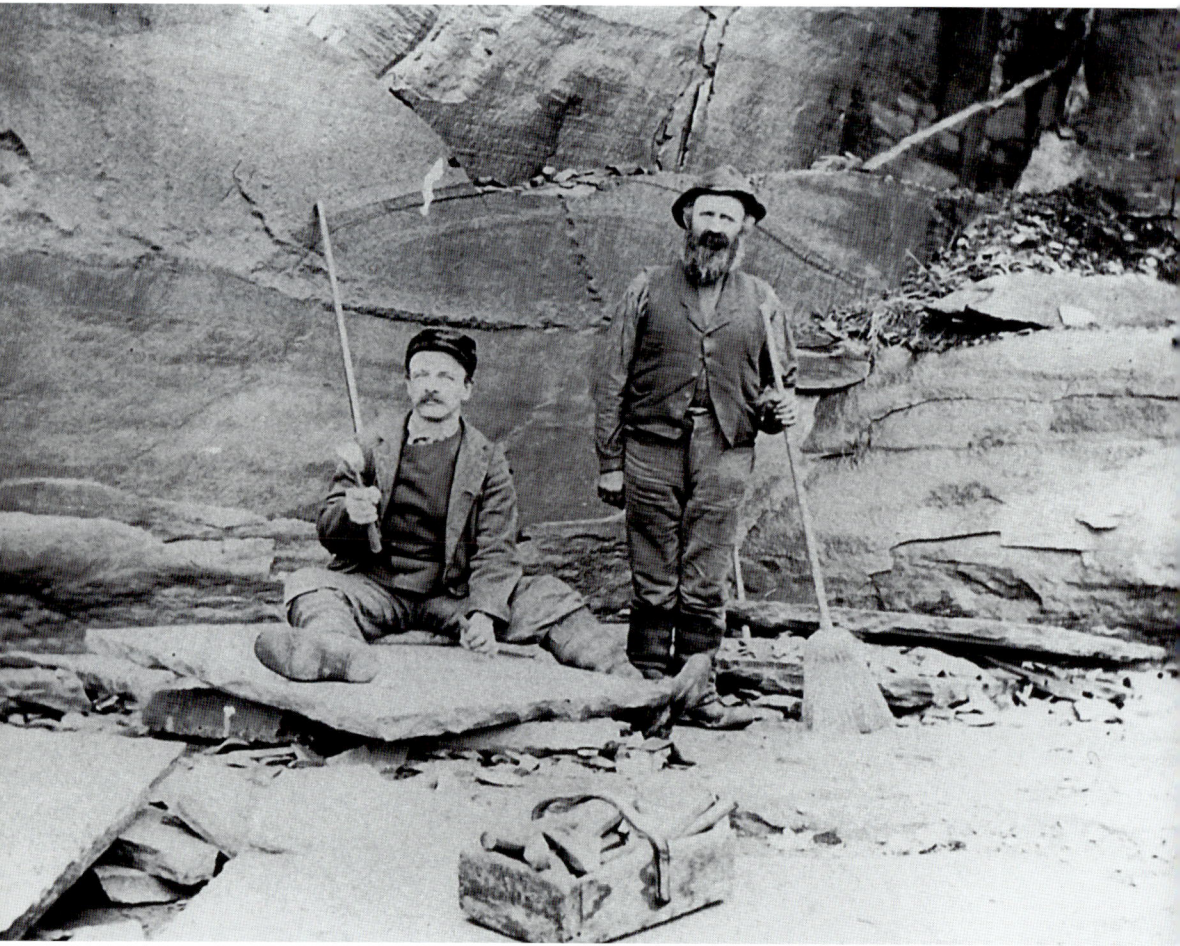

Rick Volz

Like many who were employed by IBM in Kingston, Rick Volz integrated himself into the fabric of Woodstock's community service organizations. After moving his family from Rochester to Woodstock in 1967, Volz became actively involved in little league as a coach. He also gave of his time to the Boy Scouts and Cub Scouts as pack leader and to the Woodstock Jaycees. In 1974, however, his life was tragically cut short when he was killed in a head-on collision on Route 28 between Woodstock and Kingston. In an effort to honor his life and service, the little league diamond on Dixon Avenue in Bearsville was dedicated in his name a few months later. Today, the home of Woodstock Little League still carries his name. (Courtesy the Volz family.)

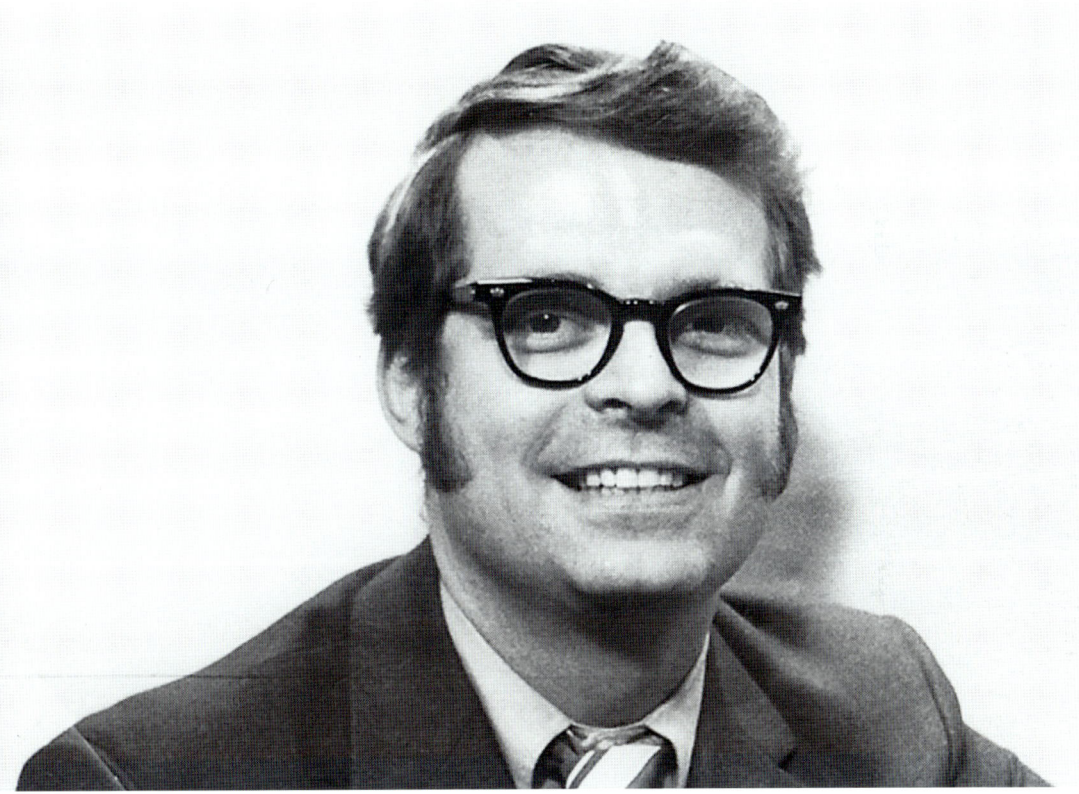

Woodstock's Fallen (RIGHT)

Following World War II, Woodstock came together as never before to create a monument honoring Woodstock's veterans and those who lost their lives in America's wars. Originally located on the village green, the memorial was later moved to its current location in the Woodstock Cemetery on Rock City Road. On the flagpole that rises above the memorial today, there are two bronze tablets presented to the town in 1949. In addition to a poem written by Archibald MacLeish on one of the tablets, the names of all Woodstockers who gave their lives for their country from the Civil War forward are included on the other. They are (Civil War) Issac Barber, Jacob Clapper, Alonzo Sylvester Lewis, Egbert Lewis, John Moe, James Mosher, Gilbert Myers, Hiram Ploss, Jacob Shultis, Philip Van Der Bogart, John Theodore Van Gasbeck, Peter Lewis Welderhouse, and Abram Whispel; (Spanish-American War) Sheldon Benjamin Elwyn; (World War I) Louis Harrison and Henry P. Longendyke; (World War II) Charles Sherwood Carnright, Eno Compton Jr., Charles Anthony Di Andrie, George De Freese, Paul Lemay, Caleb Milne IV, John Alexander Peacock, Charles Benjamin Pierpont, Roger Paul Peyre, Robert Oren Russell, Leonhard Scholl Jr., and William John White; (Vietnam War) Richard Quinn. The marker honoring Quinn, who died in Vietnam in 1970, is located at the base of the memorial.

George Wilber

Known by most as a skilled wood turner, George Wilber got his start working at the Vosburg turning mill site in Shady and, later, by working with Willis Wilber in Mink Hollow. Eventually, Wilber would set up his own shop near his home in Mink Hollow, employing as many as five people at times. Each turner had his own specialty and, whatever the order, he would create the template, purchase the lumber, cut each piece to size, and hand-turn each item. Production could include items from baseball bats to chair legs. On weekends, Wilber was no stranger to music, playing fiddle for gatherings at Doc Daley's or other barn dances in and around the Lake Hill and Shady area. (Courtesy Rowena Wilber Koester.)

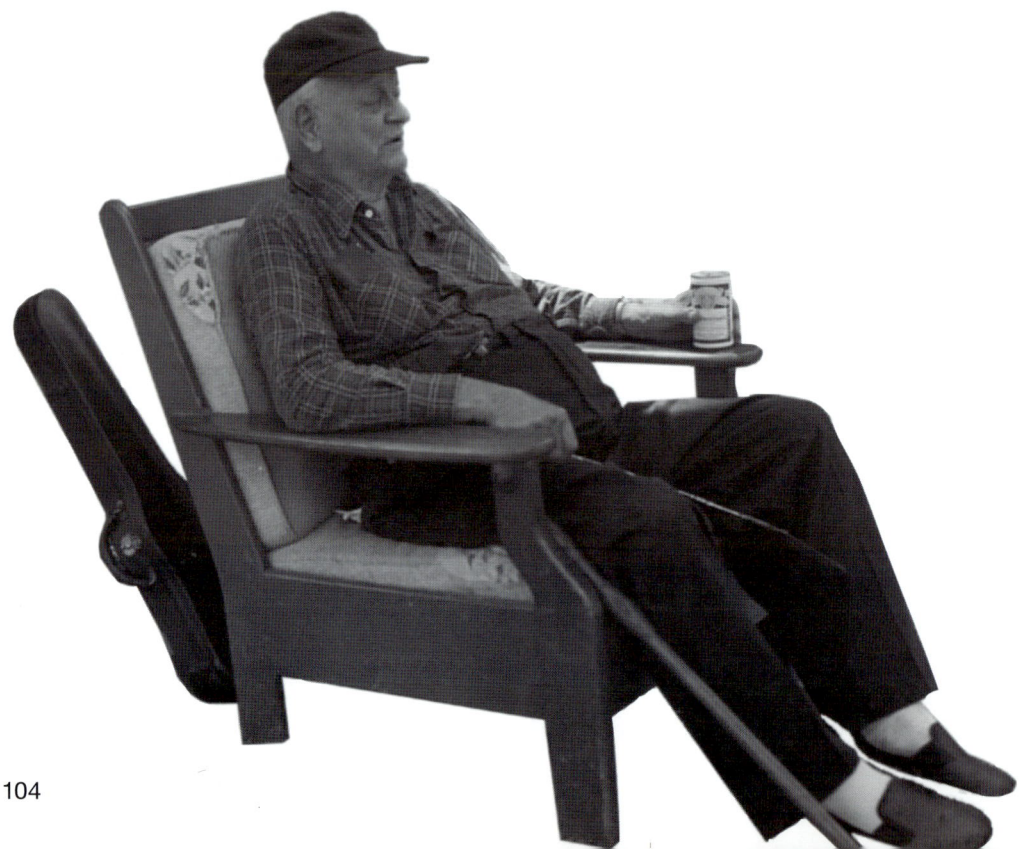

CHAPTER THREE: LEGENDS RECALLED: TALES AND STORIES THAT REMAIN

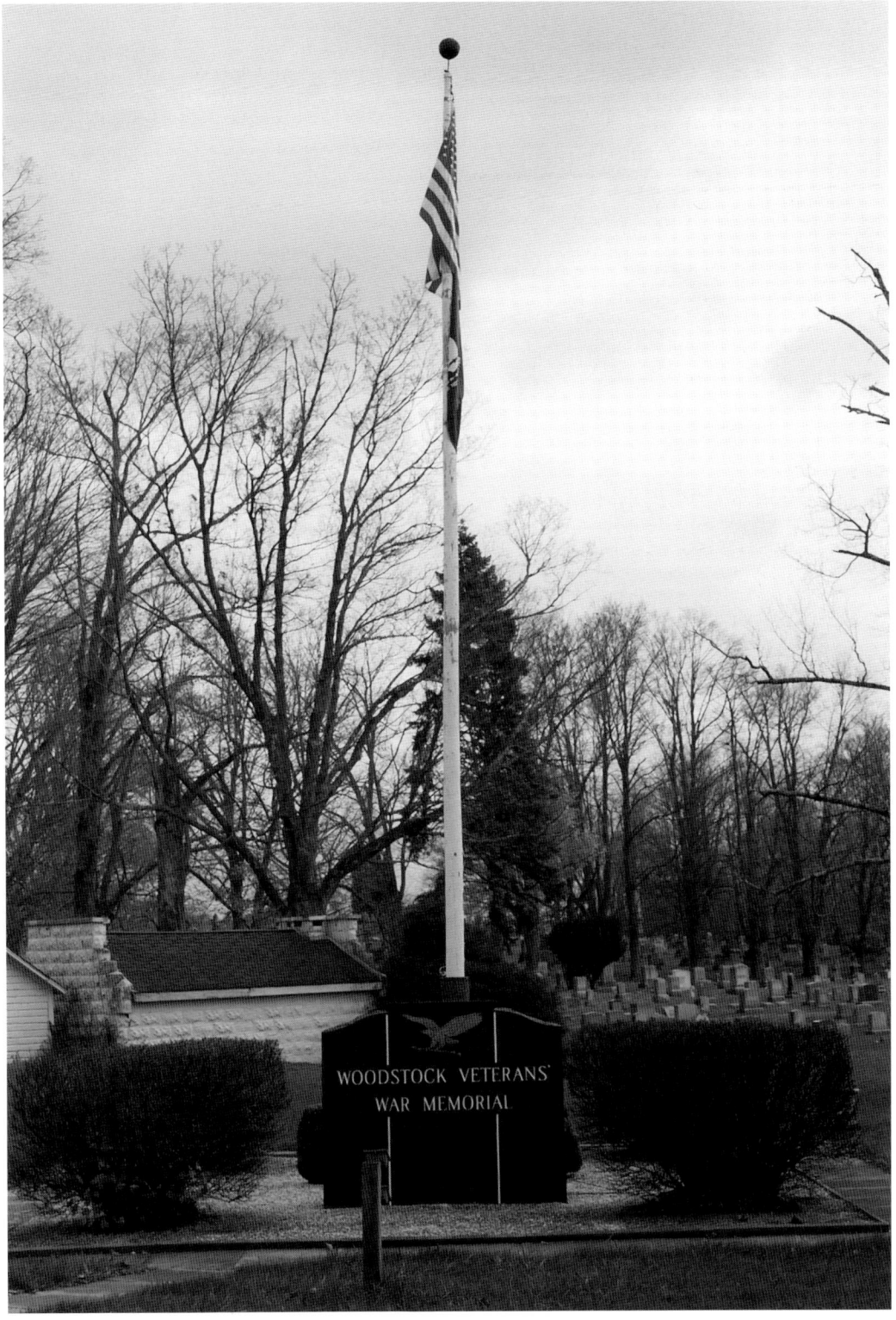

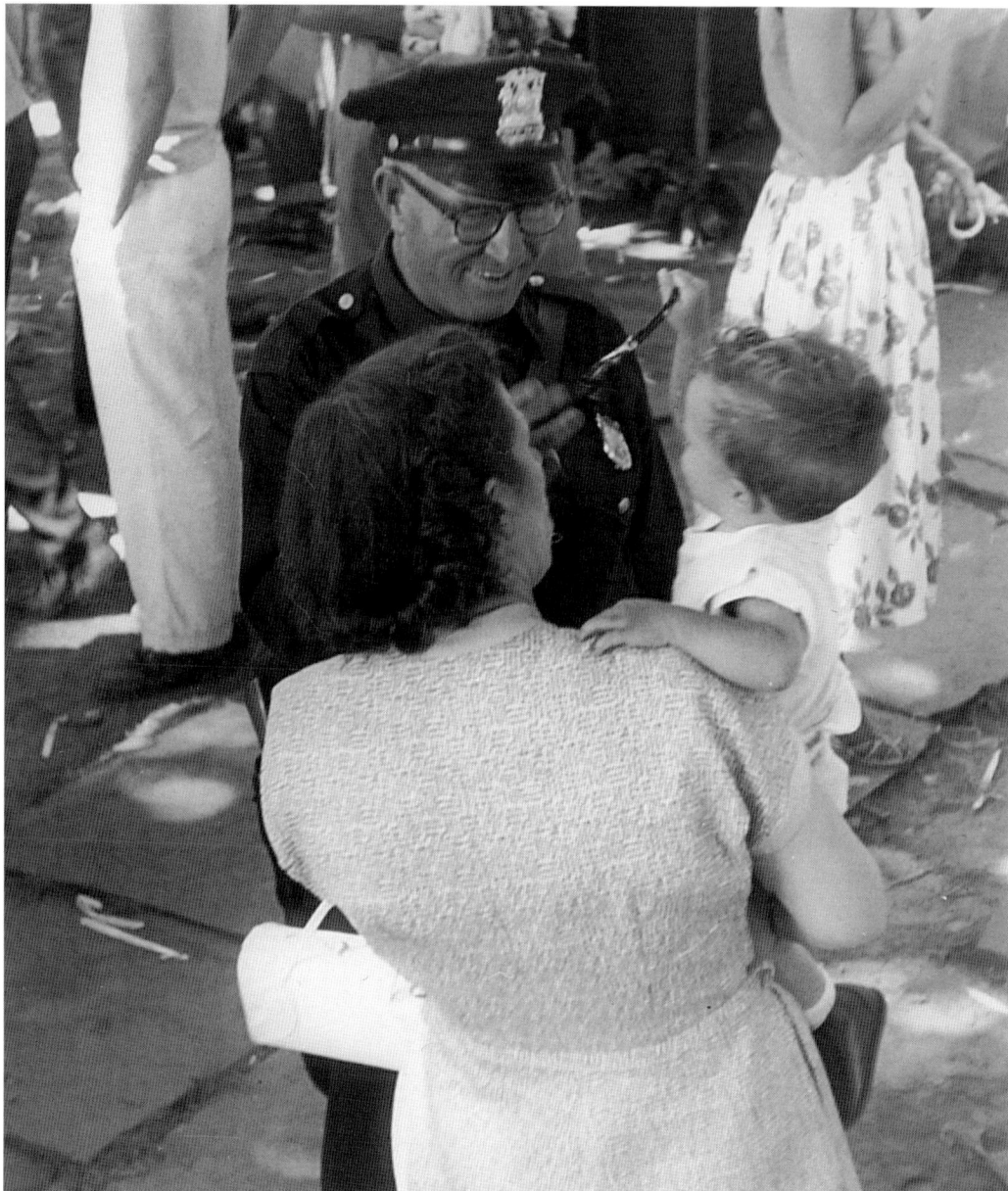

Clarence Snyder

Clarence Snyder ("Clancy the Cop") remains a legend in Woodstock even today. As chief constable in the 1950s and early 1960s, Snyder was known as a tough, authoritarian figure who cruised Woodstock streets each day in a green Mercury with a bubble light on the roof. Every afternoon, as school was dismissed, Clancy could be found at the intersection of Routes 212 and 375 performing his crossing guard duties with precision, often shouting at drivers to keep moving. Legend has it that, in his younger days, Snyder ran numbers on Coney Island and retreated to Woodstock following a run-in with the mob. Pictured here at the Library Fair, Clancy was a well-respected member of the community, even by those children who, following their Halloween antics, were made to scrub the bridge on Tinker Street. (Courtesy the Snyder family.)

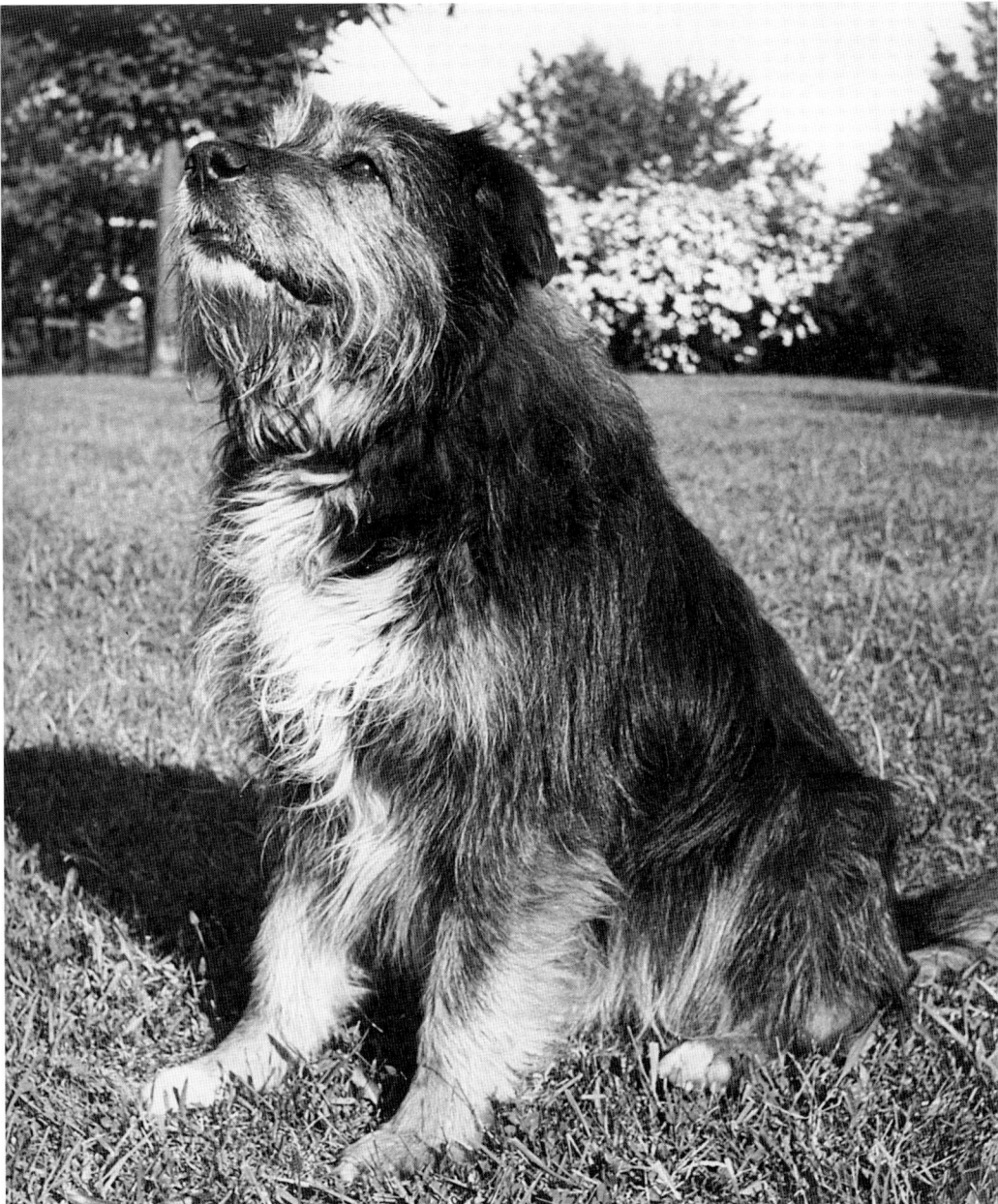

Teddy

In an era before leash laws and dog parks, Woodstock canines had a bit more independence when it came to how they spent their day. Teddy was the Allen family dog. After World War II, his "children," Victor and Elizabeth, left home to marry and set up homes of their own. At the beginning of each week, Teddy would leave his home on Neher Street and travel to Bearsville to spend time with Elizabeth. Once that visit was concluded, he moved on to Victor's home on Glasco Turnpike—a distance of approximately three miles. Along the way, Teddy became well acquainted with the homes he passed. When his travels were done for the week, Teddy returned to his Neher Street home to rest up and ponder his next excursion. (Courtesy Deborah Heppner.)

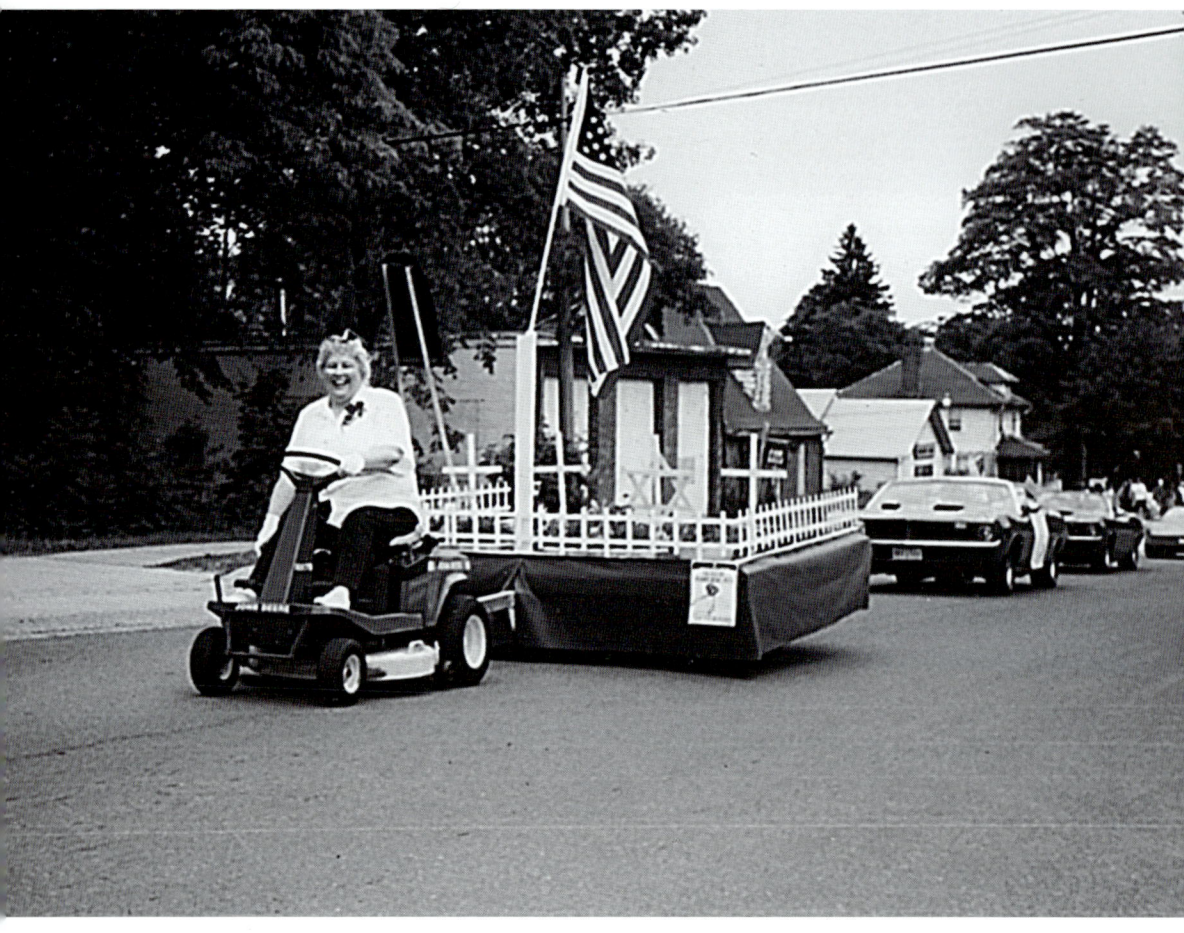

Sheron Graver
Sheron Graver was known for a warm smile and an infectious laugh. An active member of the Historical Society of Woodstock for many years, her knowledge of local history, especially the many mountain houses that dotted the area, was greatly respected. Sheron was very proud of her membership and service to the Ladies Auxiliary of the American Legion Post No. 1026 and, each year, never hesitated to be the volunteer who placed the wreath at the war memorial on Memorial Day or Veterans Day. An employee of Ametek-Rotron for many years, she also volunteered for the Rotron crew of the Woodstock Rescue Squad. Her dedication to her family, especially her mother, Martha, will be remembered by many.

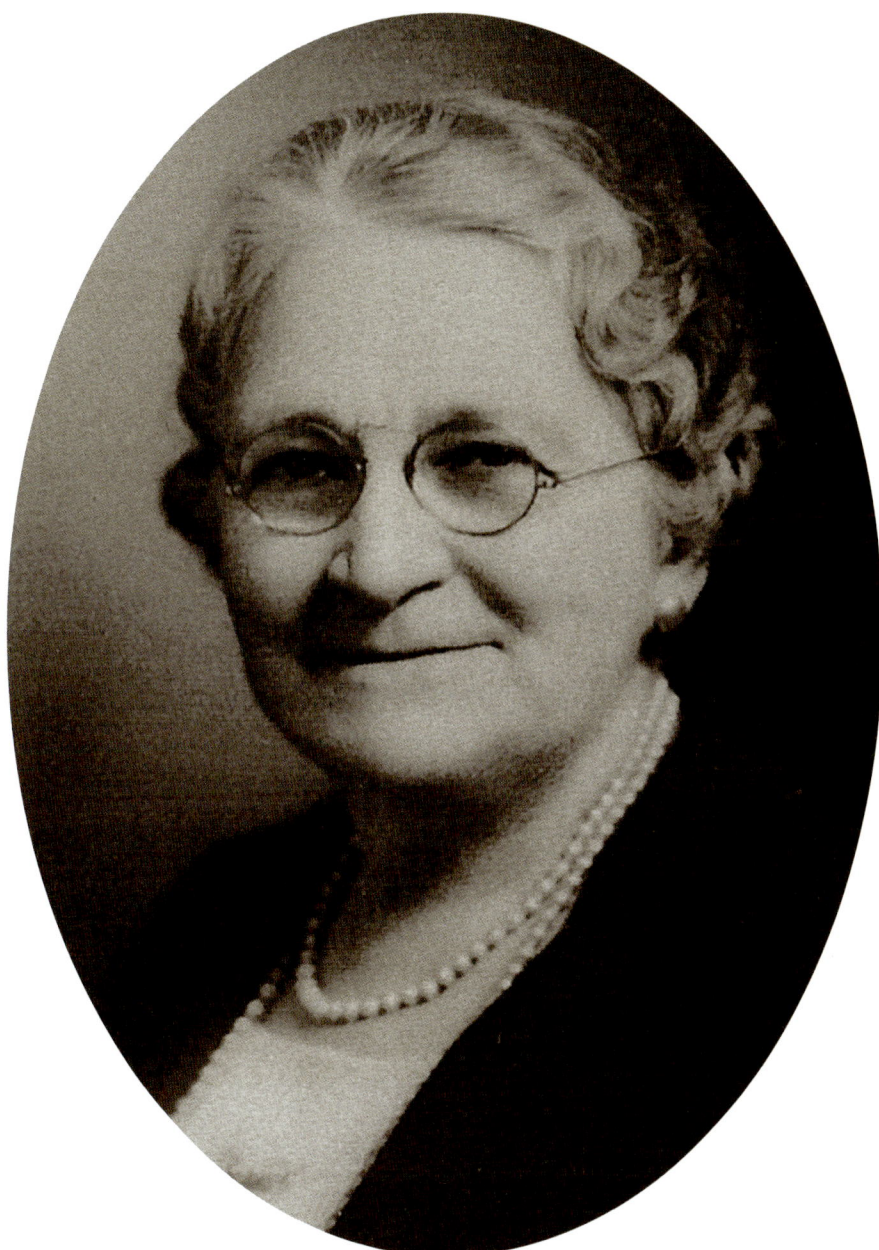

Sarah MacDaniel Cashdollar
Born on Overlook Mountain in 1871, Sarah MacDaniel Cashdollar possessed a remarkable work ethic from her earliest years. At the age of 12, she delivered milk up the mountain to the Overlook Mountain House twice a day in a horse-drawn buckboard. Later, as she and her husband, Wilbur, served as caretakers of the hotel, she would endure a fierce windstorm that toppled the hotel's chimneys, porches, and outbuildings. Following a move to town, she and her daughters operated Woodstock's first telephone switchboard on the corner of Neher and Tinker Streets. In 1922, she opened a year-round boardinghouse called the Homestead. And at age 79, she began painting and selling charming Woodstock scenes. A shy, warm lady with a desire to help others, she was beloved by friends and neighbors alike. (Courtesy Jean White.)

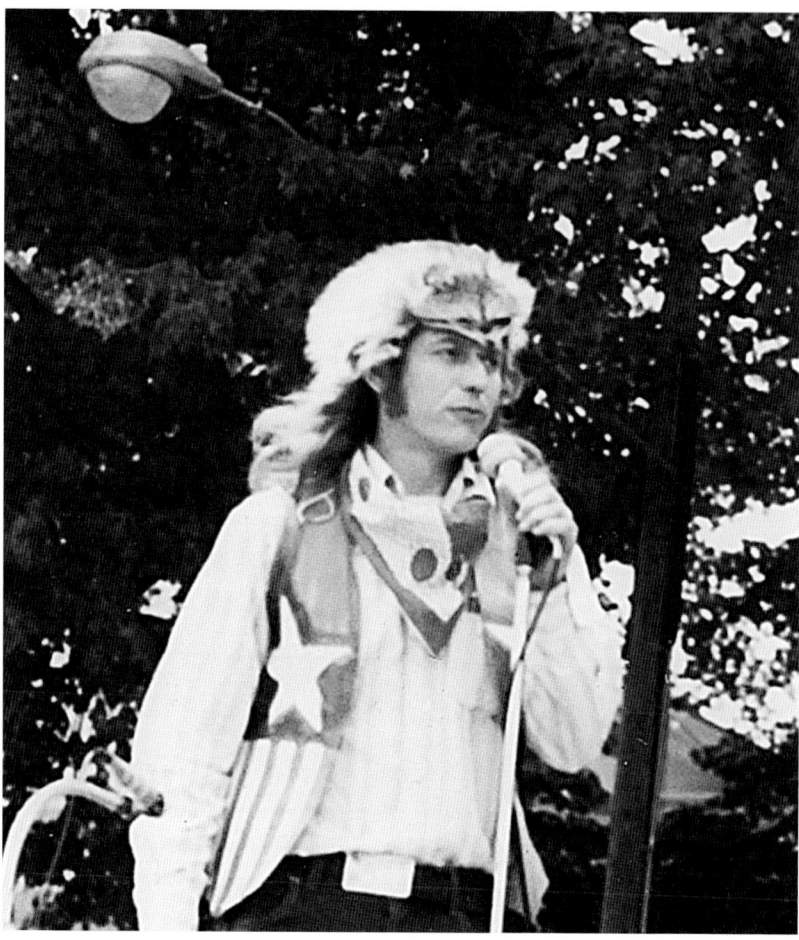

Sam Shirah

Though his life was dedicated to nonviolence, it was the tragic way his life ended in 1980 that makes the story of Sam Shirah a topic of conversation in Woodstock even today. The grandson and son of Baptist ministers, Shirah spent most of his early years as a civil rights and union activist in the South. Through his work with the Southern Mountain Project, the Student Nonviolent Coordinating Committee, and the Ladies Garment Workers, Shirah gained recognition and respect for his efforts to bring an end to racial inequality and dignity to one's work. Moving to Woodstock following the Woodstock Festival, Shirah quickly integrated himself into the community. Easily recognizable in his raccoon cap, he launched the Woodstock Independent Party as a political alternative for town voters. In addition, he served as the town's bicentennial chairman in 1976, working to coordinate town-wide activities during the celebration. When a major snowstorm hit Woodstock, Shirah, as head of a federally funded work crew, decided it would be a good idea for him and the crew to construct a giant snowman on the village green. When the inevitable outcry came, questioning if this was the best use of taxpayer dollars, Shirah and crew were forced to tear the snowman down, but not without a funeral for the snowman first. It was following a night of partying with friends that Shirah's life tragically ended. Believing that Shirah had had sex with his wife, an irate husband went to Shirah's home on Cooper Lake Road and shot him. While murders are few and far between in Woodstock, the story became even more bizarre when, immediately following the shooting, the irate husband decided that he now needed to save Shirah's life. Placing his body on the hood of the car, as there was no backseat, the man who had shot Shirah began to drive towards town in search of help. Police, however, having already been alerted, met the car on Cooper Lake Road. There, they found Shirah still on the hood of the car with his wife attempting to resuscitate him.

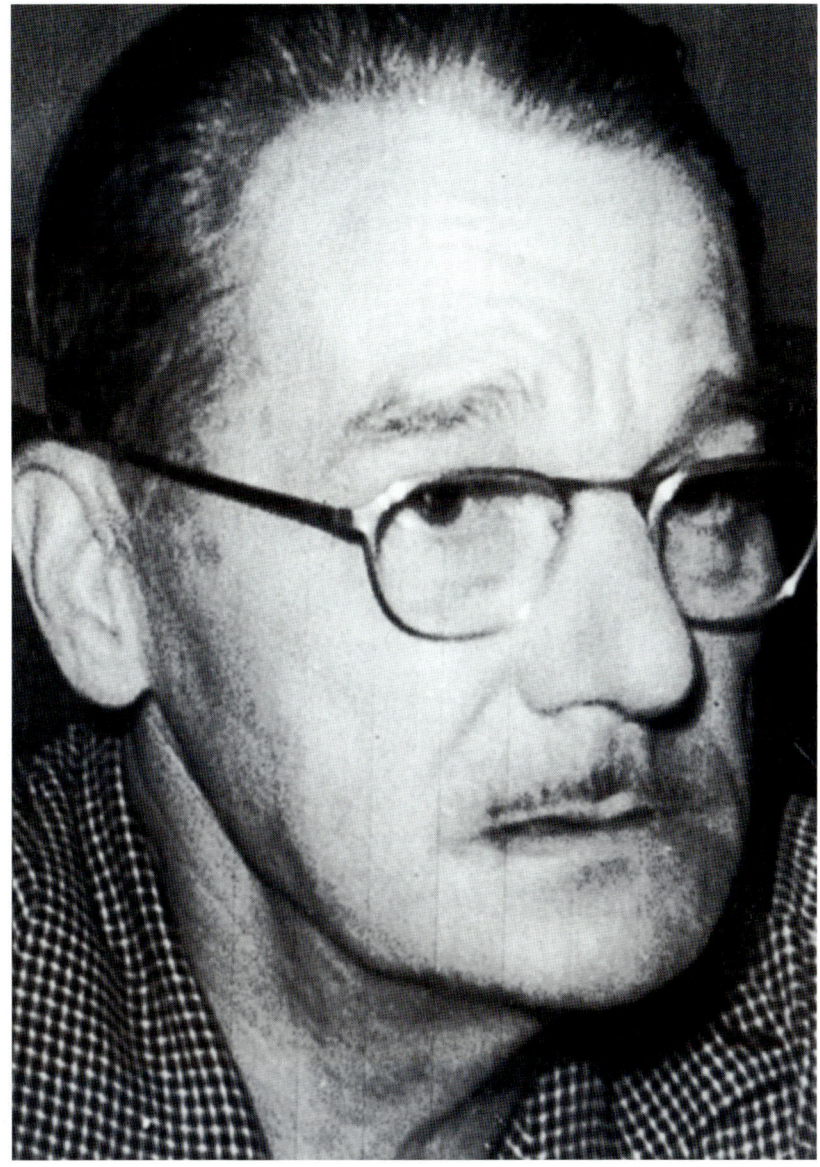

Dick Stillwell

Dick Stillwell's S.S. Seahorse was a bar, pure and simple. Located on Rock City Road, the Seahorse was a place where one went to drink after work (and through the evening). No questions were asked, and no answers needed to be given. As a result, Stillwell's establishment produced more than its share of stories in postwar Woodstock. Ironically, no story is remembered more by Woodstockers than the night Dick Stillwell died. Though he could be a generous man (he permitted local teenagers to turn the bar into a canteen during the war, for example), it was a known fact that Stillwell did not buy drinks for his customers. On one particular evening, while mixing a drink behind the bar, Stillwell collapsed. After he was carried from behind the bar and laid on the nearby ping-pong table, those gathered realized he was dead. As the customers pondered what to do next, they also realized that drinks were now on the house. And so they celebrated Dick Stillwell's life by helping themselves for the next couple of hours. When a local member of the state police was finally called, he was none too happy. No stranger to the Seahorse himself, the officer berated the crowd for having a two-hour head start on him.

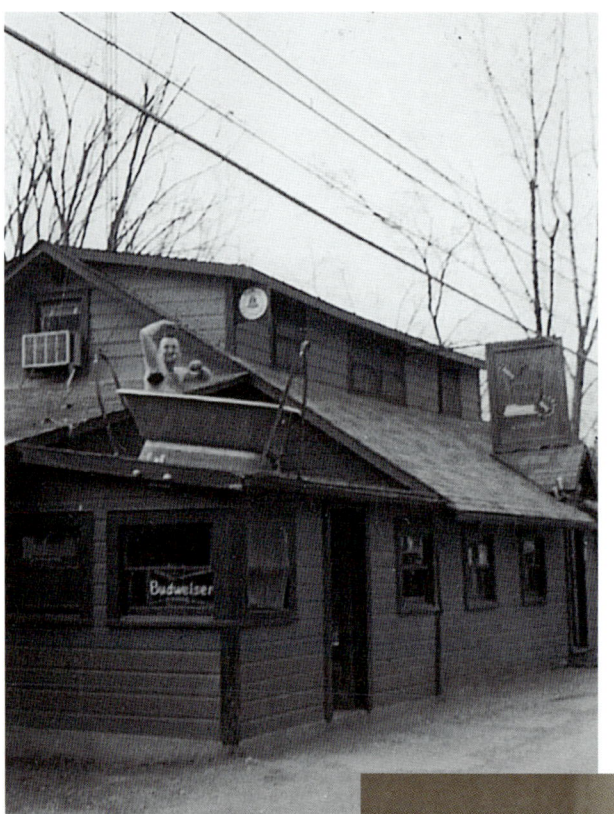

The Village Jug

For over 40 years, the same building on Rock City Road witnessed the evolution of Woodstock nightlife, housing such establishments as Buckman's, Eddie Shannon's, the Brass Rail, and the Village Jug. The Jug featured peanut nights, live bands, and Sunday softball games (with bloody marys). Stopping by, one might find a horse and rider inside or a joker in a tub on the roof. (Courtesy Denise Clark.)

Wayne Ambrosio

Most conversations about the Village Jug include the question, "Remember the guy who ate watch faces and the edges off beer glasses?" At one time, a well-dressed "IBMer," Wayne Ambrosio, was also known in the Jug as a "biker guy" who held his own in a bar fight. When he was sitting quietly at the bar, regulars understood it was best to keep it that way.

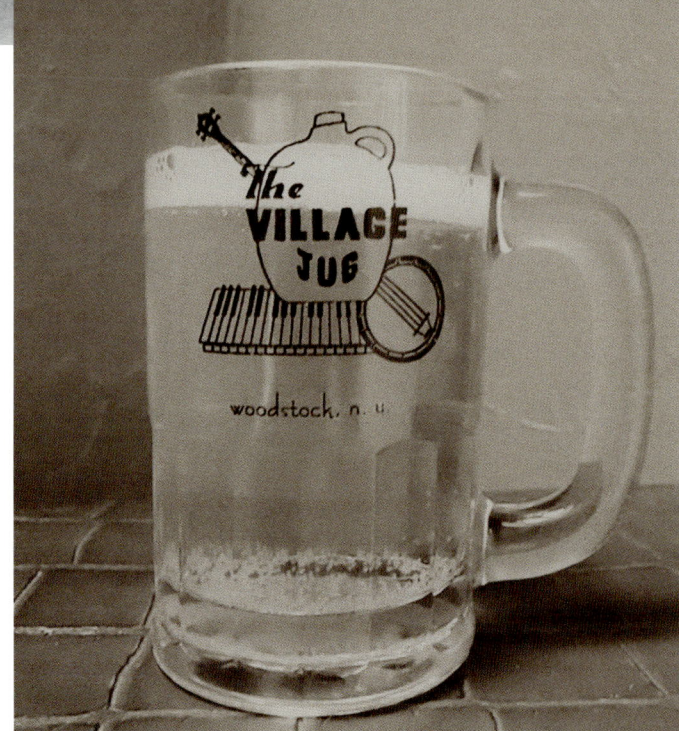

CHAPTER THREE: LEGENDS RECALLED: TALES AND STORIES THAT REMAIN

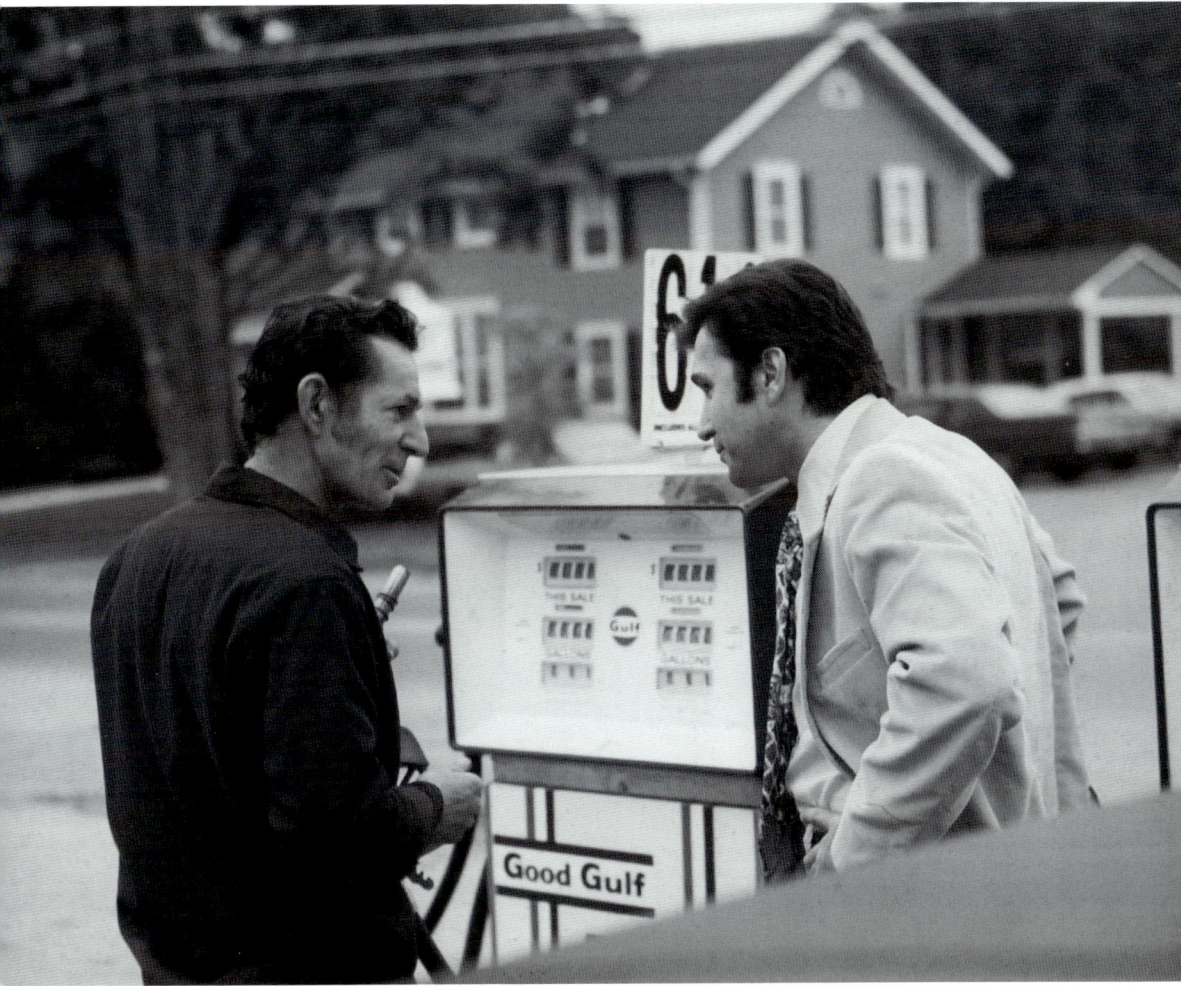

Robert Croissant
In response to a want ad for a service manager at a Kingston car dealership, Bob Croissant and his family moved from Queens to Woodstock in the early 1970s. At a time when gas prices were under $1 a gallon, Croissant, as seen in this photograph with then assemblyman Maurice Hinchey, took over the Gulf station on Mill Hill Road. Uniquely interested in town government—especially after the town turned down his request to construct a car wash—he became a public access producer and began taping town board meetings. Later, while animal control officer for Woodstock, Croissant produced a very popular local access program, *Animals without Love*. (Courtesy Rosemary Croissant.)

Andy Lee

About halfway up Rock City Road lies the Woodstock recreation field named in honor of Andy Lee. And yet not many Woodstockers know why it bears the name it does or who Andy Lee was. Andy Lee was the type of teenager who would make any town proud. An excellent student, Lee also participated in a wide variety of extracurricular activities while attending Kingston High School (as Woodstock students did during the 1950s). He served as vice president of the student council and treasurer of the junior class. Lee also excelled at football, having been selected as a member of Kingston's varsity team as a sophomore. Well-loved by his fellow students, Andy Lee was selected as both the best athlete and most popular boy by the junior class. Andy Lee's life came to a tragic end on a cold January day in 1956. While hunting with two friends, one member of the group, according to press accounts, slipped as he was about to fire upon partridges that had just taken flight. Lee was struck in the chest by the wayward round from his friend's 12-gauge shotgun. Andy Lee died before he could be taken to the hospital and was laid to rest in the Woodstock Cemetery next to the field that now bears his name.

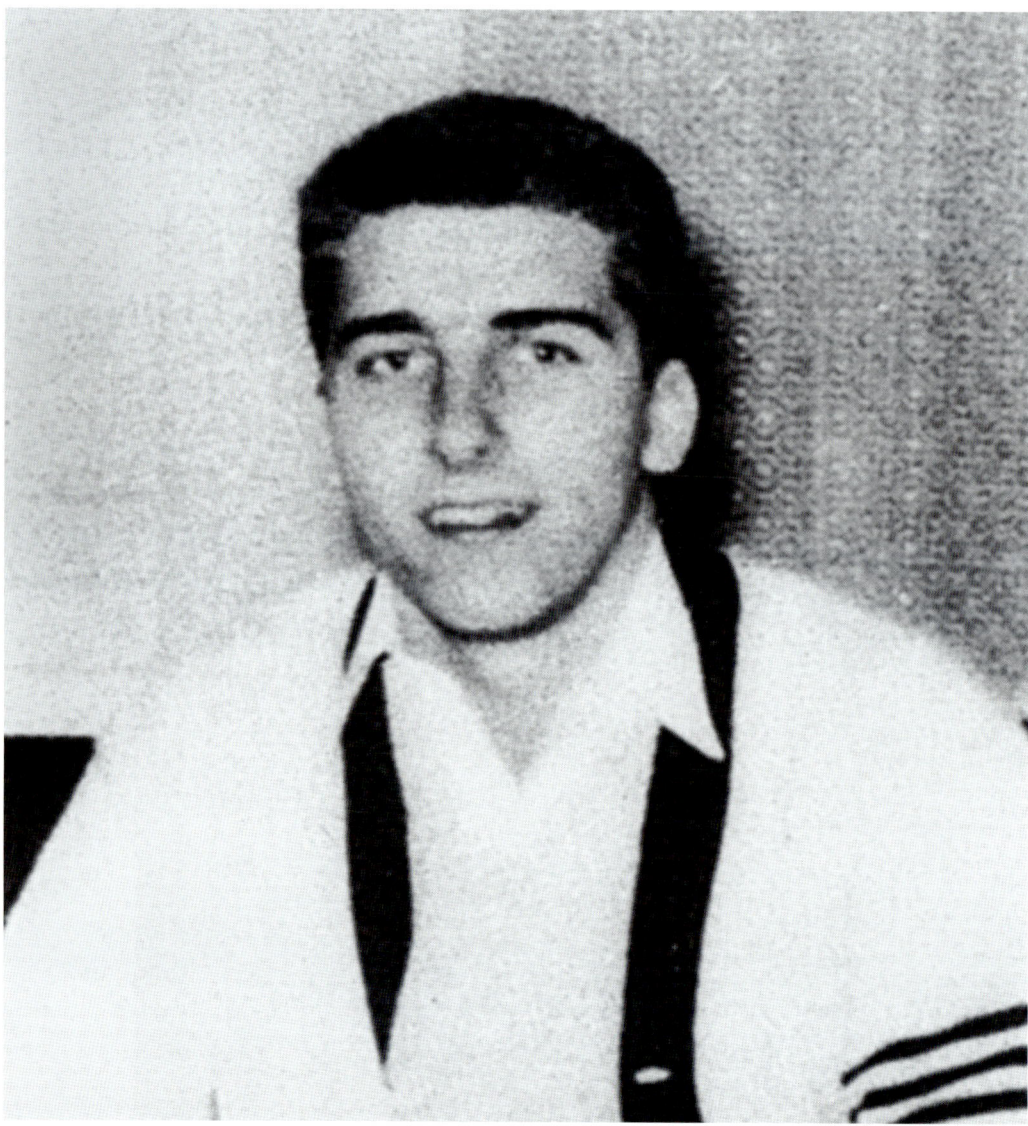

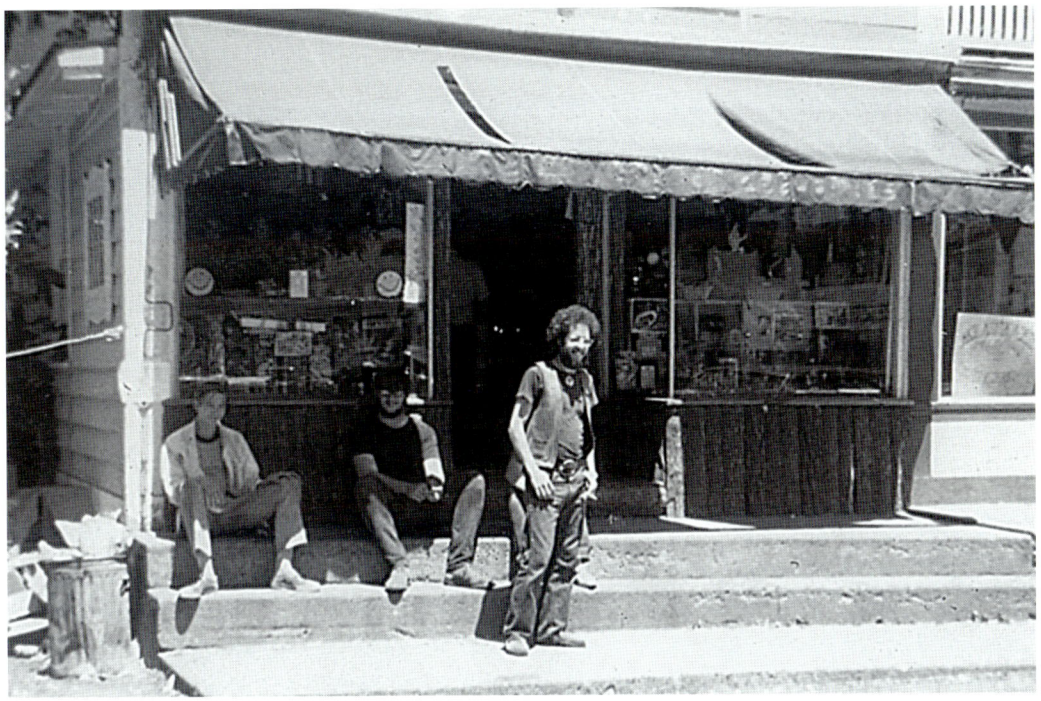

Woodstock's Head Shop

When a head shop appeared just off the village green on Old Forge Road, Woodstockers knew change was upon them. They had seen it coming as young people had, for a time, been arriving in town in search of Bob Dylan. But following the 1969 Woodstock Festival, it seemed the floodgates had opened, and a number of old-time Woodstockers were none too pleased. The head shop, opened by "Magic Markie" (center), joined an increasing number of exotic and eccentric stores in town. Shoppers were greeted by the intensity of the incense and patchouli oil and John Mayall music. More than just a place to purchase pipes, however, the head shop also became a sort of home for many of the kids, with its proprietor at times taking on the role of big brother.

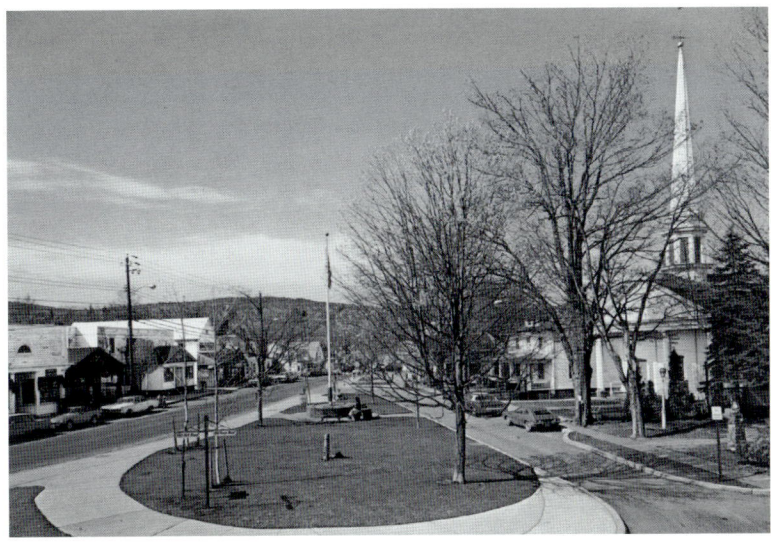

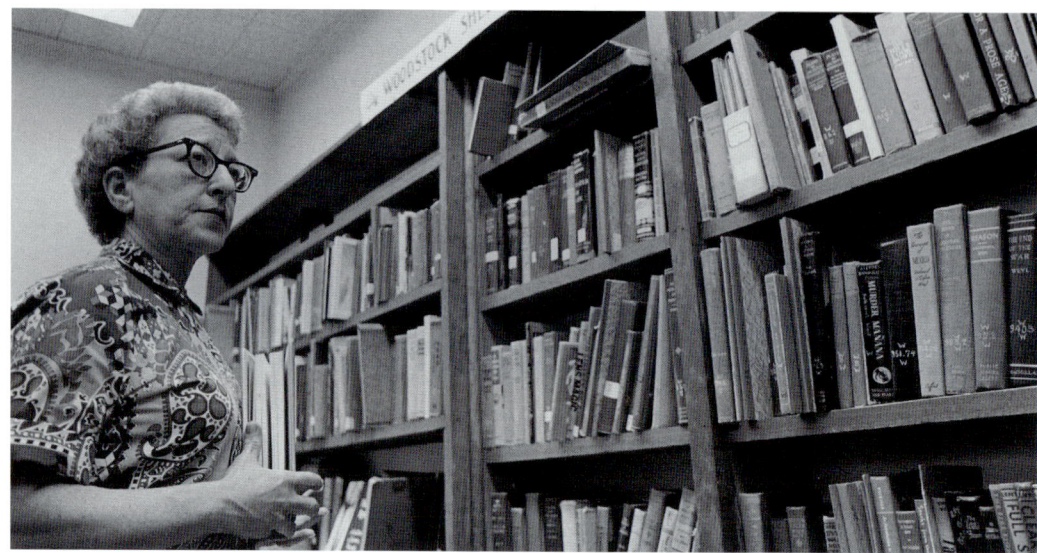

Ellin Roberts
A Vassar graduate and former Doubleday senior editor, Ellin Roberts took over the helm of the "new" Woodstock Library after the retirement of Alice Thompson in 1967. After completing library courses at Pratt, Roberts, who is recalled for her librarian persona, worked to expand and modernize the library. Preparing to expand once again, 2013 will mark the 100th anniversary of the Woodstock Library. (Courtesy Woodstock Library.)

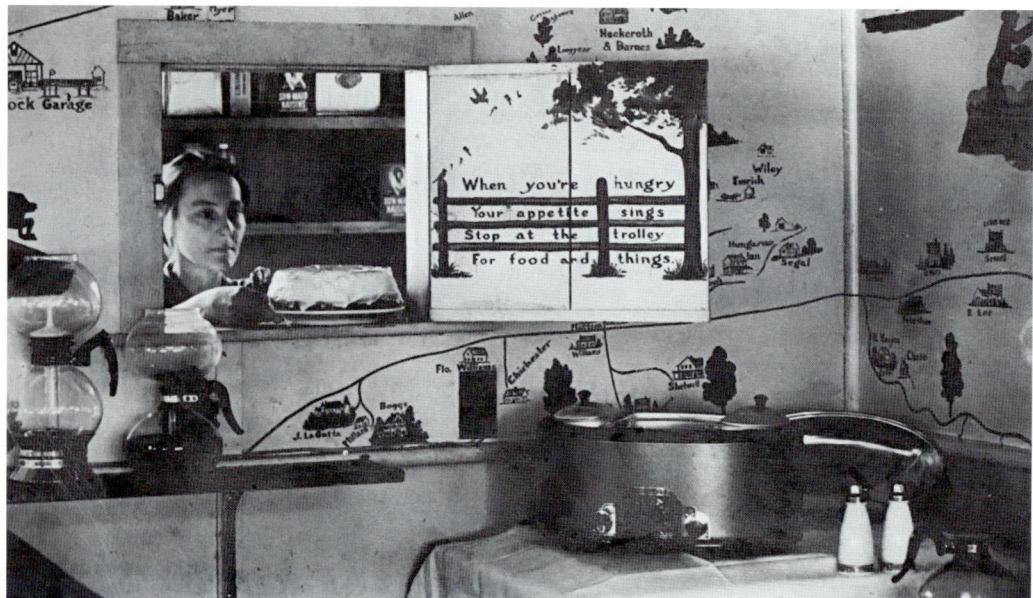

Eva Ricks Elwyn
Seen here taking a homemade cake from the kitchen of Deanie Elwyn's trolley diner, Eva Ricks Elwyn was the secret weapon of the Elwyn family. Simply put, it was her skill as a baker that helped woo customers. The decorative writing on the door to the kitchen reads, "When you are hungry your appetite sings, stop at the trolley for food and things." (Courtesy Jon Elwyn.)

CHAPTER THREE: LEGENDS RECALLED: TALES AND STORIES THAT REMAIN

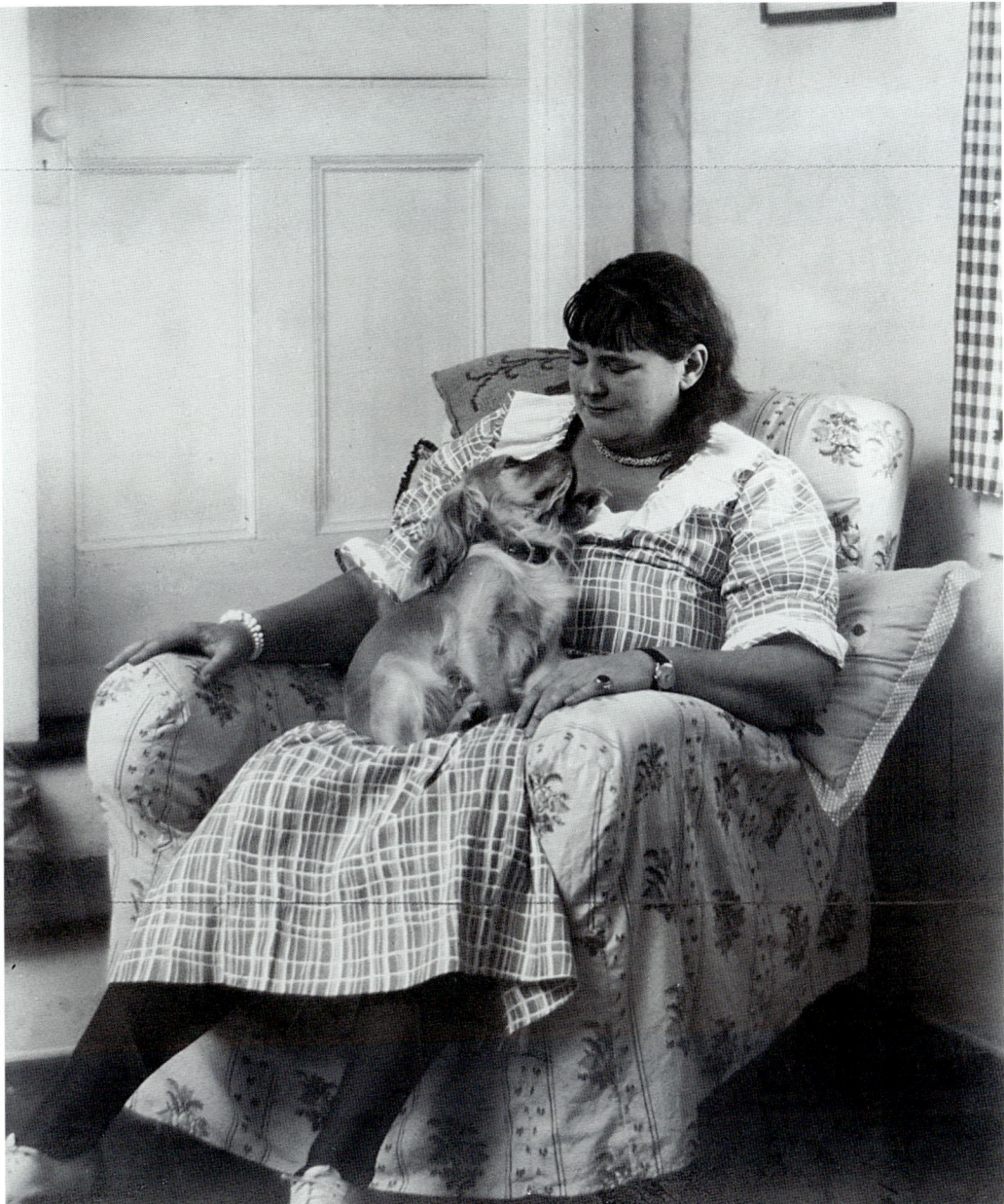

Wilna Hervey

Born in San Francisco in 1884, the six-foot three-inch, 300-pound actress appeared in a number of silent films, including her role as the "Powerful Katrinka" in the Toonerville Trolley shorts. When movie parts became less frequent, she purchased a farm in Bearsville and, with her longtime partner, Nan Mason, soon became beloved members of the Woodstock community. Both working artists, Hervey is best remembered for her enamel paintings, while Mason created both as a painter and photographer. On the social front, their parties were the talk of the town and a must-have invitation. Following World War II, working with artist Marianne Mecklem, Hervey offered the concept for the war memorial on Woodstock's village green that would honor Woodstock's war dead.

John Wolven

Most people who met John Wolven while he was working at Mower's Market on Tinker Street believed he was related to the Mowers. Pictured here on Maple Lane with Ruth Shultis Kinns and Anita Mower, John and his wife, Alice Holumzer Wolven, were Maple Lane neighbors to the Mower family. When Fred Mower took over F.B. Happy's store in 1931, Wolven came on board as a clerk and deliveryman. Though many might have looked upon the delivery of groceries as a luxury during the 30-plus years he worked for the Mowers, Wolven was always busy organizing the morning's grocery orders. Having grown up in Woodstock, he knew the town's back roads by heart and, when bad weather struck during his earlier years, winter deliveries were made by horse-drawn sleigh. (Courtesy John Mower.)

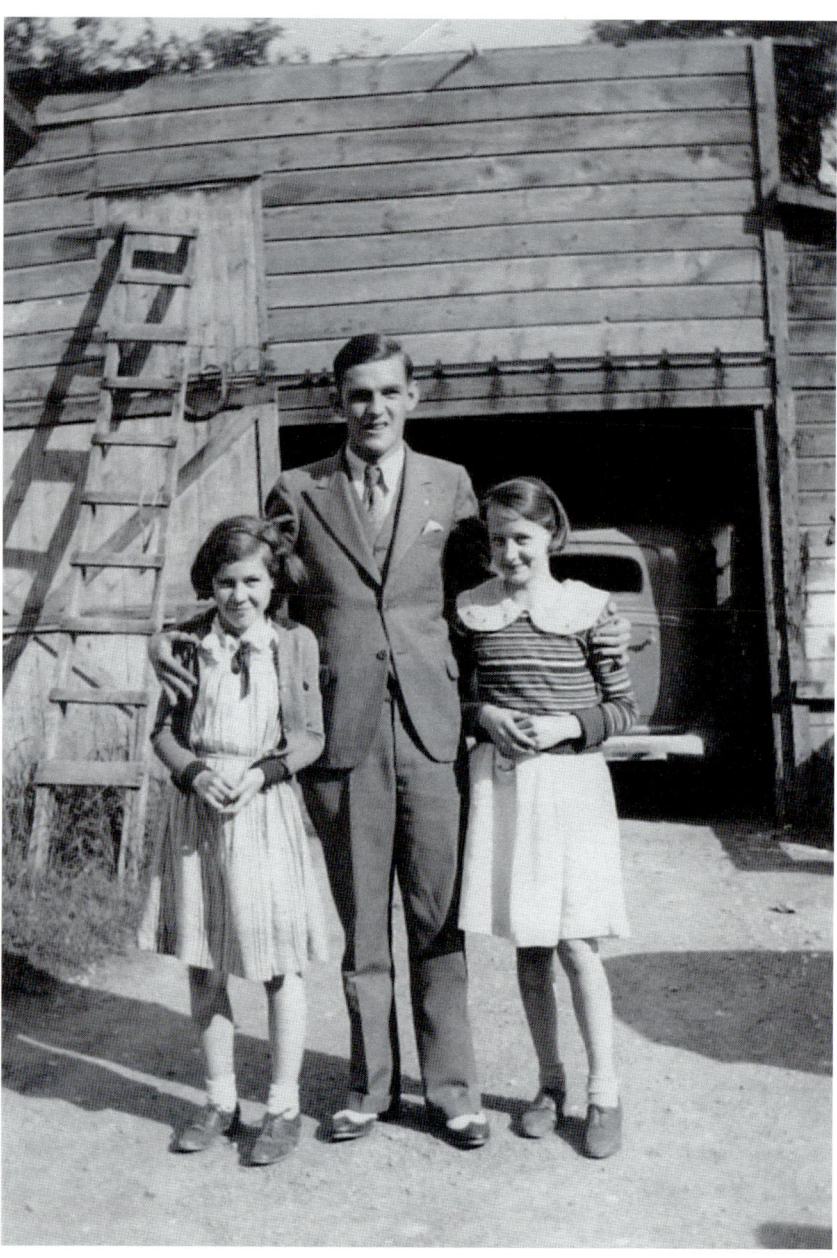

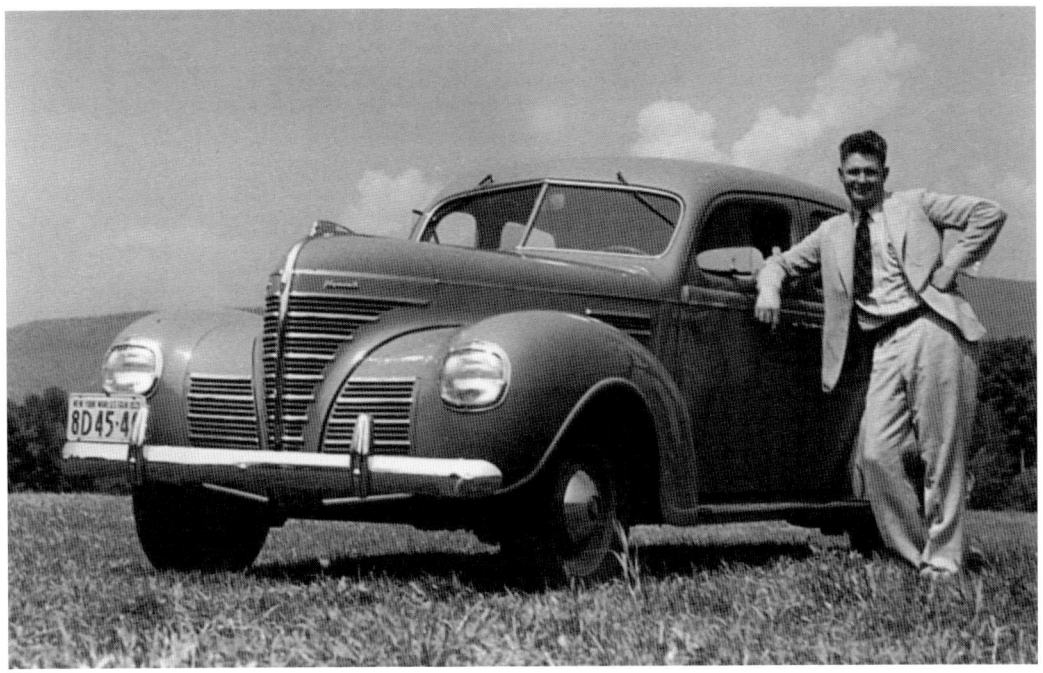

Fred Allen
Born the same year Bolton Brown first set eyes on Woodstock, Fred Allen was the son of artist Willard Allen and Woodstock dress creator Augusta Allen. Allen would go on, along with his father and half-brother Ray, to establish Allen Electric and Supply Company in 1926. Not limited to plumbing, heating, and electrical work only, Fred also sold and repaired appliances and television sets for Woodstockers over a number of years. In addition to Allen Electric, Allen also partnered with his son Victor Allen, Deanie Elwyn, Bill Allen, and his son-in-law Harry Kennedy to build and operate Woodstock Lanes in Bearsville. Fred Allen remains a bit of a legend today at the Woodstock Golf Club, where his creative scoring was often the subject of much discussion. (Both, courtesy Deborah Heppner.)

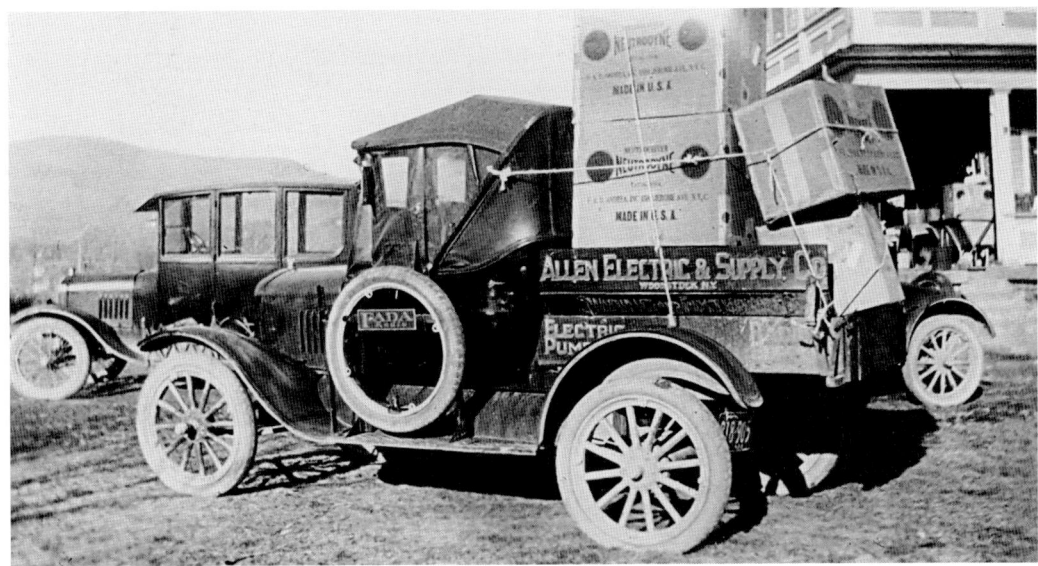

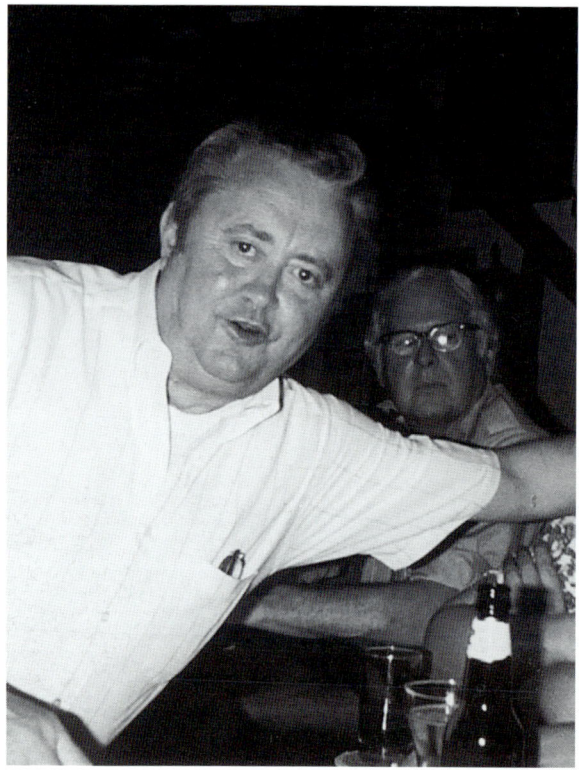

The Woodstock Pub

Jimmy Scales of Doolin, County Clare, and his wife, Maureen, opened the Woodstock Pub in 1972. The couple and their staff re-created the merriment and buzz that recalled the days when Bill Dixon presided over the Irvington. Looking for a place to keep warm on Christmas Eve? Locals knew enough to grab a seat at the bar by 4:00 p.m., for once the crowds arrived in town to greet Santa, the pub would be jammed. On St. Patrick's Day, Maureen and her daughters could be found performing Irish step dancing in between serving plates and plates of corned beef and soda bread. If one weren't engaged in sharing a round of blarney with Pat Murphy or Jim Barlow at the bar, then one was sitting on the porch, sipping a beer and watching the world go by.

JAMES AND MAUREEN SCALES CORDIALLY INVITE YOU TO AN EVENING OF TRADITIONAL IRISH MUSIC AND A BUFFET OF CORNED BEEF & CABBAGE AND IRISH SODA BREAD WILL BE SERVED ON

ON SAT. DEC. 5TH

AS THE

WOODSTOCK PUB AND RESTAURANT

CELEBRATES ITS

TWENTIETH ANNIVERSARY

CHAPTER THREE: LEGENDS RECALLED: TALES AND STORIES THAT REMAIN

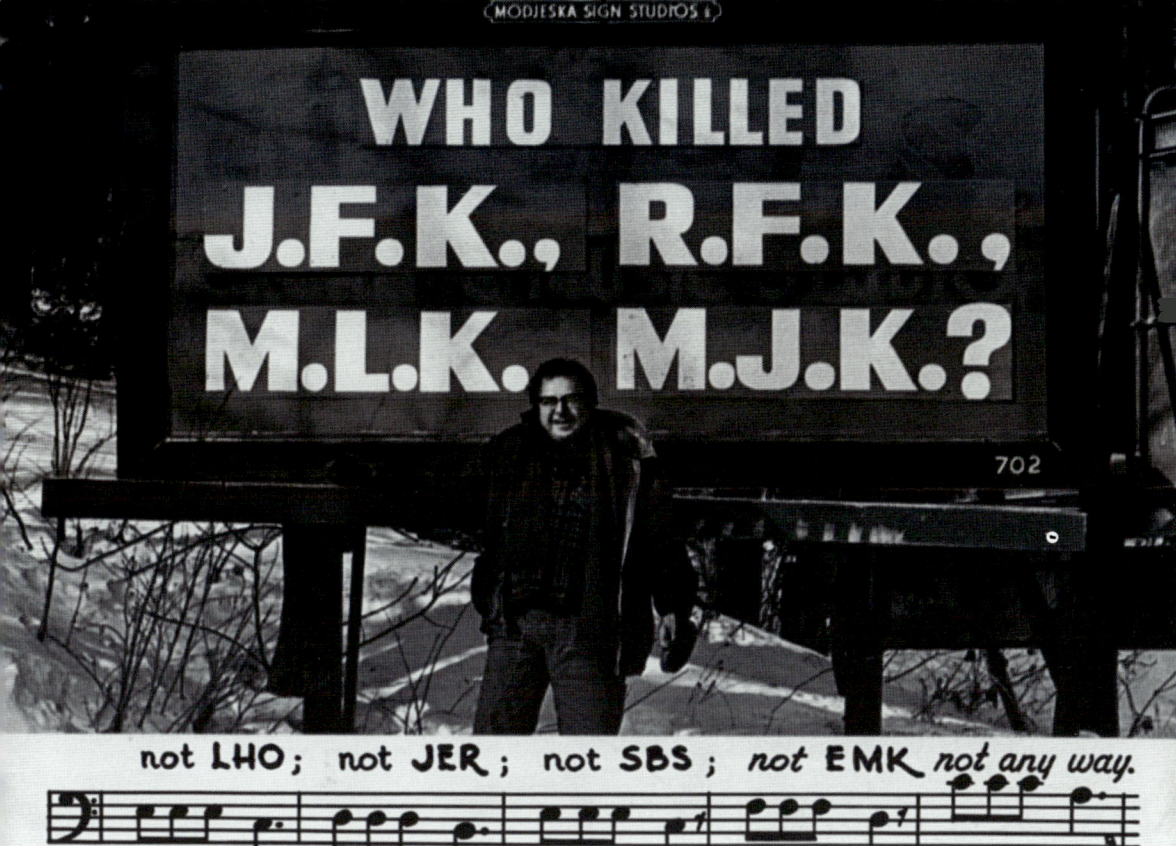

Rush Harp
Rush Harp, Woodstock's self-proclaimed "assassinologist," found himself stranded in Woodstock in the late 1950s during a blizzard. Unable to return home to New York City, he simply stayed. Described as kind, loveable, and considerate, he was a man of many financial fortunes that seemed most easily spent on others. A lifetime member of the National Rifle Association, it was his detailed knowledge of guns that contributed to his belief that the Kennedy assassination was part of a conspiracy and could not have been carried out by Oswald alone. In the years that followed, he expanded his conspiracy theories to cast an even wider net. No stranger to helping others, Rush Harp was a mainstay on the night shift for the Family crisis hotline. Ever the optimist, when asked how he was doing, his reply was "supreme." (Courtesy Frank Engel.)

LEGENDARY LOCALS

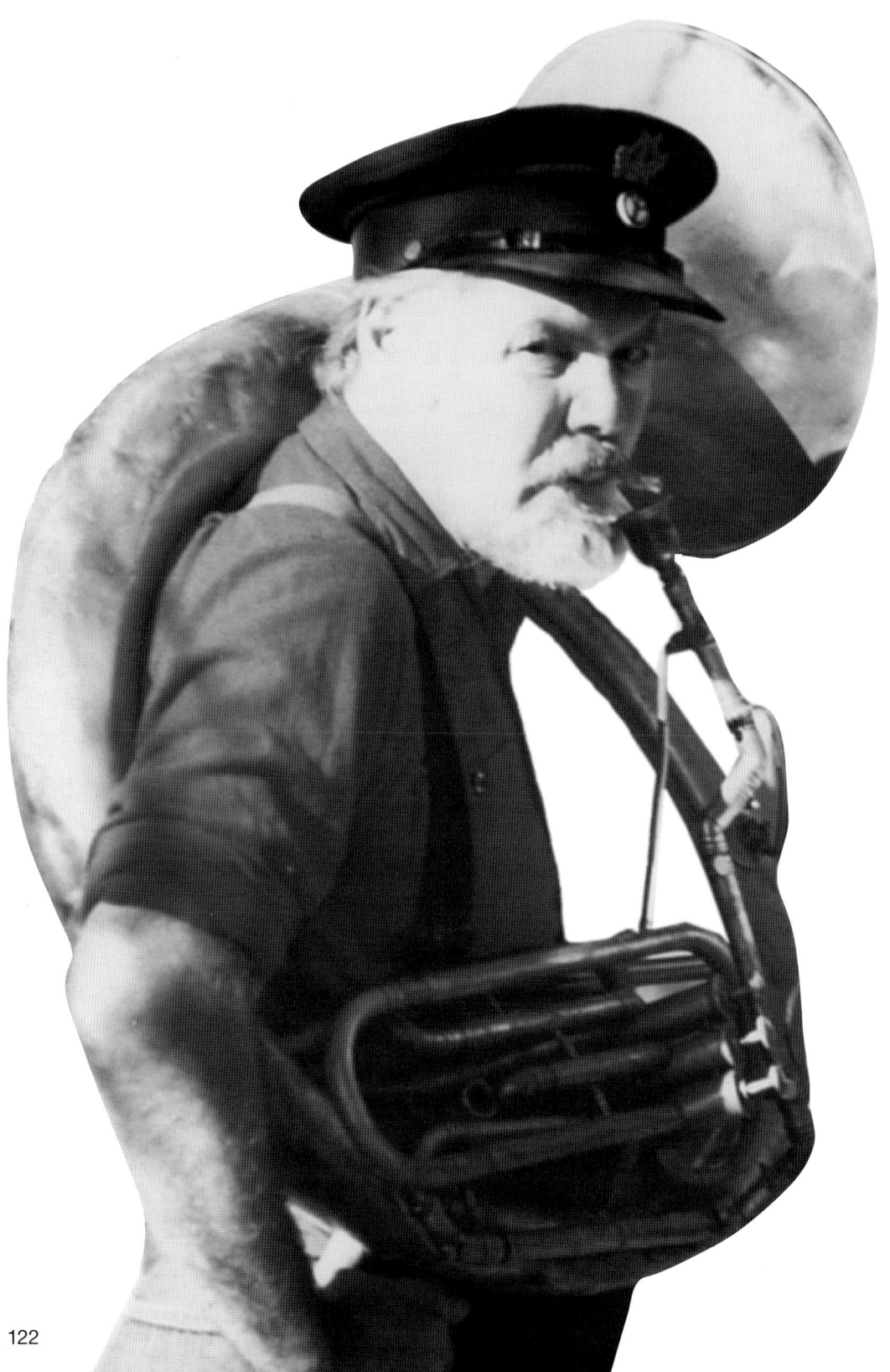

CHAPTER THREE: LEGENDS RECALLED: TALES AND STORIES THAT REMAIN

Holley Cantine (LEFT)
On the world stage, Holley Cantine was a pacifist and an anarchist. Along with Dachine Rainer, he served as editor of *Retort*, an anarchist journal. He also edited *Prison Etiquette*, featuring writings from conscientious objectors during World War II. Multilingual, Cantine translated such volumes as *Nineteen-Seventeen* and *The Unknown Revolution* for the Libertarian Book Club in the 1950s. On the Woodstock stage, Cantine was equally as versatile. His locally produced newspaper, the *Wasp*, strongly objected to commercialism in Woodstock and the increasing number of tourists occupying Woodstock sidewalks, whom he called "trudgers." As a result, the *Wasp* was banned by some local businesses. Holley Cantine was also a musician. His Woodchuck Hollow Brass and Woodwind Band performed at many local functions. Though technically not very good, their oompah music was well loved. (Courtesy Jay Wenk.)

Woodstock Ladies Home Bureau
In the 1950s and early 1960s, women in Woodstock came together to form their own version of the Ladies Home Bureau. Widely found in towns across America at the time, the Ladies Home Bureau served as a counterpart to local men's organizations such as Rotary. Used as a means of fellowship and support, women in Woodstock met regularly in each other's homes to create crafts, aid charities, share recipes, and no doubt to lend their opinions on the state of Woodstock's political, cultural, and social scene. Here, members of the bureau are shown meeting to commemorate their organization in 1957. While the names of all the women are not known, included in the photograph are Libby Kennedy, Cookie Neher, Pat Hastie, Jane Allen, Ruth Kinns, and Ginny Holdridge.

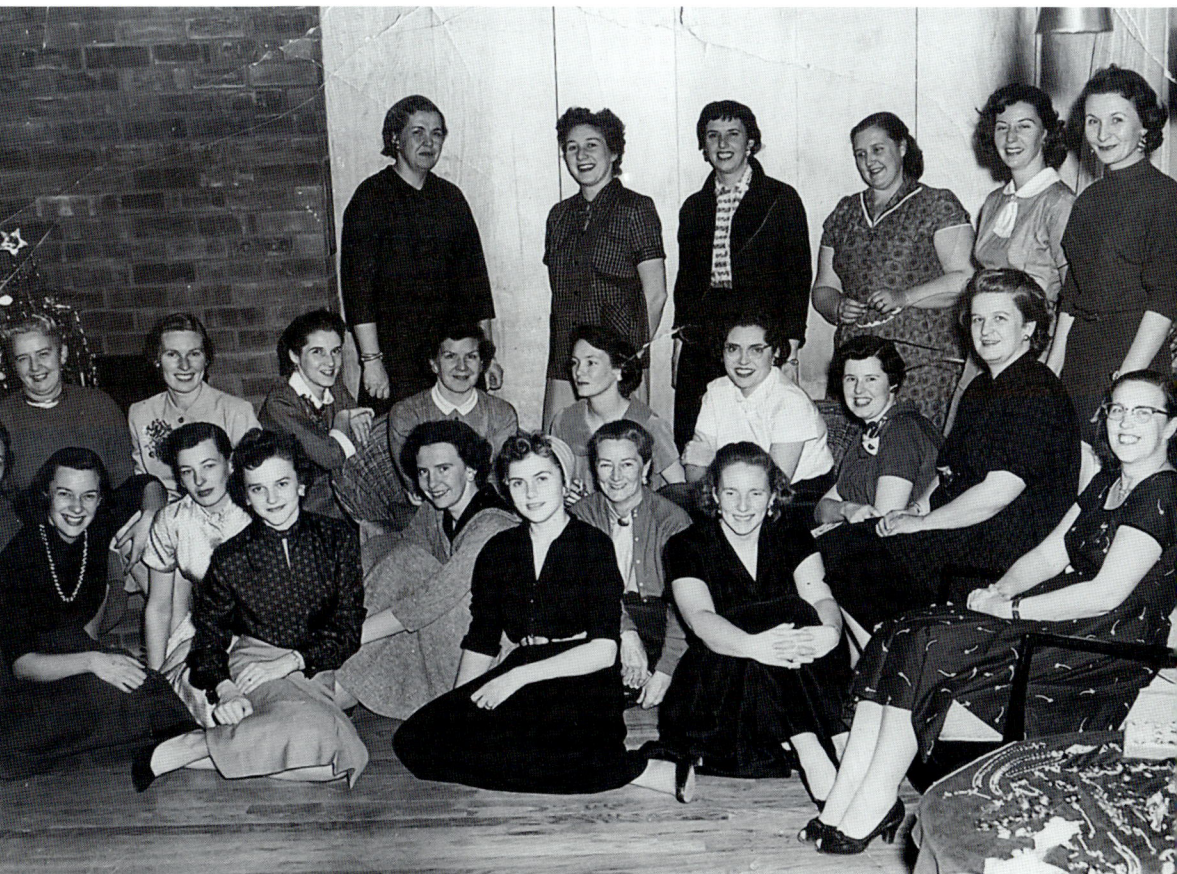

Gretchen Smith Mount and Mary D. Smith

The daughters of artist Judson D. Smith and Mary Dufresne Smith, Gretchen (left) and Mary arrived in Woodstock at a young age. Originally from Michigan, the family settled into an idyllic country life in a rambling farmhouse that once belonged to the Riseley family. In the summer of 1925, with formal training at Columbia behind her, Gretchen began teaching and eventually became director at Children's House in Woodstock, founded by Zoe Bateman in 1918. Following her work at Children's House, Gretchen and Mary opened their own country school in the Smith home on Ohayo Mountain Road. Together, the sisters turned their school into a local institution. Even today, students recall their experience at the Country School as being warm, thoughtful, and full of learning. (Both, courtesy Judson Smith.)

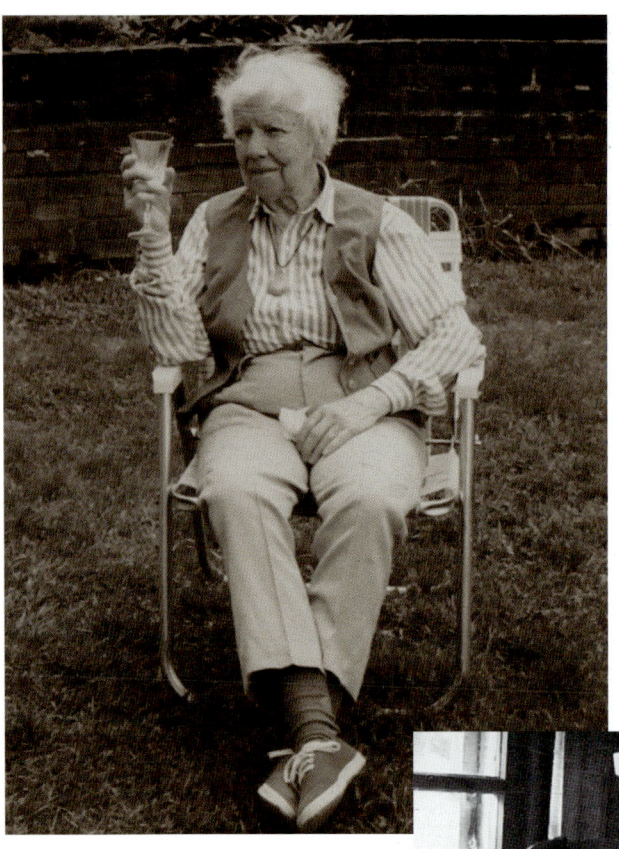

CHAPTER THREE: LEGENDS RECALLED: TALES AND STORIES THAT REMAIN

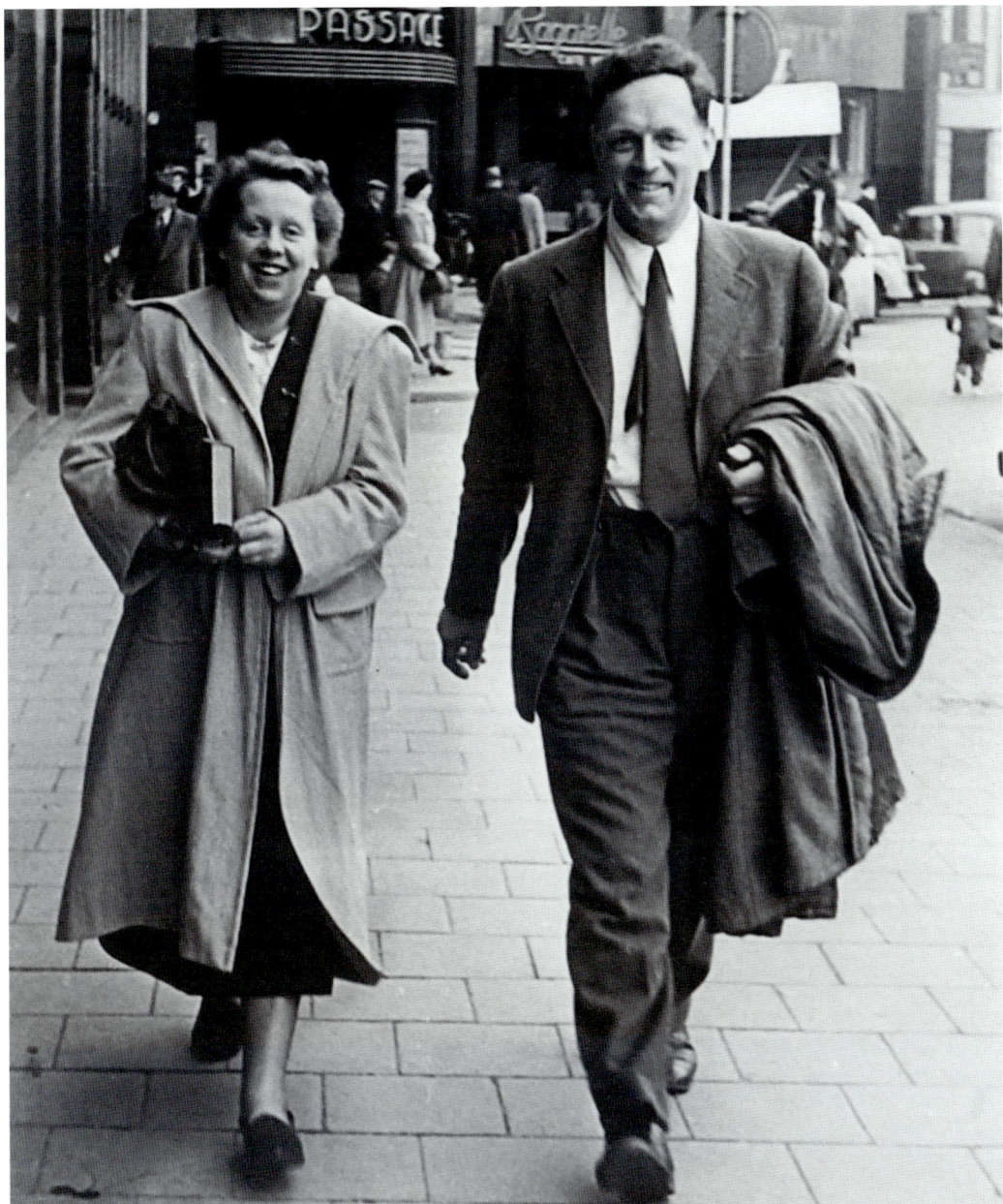

Johtje and Aart Vos
Johtje and Aart Vos moved to Woodstock in 1951 from their native Netherlands. Their ties to Woodstockers, including the Brokenshaws, Van Rijns, and Wim Cramers made it an easy decision. The couple's remarkable story includes risking their lives sheltering Jewish friends and neighbors during the Nazi invasion of the Netherlands—a story that began with a simple knock on the door one night and a Jewish couple asking for shelter and rest as they fled the Germans. To honor their heroic efforts, Rabbi Meeds of the Israeli Consulate bestowed upon the couple the designation "Righteous People" in 1992. Always maintaining a humble attitude regarding their extraordinary service during the war, Johtje and Aart went on to establish a summer camp known as Peter Pan Farm on Glasco Turnpike. (Courtesy Barbara Vos Moorman.)

INDEX

Adams, Jane, 12
Allen, Augusta, 83, 119
Allen, Bill, 119
Allen, Fred, 119
Allen, Jane, 29, 123
Allen, Ray, 119
Allen, Victor, 29, 119
Allen, Willard, 83, 119
Ambrosio, Wayne, 112
Baehr, Christian, 4, 15
Baehr, Wihelmina, 15
Baldwin, Pauline Lane, 98
Balmer, Ed, 66
Balmer, Margot, 66
Barlow, Jim, 120
Baumgarten, Ludwig, 56, 59
Baumgarten, Rudolf, 59
Black, Marc, 78
Bolton, Clarence, 57
Bolton, Louise Cashdollar, 57
Breitenstein, Barbara, 19
Briand, Aristide, 18
Bromberg, Jane Dow, 55
Bromberg, Manuel, 55
Broun, Heywood Hale, 54
Brown, Bolton, 11, 12, 21, 119
Bullard, Marion, 9, 31
Burg, Dr. Norman, 19
Burg, Sandy, 19
Buttrick, Helen, 101
Buttrick, Philip, 101
Cadden, Valerie, 9, 35
Cantine, Holley, 4, 85, 122
Carlson, John, 25, 38
Carlson, Margaret, 25
Cashdollar, Albert, 10, 30
Cashdollar, Carol, 53
Cashdollar, Roger, 53
Castle, Minerva, 97
Castle, William, 97
Comeau, Martin, 25, 26
Cramer, Aileen, 39
Cramer, Florence Ballin, 39
Cramer, Konrad, 39
Croissant, Robert, 113
Cunningham, Calvin, 20

Daily, Catherine, 15
Danko, Rick, 74
DeLisio, Robert, 52
DeLisio, Tony, 77
DeLisio, Wiggy, 77
DeLisser, R. Lionel, 89
Downer, Dr. Mortimer, 12
Drury, "Sally," 34
Dylan, Bob, 13, 42, 64, 74, 115
Eames, Edgar, 25
Eames, Kate, 25
Eames, Marion, 25, 26
Elwyn, Alexander, 75
Elwyn, Allen "Deanie," 41, 51, 92, 116, 119
Elwyn, Bertha, 67
Elwyn, Eva Ricks, 51, 116
Elwyn, Grant, 24
Elwyn, John M., 75
Elwyn, Larry, 79
Elwyn, Robert, 43
Elwyn, Washington, 57
Elwyn, William S., 67
Ernst, John, 90
Esposito, Michael, 78
Evers, Alf, 8, 9, 16, 47, 99
Father Francis, 41, 45
Feeley, Pamela, 94
Forno, Barbara Shultis, 33, 53
Forno, Joe, 33, 53
Fuller, Henry, 21
Gillman, Jerry, 23
Gillman, Sasha, 23
Gordon, Harris, 44
Grant, Ulysses S., 91
Graver, Sheron, 108
Grossman, Albert, 4, 9, 13
Grossman, Sally, 13
Gurland, Audrey, 53
Gurland, Ed, 53
Haile, Winnie, 57
Hall, Dr. Larry, 48
Haney, Bob, 52
Harder, Bill, 17
Harder, Carol, 17
Harder, Clayton, 80

Harder, Marge, 68
Harp, Rush, 121
Harrison, Birge, 38
Hastie, Pat, 76
Hastie, Walter, 34
Helm, Levon, 74
Herrick, Fordyce, 50
Herrick, Griffin, 10
Hervey, Wilna, 4, 117
Hilton, Richard, 19
Hinchey, Maurice, 113
Hoag, Bessie "Jean," 59
Holdridge, Ginny, 123
Holdridge, Joe, 85, 86
Hollander, Brian, 23
Hopkins, Harry, 27
Hornbeck, Mescal, 36, 84
Huffine, Dave, 96
Hutty, Warren, 34
Keefe, Jane Neher, 54
Keefe, Joe, 54
Kennedy, Harry, 119
Kennedy, Libby, 123
Kingsbury, Dr. John, 27
Kinns, Ruth Shultis, 118, 123
Klementis, Luke, 4, 95
Koehn, Priscilla Hastie, 76
Landi, Elissa, 43
Lapo, Bernie, 24
Lasher, Victor, 29, 56
Leaycraft, Edgar "Pete," 47
Leaycraft, Winifred, 47
Lee, Andy, 85, 114
Livingston, Madame, 99
Livingston, Robert, 7, 28, 97
Longyear Emily, 71
Longyear Janet, 71
Longyear, Kathy, 73
Longyear, Stan, 73
Longyear, Stanley " Sonny," 72
Longyear, Stanley Brinkerhoff, 30, 71, 72
Lubinsky, Bill, 87
MacDonald, Betty, 78
Magee, Rosie, 82
Magic Markie, 115

Marvin, Lee, 94
Mason, Nan, 117
Matteson, Jim, 95
McCall, Jane Byrd, 11
Mead, George, 4, 9, 21
Mecklem, Marianne, 117
Mercer, Sam, 41, 61
Milliken, Albert, 43
Milo, Capt. Salvo, 21
Moorman, Barbara Vos, 19
Morris, William, 11
Moskowitz, Al, 53
Moskowitz, Vivian, 53
Mount, Gretchen Smith, 81, 124
Mower, Anita, 118
Mower, Anne, 76
Mower, Fred, 118
Murphy, Pat, 120
Neher, Clark, 54, 34
Neher, Cookie, 123
Nessel, Clementine, 96
Newgold, Gabriel, 67
Newgold, Morris, 69
Park, Ann, 76
Peckham, Rev. William, 58
Peper, Florence, 68
Peper, Henry, 68, 69
Peper, John, 68
Peper, Will, 69
Pierpoint, Bill, 96
Pierpoint, Charles, 96, 105
Pike, John, 4, 24, 96
Povill, Ellen, 60
Prosky, Murray, 52
Rainer, Dachine, 122
Reynolds, Dodie Maclary, 70, 76
Reynolds, Ken, 70
Reynolds, Olive, 10
Reynolds, William, 59
Rick, Ami, 99
Rick, Jonathan, 99
Rick, Philip, 99
Ricks, Peter, 100
Riley, William, 63
Riseley, Edith, 62
Roberts, Ellin, 116
Rodney, Courtney, 25
Rose, Elizabeth Busch, 92
Rose, Malcolm, 65
Rose, Will, 79
Rosenblum, Edgar, 44
Ruskin, John, 11

Sanders, Ed, 52
Santa Claus, 2, 86
Scales, Jim, 120
Scales, Maureen, 120
Schmidt, Clarence, 93
Schwarz, Betty, 53
Schwarz, Kermit, 53
Schwarz, Rose Sheehan, 53
Scism, "Flo" Odell, 92
Shirah, Sam, 110
Shotwell, Dr. James T., 8, 18
Shultis, Lester, 63
Shultis, Neva, 48, 81, 89
Shultis, Wesley, 15
Simmons, Birge, 15
Simpson, Ruth, 60
Slayton, Freda, 40
Slayton, Sidney, 40
Smith, Judson D., 124
Smith, Anita, 49, 101
Smith, Mary D., 124
Smith, Mary Dufresne, 124
Snyder, Clarence, 106
Spinelli, Elizabeth DeLisio, 77
Spinelli, Philip, 77
Stern, D.J., 60
Stillwell, Dick, 111
Stolpinski, Paul, 51
Striebel, John, 96
Sweeney, Kevin, 32
Teddy, 107
the Jug, 112
Thompson, Alice, 115
Tiano, Charlie, 50
Todd, Rev. Harvey, 58
Toms, Olive, 81, 84
Traum, Artie, 42
Traum, Happy, 42
Traum, Jane, 42
Twaddell, Jim, 91
Van De Bogart, Aaron, 22
Van De Bogart, Jane, 22
Van Debogart, Catherine, 89
Van Debogart, John, 89
Van Kleeck, Bert, 88
Van Kleeck, Clara, 88
van Rijn, J. Constant, 37, 125
Van Valkenburg, Ray, 66
Van Wagenen, Walter, 34, 53
Varney, Dorothy, 46
Varney, Elbert, 46
Volz, Rick, 80, 85, 103

Vos, Aart, 125
Vos, Johtje, 125
Waterous, Mary, 64
Waterous, William, 64
Wein, George, 13
White, Hervey, 4, 9, 11–13, 43, 58, 69
Whitehead, Jane, 75
Whitehead, Peter, 11
Whitehead, Ralph Radcliffe, 4, 9, 11–13, 21, 38, 50
Wicks, Arthur, 30
Wigram, John, 4, 28
Wilber, George, 104
Wilber, William H., 67
Wilson, Ken, 30
Wilson, Lew, 30
Wilson, Woodrow, 18
Woodstock's fallen, 104
Wolven, Alice Holumzer, 118
Wolven, Arthur, 43
Wolven, John, 118

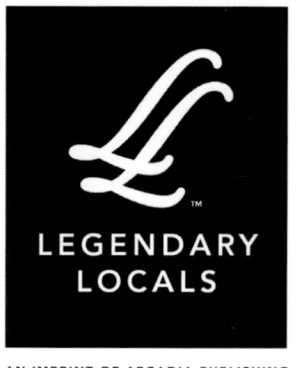

AN IMPRINT OF ARCADIA PUBLISHING

Find more books like this at
www.legendarylocals.com

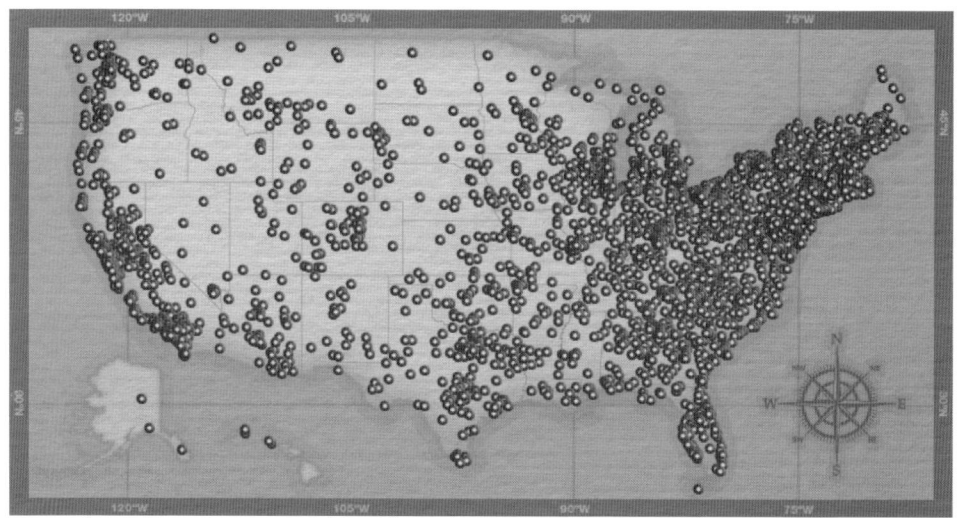

Discover more local and regional history books at
www.arcadiapublishing.com

Consistent with our mission to preserve history on a local level, this book was printed in South Carolina on American-made paper and manufactured entirely in the United States. Products carrying the accredited Forest Stewardship Council (FSC) label are printed on 100 percent FSC-certified paper.

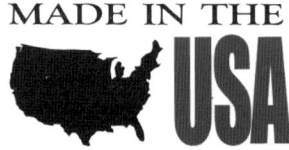